EARLY 20TH CENTURY DEVELOPMENTS
IN AMERICAN ACCOUNTING THOUGHT

THE DEVELOPMENT
OF CONTEMPORARY
ACCOUNTING THOUGHT

EARLY 20TH CENTURY DEVELOPMENTS
IN AMERICAN ACCOUNTING THOUGHT
A Pre-Classical School

Edited by
Gary John Previts

With An Introduction

ARNO PRESS
A New York Times Company
New York • 1978

**Publisher's Note: This book has been reproduced
from the best available copies.**

Editorial Supervision: LUCILLE MAIORCA

———◆———

Reprint Edition 1978 by Arno Press Inc.

Arrangement and compilation copyright © 1978
    by Arno Press Inc.

"Treatment of Maintenance and Depreciation Accounts
    in the New Classification of Accounts by
    Interstate Commerce Commission" was reprinted
    by permission of Price Waterhouse & Co.

THE DEVELOPMENT OF CONTEMPORARY ACCOUNTING THOUGHT
ISBN for complete set: 0-405-10891-5
See last pages of this volume for titles.

Manufactured in the United States of America

———◆———

PV

Library of Congress Cataloging in Publication Data

Main entry under title:

Early 20th century developments in American accounting
    thought.

    (The Development of contemporary accounting thought)
    Reprint of 17 articles published in various journals
between 1880 and 1929.
    1. Accounting--United States--History--Addresses,
essays, lectures. I. Previts, Gary John. II. Series.
HF5616.U5E15   657'.0973   77-87316
ISBN 0-405-10929-6

Editor's Introduction

Significant influences upon the development of financial accounting
thought can be traced to the writings of a group of professional accounting
pioneers of the period 1900 to 1920. In particular, William Morse Cole,
Arthur Lowes Dickinson, Paul-Joseph Esquerré, Henry Rand Hatfield, Roy
Bernard Kester, Robert Heister Montgomery, Charles Ezra Sprague and John
Raymond Wildman, among others, enunciated basic concepts which are believed
to have transformed earlier accounting notions into those which now have
evolved to serve as a classical foundation for subsequent advances in
accounting theory.

Professional financial accounting in America made important strides
toward maturity during the first decades of this century. Among leading
members of the young profession, several men appeared most qualified in
position, ability and experience to serve as authoritative spokesmen for
accounting's Preclassical era. This era preceded the age of Classical
American Accounting thought, most often identified with the activities
of W. A. Paton, E. L. Kohler, G. O. May and A. C. Littleton.

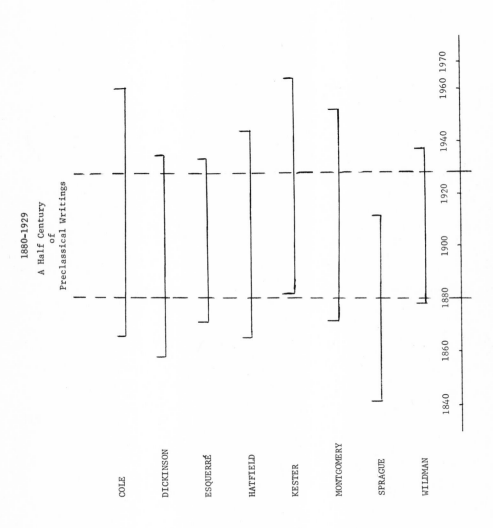

Figure 1. Life spans of some Preclassical accountants.

These eight "Preclassical" writers have been chosen to represent the period because they were devoted professionalists; most are known to have held important offices or committee posts within professional and academic groups. Almost all were active as practitioners or consultants and were noted academicians as well, holding teaching positions at several levels, including accounting professorships at major universities for long periods. Usually these men were among the first accounting professors at the collegiate institutions with which they were associated.

This uncommon blend of professionalist-practitioner-professor is the hallmark of the Preclassicist. Prior to this period the academic and professional prominence of accountancy had not advanced far enough to warrant accountants' claim to this triad of distinctions. Later as accountancy became more specialized between teaching and practice it was highly unusual to find men with all these active credentials.

Biographical Material

WILLIAM MORSE COLE (1866-1960)

Born in Boston on February 10, 1866, Cole received a high school education in Portland, Maine, and attended Portland Business College. He earned an A.B. (1890) and an A.M. at Harvard, the institution at which he would become associated as a faculty member.

Prior to becoming an instructor of political economy at Harvard, Professor Cole worked as a clerk-bookkeeper for several wholesalers and as an auditor for two corporations. His first known manuscript coincides with the start of his academic career. In 1890 he prepared an article entitled "Cooperative Insurance and Endowment Schemes," for publication in the Quarterly Journal of Economics.

Before the business school opened at Harvard he offered a course in accounting principles to seniors at the college. No credit was given for the work as it was considered a vocational training course. When the first faculty of the Business School was appointed in 1908, Cole was among its members, serving as an assistant professor. In 1913 and 1916 he received promotions, and upon his retirement in 1933 he held the rank of Professor Emeritus of Economics and Social Philosophy. What is believed to be his last article, "Our Outdated Accounting," appeared in the July, 1933, issue of the Harvard Business Review.

Though not active as a CPA, Cole maintained ties with the practitioners, and was an honorary member of the Massachusetts Society of Certified Public Accountants. His career of service outside accounting included teaching English and composition. At that time, under the pseudonym Christopher Craigie, Cole wrote An Old Man's Romance (1895). From 1894-1895 he was secretary for the Massachusetts Commission for the Unemployed and during World War I he held a commission as a Captain in the Quartermaster Corps.

Cole married in 1898 and raised two daughters, Catriona and Elizabeth. In 1909 he wrote a major nonaccounting work The American Hope, a commentary on the principles of American life as he viewed them.

Cole's classroom techniques were recalled by Mark Walker who said:

> Many of Professor Cole's Business School students will remember his precise speech, his refusal to use or to attempt to understand slang expressions, his meticulous explanations and his impatience with slovenliness and carelessness.

Accounts: Their Construction and Interpretation, Cole's important financial accounting treatise, appeared in 1908 and was revised in 1915. Fundamentals of Accounting a widely used textbook which he coauthored with Anne Geddes was published in 1921. Professor Cole authored books and many articles on the subject of institutional and hospital accounting and cost accounting.

His death on December 15, 1960, ended a career of service of which over forty years had been spent teaching accounting.

ARTHUR LOWES DICKINSON (1859-1935)

Arthur Lowes Dickinson was born in London, England on August 8, 1859. Much of what is known of his ancestry is through the biography of his brother, Goldsworthy Lowes Dickinson, the noted poet and writer. The Dickinson family included three sisters in addition to the brothers.

Dickinson was educated at Charterhouse School and Cambridge, graduating in 1882 as a Wrangler in Mathematical Tripos, the highest honors in mathematics at the school; in 1888 he received an M.A. At Cambridge he was tutored by John Neville Keynes. Later when Dickinson was living in America he was host to the son of his former tutor, John Maynard Keynes and introduced the young Keynes to George O. May.

In her study of Dickinson's career, Mary Murphy states:

> When Arthur Lowes Dickinson came down from Cambridge in 1882, he considered with some care the various occupational avenues open to a young Englishman possessed of the additional qualification of a First in mathematics. Many fields beckoned to him, both at home and in the Empire. . . .
>
> After deep consideration of all occupations open to him, Dickinson selected for himself a fledgling profession -- public accountancy. This profession, because of rapidly expanding business opportunities, offered him a promising field for a career, and afforded him the chance of using his mathematical training in an occupation dedicated to public service.

Dickinson was first prizeman of the 1886 Institute examinations and began to practice as a chartered accountant in 1887. On May 17, 1887, he delivered his first paper, "Life Assurance Accounts." He and Mary Jennings were married in 1888 and they raised two daughters, Mary and Dorn.

Under an arrangement with the controlling English firm, Dickinson was
sent to the United States in April, 1901, to assume the senior partnership
of the American accounting practice which was to become Price, Waterhouse
& Company. During the twelve years Dickinson resided in America he embraced
the country as his own, obtaining citizenship in 1906 and establishing his
professional credentials in Illinois (1903) and New York (1913) by obtaining
his certificate as a public accountant.

Dickinson acted to unite the many independent state accounting groups
by sponsoring the Federation of Societies of Public Accountants in America
and serving as President in 1904. In the best tradition of the British
profession Dickinson, through his efforts and example, played an important
part in encouraging accountants to build strong ties with academicians and
other professionals.

In 1904 the Federation undertook sponsorship of the Congress of
Accountants, the first attempt at a national and international meeting of
North Atlantic accounting professionals. Dickinson was instrumental in
assuring the meeting's success and delivered the significant paper "Profits
of a Corporation."

During 1905 Dickinson served as secretary of the American Association
of Public Accountants (which was to absorb the Federation). He was a member
of many other professional groups including the New York State Society of
CPAs, the Royal Statistical Society (England) and the Institute of Actuaries
(England).

One of his first contributions as an American practitioner was to devise
a unique format for the annual accounts of the United States Corporation, a

milestone in the advance of adequate disclosure in corporate financial
statements.

The strain of developing a national practice and the efforts put forth
in behalf of the profession during his decade of leadership and participation
in the American profession led Dickinson to resign his senior partnership in
New York and return to England in 1913, shortly before the outbreak of World
Was I. In England he continued to work in behalf of the public interest and
the profession, receiving knighthood from King George in recognition of his
services to that country during the war.

While he lived in England Dickinson's presence continued to be felt in
America. The publication of his book Accounting Practice and Procedure (1914)
and several other contributions to the literature, combined with occasional
visits to the states, kept him abreast of the American accounting scene.
His retirement in 1923 was acknowledged internationally in tribute to his
leadership and influence. He continued even after retirement to add to his
record of public service by accepting a government appointment to investigate
the condition of the railways in India.

During his retirement Dickinson found time for several return visits to
New York and until his death on February 28, 1935, he was in constant touch
with the profession. In tribute to Dickinson, Maurice Peloubet remarked:

> He was first of all a practical professional accountant. He
> was the advisor of many of those responsible for the conduct of
> some of our largest industries. In the period of consolidation
> and reorganization of corporations at about the turn of the century,
> his influence was felt in many of the most important of these.
> Beyond this, however, he was a profound scholar and a clear and
> illuminating writer.

This natural scholarly ability never drew Dickinson into the classroom
formally as professor or instructor. However, in 1929 the Arthur Lowes

Dickinson Fund was established at the Harvard Graduate School of Business in recognition of Sir Arthur's contributions to American accountancy. The income from this fund has been used to conduct research and for the appointment of a distinguished accountant to serve as the "Dickinson Lecturer", and more recently as Dickinson Professor.

In 1951 Dickinson was inducted into the Accounting Hall of Fame at the Ohio State University. The nominating remarks stated:

> He brought to his task much more than theoretical and practical training in accounting, he brought a broader intellectual background, a rugged integrity, an eager desire to advance the profession and a personality that commanded respect and inspired those with whom he worked.

PAUL-JOSEPH ESQUERRÉ (1872-1934)

Born in Plaisance, Gers, France, on May 16, 1872, Esquerré was a student at the Lyceum of Auch, the Academy of Toulouse and the University of France. He held a B. ès L. and earned his CPA certificate in New York (1911). In 1893 he had come to America to work as a bacteriologist at the New York Pasteur Institute. Previously he had served with the French Army (2nd Regiment Zouaves) in Algiers.

On July 10, 1905, he was hired by the firm of Haskins & Sells, probably in connection with the audits of insurance companies instigated by the Armstrong investigation, for he had acquired his accounting skills working in the insurance field. Before leaving to begin a teaching career at NYU Esquerré was promoted by the firm and a note on his resignation form indicates that he had worked satisfactorily and would be reemployed upon request.

It has been said of Esquerré that he was primarily a teacher. He said it was his function to make his students "think like accountants". In 1917 Esquerré became a faculty member of the City College of New York where he taught accounting theory and problems. Between his positions on the

faculties of the New York schools he had undertaken the development of his

own school, The Esquerré Postgraduate School of Accountancy, which Peloubet

recalls as offering ". . . the first really successful . . . [review] course

for the CPA examination. . . ."

A 1913 article by Esquerré, "Goodwill, Patents, Trademarks, Copyrights

and Franchises," was selected by Moonitz and Littleton as one of the signif-

icant accounting essays of the period. They noted that it ". . . raises

the relevant issues concerning intangibles in a clear and forthright manner."

Esquerré's book, Applied Theory of Accounts (1914) was widely used

and later reissued as Accounting (1927). This work may have been significant

for its nonconformity of view above all else. As the publisher remarked

regarding the later edition:

> In this . . . book [Esquerré] turns his guns on the conven-
> tional ways of handling a number of major problems, as statement
> preparation and valuation procedure. He shows where in his
> estimation, existing practice falls short and advances sound,
> refreshingly flexible methods which he feels accomplish better
> the objectives in view.

Of what is known of Paul-Joseph Esquerré there seems to be evidence

that he was a colorful individual with a "Napoleonic flair." An original

thinker, he provided a continental influence on early accounting thought in

America.

Esquerré was a member of the American Institute and the New York Society.

Homer Pace, editor of The American Accountant, commented on Esquerré's role

among professional groups as follows:

> His humor, satire and constructive thinking have enlivened
> many a meeting of the New York State Society of Certified Public
> Accountants, and his fame has extended far beyond the environs of
> this metropolis.

One of his last works, on the topic of depreciation, appeared in 1928. He died at the age of 62 on August 15, 1934, and was survived by his wife, Alice Macdona Esquerré.

HENRY RAND HATFIELD (1866-1945)

Hatfield was born in Chicago on November 27, 1866, the same year as Cole. He was raised in a religious environment, the son of the Rev. Robert W. and Elizabeth (Taft) Hatfield. In 1892, he received a bachelor's degree from Northwestern and in 1897 he earned his doctorate at Chicago.

From 1886 to 1890 he was affiliated with the municipal bond business. He began his teaching career at Washington University (St. Louis) where he remained as an instructor in political economy until he returned to the University of Chicago. At Chicago he served as an instructor from 1898 to 1902 and as an assistant professor and Dean of the College of Commerce and Administration (1902 to 1904).

He moved west in 1904 and from that date until his death except for brief summer teaching at Columbia he was associated with the University of California (Berkeley) rising to the position of Dean of Faculties. As an accounting instructor, Hatfield was apparently an innovator as noted by C.E. Allen:

> It is interesting to know that as early as 1902 a departure from the regular method of teaching the elementary course was made by a well-known teacher of accounting [Professor Hatfield]. In this course accounts were studied and interpreted from the point of view of the businessman rather than of the professional bookkeeper.

Hatfield's most memorable work is not necessarily his most theoretically important. His "An Historical Defense of Bookkeeping," a fondly regarded effort tracing the heritage of accountancy, came long after his major

treatise Modern Accounting (1909). "Defense" was given as a speech before
the American Association of University Instructors in Accounting on December 29,
1923. It is oft quoted and was also chosen by Moonitz and Littleton as a
significant essay of the period. In 1927, Modern Accounting was reissued
under the title of Accounting after substantial updating and revision. The
appeal of this work continues to the present day, with a 1971 reprint offered
by the Scholars Book Co.

Hatfield apparently spoke and wrote German fluently and enjoyed travel
on the Continent. One of the products of his trips abroad appears to have
been his earliest article length manuscript 'Zwei Pfadfinder' (Two Pathfinders)
published in Germany in 1909 on the subject of the accounting contributions
of Jones and Foster, two nineteenth century American writers.

Hatfield was among the college professors who gathered at the Deshler
Hotel in Columbus, Ohio, in December, 1916, to organize a national association
of college instructors in accounting. He served that organization as the
first Vice President and as President during the third year. Among his
other professional activities Hatfield served as Vice President of the
American Economics Association in 1918, as a Senator of Phi Beta Kappa, 1923
to 1928, and in 1929 was appointed the United States representative to the
International Congress on Commercial Education in Amsterdam.

His service to the accounting profession was highlighted by participation
with Thomas Sanders of Harvard and Underhill Moore of Yale during the 1930s
in the preparation of A Statement of Accounting Principles, an early attempt
to formulate the basic concepts upon which accountancy functioned in the
American business community.

His interest in accounting history, as evidenced by "Defense," was a source of inspiration to many including A.C. Littleton who dedicated his own important research Accounting Evolution to 1900 to Professor Hatfield in recognition of the latter's influence.

Hatfield received many distinctive honors during his lifetime. In 1951 he was elected to the Accounting Hall of Fame with these remarks:

> Professor Hatfield was an inspiring teacher, gifted author and one whose keen insight and independent thinking were potent influences in the early development of accounting theory.

Hatfiled married in 1898 and had two sons, Robert and John, and one daughter, Elizabeth. His later works include "Replacement and Book Value," which appeared in the Accounting Review in 1944. Hatfield died on Christmas day, 1945, a month before his seventy-ninth birthday.

Several years after his passing he was remembered by Maurice Peloubet in these words:

> Professor Hatfield is the type of the pioneer scholar and the formative writer in accountancy. It is to men like him that we owe the development of the large and varied accounting literature we have today and the educational opportunities which enable us to train men for the ever increasing difficulties and complexities of the profession.

ROY BERNARD KESTER (1882-1965)

Kester, born in Cameron, Missouri, September 11, 1882, is the junior member of the accountants selected to represent the Preclassical period. He received an A.B. in 1902 from Missouri Wesleyan College. "Kester also studied at Colorado College in Colorado Springs in 1906 and at the University of Chicago in 1907. He received a B.C.S. (1911) and an M.A. (1912) at the University of Denver and received his doctorate at Columbia in 1919. His dissertation topic was A Study in Valuation of the Commercial Balance Sheet.

Kester's teaching career began as an instructor in mathematics at

Missouri Wesleyan in 1902. Later he taught in Denver and East Denver High School and finally at the University of Denver. From 1915 until his retirement in 1949 he was on the Columbia University faculty, serving twenty-seven of those years as full Professor of Accounting.

Kester's practical experience included several years in Denver as a public accountant, having received his certificate in Colorado in 1914. After 1917 he was associated with the firm of Boyce, Hughes and Farrell in New York and served continually in the capacity of a consultant, including important assignments with the Federal government.

Being the youngest of the Preclassicists, many of Kester's publications overlap into the Classical era -- the years identified with the influence of May, Paton, Kohler and Littleton, but his major work Accounting Theory and Practice is clearly a product of Preclassical thinking. One of Kester's first articles appeared in 1920 in the Spice Mill a journal of the spice and coffee trade. Professor Kester married in 1915 and had a daughter; his wife died at an early age leaving him a widower before 1920.

His wide influence within the early profession can be appreciated from the list of important assignments he undertook. For example, as early as 1920 he was appointed to chair the National Association of Cost Accountants' special committee investigating the topic of interest cost.

A paper he delivered at the 1920 program of the American Association of University Instructor's meeting was noted by Scovill as the forerunner of the important role Kester would play in the development of that organization, as Vice President from 1922 to 1924 and as President in 1925. Prior to coming east, Kester had served as President of the Colorado State Board of Certified Public Accountants and from 1925 to 1928 he was research director of the National Association of Cost Accountants. He also served on the committee on accounting procedure of the American Institute. His influence upon accounting instruction is apparent when considering the number of editions of his popular texts. Originating in 1917, his Advanced Accounting was last revised in 1946 and Principles of Accounting in 1939.

In 1957 he was inducted into the Accounting Hall of Fame. His last noted article "Sources of Accounting Principles," appeared in the Journal of Accountancy of 1942 and was selected by Moonitz and Littleton as a significant accounting essay.

Professor Kester died in 1965.

ROBERT HEISTER MONTGOMERY (1872-1953)

Like Hatfield and Sprague, Montgomery was the son of a minister. Born in Mahanoy City, Pennsylvania, September 21, 1872, young Montgomery moved often as the needs of his father's calling demanded. He received his formal education in public schools and night schools.

On Monday morning, February 4, 1889, sixteen year-old Robert H. Montgomery entered the building at 58 Walnut Street, Philadelphia to take up his dities as an office boy in the employ of John Heins, public accountant. Nine years later Montgomery had risen to the level of partner in the newly formed firm Lybrand, Ross Brothers and Montgomery. Today that firm is among the largest in international public accounting practice -- Coopers & Lybrand.

In 1899 he became a charter member of the Pennsylvania Institute of Certified Public Accountants, having received his certificate under the laws of that state. During the Spanish-American War he volunteered and served in the Puerto Rican Campaign. Again in 1917 he was called upon to serve in the military with the rank of Lieutenant Colonel. His duties limited him to the

home front as a planner with the War Industries Board even though he made
several attempts to obtain an overseas transfer.

Between his periods of military service Montgomery supplemented his
interest in accounting by undertaking the study of law. In 1900 he was
admitted to the Bar in Pennsylvania. This legal background and his auditing
experience were readily adaptable to meet the complications which arose when
national tax laws were enacted in 1909 (excise) and 1913 (income). After
the war when the permanent character of the income tax became apparent
Montgomery continued to provide leadership in tax accounting. Professor
Roberts' study of Montgomery states:

> The emergence of Montgomery as an authority on accoutning
> can loosely be placed during the period 1904 to 1914. He first
> attracted widespread attention with his presentation of a paper
> at the Congress of Accountants in 1904. The next year he edited
> and published an American Edition of Dicksee's Auditing: A
> Practical Manual for Auditors.

Also in 1905 Montgomery contributed an important article to the initial
issue of the Journal of Accountancy on the topic of professional ethics.

When the Pennsylvania Institute began evening classes for accountants
in September, 1902, Montgomery taught the accounting theory portion of the
course. This was the start of a teaching career which saw him lecture at
the University of Pennsylvania and New York University during the years
1904 to 1906. Montgomery recalled:

> Evening courses in accounting were established at Columbia
> University in 1910. I assumed the task of teaching the first
> class and of obtaining instructors to take over all additional
> classes.

> In due course as the number of classes increased I was
> made full Professor of Accounting in 1919. . . .

From as early as 1899 Montgomery worked to promote the professional
organizations of American accountancy. He was the President of the American

Association of Public Accountants (now the American Institute) from 1912
to 1914; of the New York Society of Certified Public Accountants, 1922 to
1924; and of the American Institute from 1935 to 1937. His interests, as
did Hatfield's, transcended the American profession. In 1926 Montgomery
headed the New York delegation to the International Accounting Congress in
Holland. In 1929 he served as President of the Third International Congress
in New York City.

Montgomery was a dedicated collector of early accounting texts and books
of account. In 1926 he donated his collection to the Columbia University
library. It is a group of works which represent several centuries of
accounting thought and serves as an important research source. Montgomery's
distinguished service to his country and the profession was recognized in
1949 with the award of the American Institute's Gold Medal. In 1951, along
with Paton and May, he was one of the charter inductees to the Accounting
Hall of Fame. The Hall of Fame citation read: "As one who was steadfast in
the demand for high ethical standards and as a teacher and author, Colonel
Montgomery was one of the Founders of the profession of accounting in the U.S."

Montgomery died May 2, 1953, in his Miami home at the age of eighty,
being survived by his wife.

CHARLES EZRA SPRAGUE (1842-1912)

Charles E. Sprague, senior member of the Preclassical group, served a
variety of professions during his lifetime. Born October 9, 1842, in Nassau,
New York, he was the son of the Rev. Ezra Sprague and his second wife.

In the fall of 1856 Sprague enrolled at Union College, Schenectady, as
a freshman; the youngest student [age 14] to be admitted to the freshman class
up to that time. He was a brilliant pupil winning all the prizes for which

he was eligible and was elected to Phi Beta Kappa at graduation in 1860. In
1862 he received a Master of Arts degree from the same school. In 1893 he
was awarded an honorary Ph.D. also from Union.

Having taught at Greenwich Union Academy after graduation, he enlisted
in the Union Army in May, 1862, in the early part of the War between the
States. His letters to his mother which are included in the biography by
Helen Scott Mann, provide a valuable insight of young Sprague as he witnessed
the bloodshed of that period.

> "I was not so lucky this time" read a short note by Sprague.
> Rebel fire had torn a hole in his left shoulder at Little Round
> Top. . . .

> The title "Colonel" by which he was known for so many years
> came to him for his "gallant and meritorious service at the Battle
> of Gettysburg. . . ."

> On December 30, 1968, he was made a brevet colonel in the
> New York Volunteers in recognition of his courage and sacrifice.

Upon discharge from active service in 1864 and until 1870 he taught at
various military academies in New York State and authored a number of articles
on military tactics. Later he was asked to assist the commandant of the
U.S. Military Academy (West Point) in revising the book of tactics used there.
In 1866 he married Ray Ellison of New York City; they had four daughters;
two died before reaching their twenty-first birthdays.

His career as a banker began in 1870. Partially because of his skill
as an interpreter his application for a clerk's position at the Union Dime
Savings Bank in New York City was accepted. He rose through several positions
to become President of that institution in 1892.

As early as 1880 he was involved in the publication of financial news.
In August of that year he assumed the editorship, along with Seldon Hopkins,
of the Book Keeper, a fortnightly business publication.

Between 1880 and 1900, Sprague's influence on American accountancy, then in its formative stages, became pronounced. His efforts to provide a continuing number of stimulating articles on the problematic aspects of practice were but one example of his role. In 1895 when public accountants in New York were soliciting passage of the very first CPA law:

> Col. Sprague took the draft of the bill to Albany, and there was his friend Mr. Melvil Dewey, the . . . Secretary of the Regents of the University of New York, whose counsel was eagerly sought and very useful.

In an analysis of the evolution of the CPA movement George Wilkinson adds:

> I wish to emphasize that the program . . . which . . . was later embodied into law was initiated by three men whom we should revere. . . Major Henry Harney . . .; Colonel Charles Sprague . . .; Honorable Melvil Dewey. . . .

Upon passage of the law Sprague served on the first Board of CPA Examiners which was appointed by the Regents of New York. As a CPA (certificate #11) Sprague was active in the affairs of professional groups. He was President of the Institute of Accounts (now defunct) and it is believed he did much to promote the publication of <u>Accountics,</u> a pioneering professional accounting magazine first issued in April, 1897.

When the New York University School of Commerce, Accounts and Finance commenced operation in 1900, Sprague was appointed to the faculty to teach the theory of accounts, and he established a wide repution as an accounting teacher and author during the first decades of this century. In 1902 Professor Sprague offered a course entitled "Philosophy of Accounts." In this, accountancy was considered from the standpoint of science. Illustrations were fully used but emphasis was upon the philosophy of the subject as a phase of economic theory.

As an author he wrote two accounting classics, <u>The Accountancy of Investment</u> (1904) and <u>The Philosophy of Accounts</u> (1907).

In addition to his multiple vocations as a soldier, banker, teacher and accountant Sprague was also a linguist. He is reported to have spoken sixteen languages and, as an avocation, was an American authority on Volapük (world's speech) and Esperanto, two of the so-called universal languages. Volapük was devised in the 1870s by the German priest Johann Martin Schleyer and adopted by Sprague in some parts of his own vocabulary. The simplified prose noted in his writing is the by-product of this influence. In 1902 he prepared a <u>Handbook on Volapük</u> in an attempt to draw serious attention to the commercial applications to which the language could be put.

Sprague's death on March 21, 1912, came after a short illness from pneumonia. He was admitted to the Accounting Hall of Fame in 1953.

JOHN RAYMOND WILDMAN (1878-1938)

A direct descendant of William Brewster of Mayflower fame, John R. Wildman was born in Yonkers, March 15, 1878. He entered Yale University, but when the Spanish-American War came he elected to enter government service, being assigned as a hospital steward in the Puerto Rican Regiment. Later he entered the employ of the Department of Education of Puerto Rico on August 15, 1900, as a bookkeeper and became disbursing officer and Chief of the Division of Disbursements and Accounts. As such he was charged with the supervision of the accounting for forty-six school boards and the devising and installing of a system of accounts for them.

Upon returning to New York in 1905 he applied to Haskins & Sells for employment. There was no immediate opening, but in July, 1905, the requirements of the Equitable Life Assurance Society engagement led to his employment on

July 24, 1905, as an assistant accountant at $25.00 a week.

Wildman enrolled in accounting courses at New York University in 1906, taking the work at night. He graduated in June, 1909, the recipient of the accounting prize, with a B.C.S. (cum laude) and was offered an appointment as instructor in accounting which he accepted effective August 30th. Earlier that same year he had taken and passed the CPA examinations. In 1911 Wildman received the degree of Master of Commercial Science also from NYU.

Wildman is the personification of the attributes cited above as hallmarks of the Preclassicist. He was a professionalist, a respected practicing accountant and an inspiring and popular teacher. His classroom manner is described by Maurice Peloubet:

> In the college year 1912-1913 I took a course in cost accounting under John Raymond Wildman. . . . Professor Wildman was a man of great dignity and impressive presence, but was at the same time a well-liked and popular teacher with the under-graduates. . . .
>
> One of Professor Wildman's characteristics or gifts was the ability to write on complex subjects with great clarity.

His influence extended beyond New York University through his books and his many articles on accounting. Wildman's major works include <u>Principles of Accounting</u> (1913), <u>Cost Accounting</u> (1913), and <u>Principles of Auditing</u> (1916). Several early issues of the <u>Journal of Accountancy</u> contain the series "Department of Practical Accounting," a problem oriented sequence of discussions prepared by Wildman to provide instruction in problem solving and ". . . to show the application of accounting principles."

He continually made addresses to businessmen, bankers and lawyers with the intention of encouraging a stronger interest in formal commercial education, particularly as it related to accounting.

Professor Wildman was one of the founders of the American Accounting

Association. The Association's formative meeting was held in Columbus, Ohio, in 1916 with about seventeen in attendance, including Professor Hatfield. Wildman was elected the first President.

Mr. Wildman rejoined Haskins & Sells on January 16, 1918, charged with organizing the H & S research and training unit. On December 1, 1918, he was admitted to partnership; however, he continued to be Professor of Accounting at NYU until 1923. One of his innovations upon returning to the firm was to sponsor the publication of an intra-firm magazine, The Haskins & Sells Bulletin, which was first issued in March, 1918. Printed monthly and usually containing eight pages, it was a compendium of firm policy statements, theoretical vignettes, practical audit advice and personnel news. As one of the first such publications it was a credit to Wildman's foresight and evidenced his respect for the power of the printed word as a means of strengthening the internal operation of a growing professional organization.

Wildman pioneered technical research and innovation in practice. As early as 1926 he outlined a research program designed to eliminate the arbitrary apporaches which appeared as the result of purely pragmatic applications in accounting practice. Earlier, in 1924, he had served as chairman of the New York Society's special technical committee which was considering the feasibility of various forecasting duties which had been proposed for accountants.

Wildman was a prolific but careful writer. His later works in particular evidence the product of an orderly and mature approach to accounting. He abhored publication for publication's sake, commenting to his colleagues that ". . . there was a great deal of trash on the market . . ." because of the lack of critical thinking before writing for print.

Wildman's personality has been variously described. For example,

Dean John T. Madden of NYU recounted: "Mr. Wildman was always a hard worker, dominant yet quietly so, aggressive but never unpleasantly, tense but not appearing so, with a doggedness that survived all discouragements that beset his path toward the objective he was seeking to attain." Dr. Joseph J. Klein, a contemporary of Wildman, made reference to what must have been Wildman's attention to detail, suggesting that Wildman was always proper and somewhat of a "stuffed shirt." To the contrary, Howard C. Greer pointed out, ". . . he had red hair and a flamboyant demeanor -- [he] once said in a meeting that a newspaper headline reading WILD MAN AT LARGE must have referred to him."

Whether "flamboyant" or a "stuffed shirt" Wildman left his mark on his co-workers, fellow practitioners and students. Two of the young men he was directly responsible for recruiting to work for Haskins & Sells, Arthur B. Foye and John W. Queenan, later became succeeding managing partners of that large international accounting firm.

Wildman was very closely associated with the undertaking of The Statement of Accounting Principles. Foye notes that when the ". . . Haskins & Sells Foundation projected the 'Statement of Accounting Principles' in July, 1935, Mr. Wildman through his knowledge of and acquaintance with distinguished educators . . . arranged for Professor Thomas H. Sanders . . . and Professor Henry Rand Hatfield . . . to be two of the three independent authorities."

Regarding Wildman's role in the project, Sanders added:

> The work which the Foundation has entrusted to the committee has required frequent and intimate association between Mr. Wildman and myself. Although I have for years known and admired his ability and character . . . I have been constantly surprised by his penetration, understanding and unfailing sound judgement.

The death of his wife of thirty years, Louise M. Wildman on October 18,

1932, was a severe emotional shock and caused him to submit to an extended
period of rest. Later he remarried but further illness led Wildman to
request that his retirement be commenced June 1, 1936, at the age of fifty-
eight. He died on September 21, 1938.

The Historical Relevance of Preclassicism

Within the mill race of changing events which typified the early
twentieth century American economy, accountants groped for the fundamental
precepts which would provide a basis for defining and discharging the growing
burden of responsibilities which they were being called on to accept.

The eighteen items selected to be reprinted in this anthology represent
some of the unique and not widely read works of eight of the most prominent
Preclassical writers. Little needs to be said about their more popular and
well known writings, but most students of the history of accounting thought
have been unacquainted with the broader spectrum of their works as evidenced
by these selections.

The theoretical feats of this era are rooted in the concepts advanced
by a group which has been designated the Preclassical school of American
financial accounting thought. The identification of this school aids in
affirming the importance of research into the history of accounting thought
by serving to preserve a link in the chain of accounting's theoretical
heritage. These readings provide us with capsule perspectives of the
accounting thought of this early school of important writers. In revealing
these writings a possible pattern for study of the development of American
accounting thought is suggested. For in being able to identify the

Preclassical lineage of many modern notions today's thinkers should be better capable of discriminating between what is a unique contemporary contribution and what may be largely réchauffé.

A Review of Positions

A summary of the important contributions of the eight Preclassical writers now seems in order.

COLE

One of the pioneer authors of professional financial accounting, Cole devoted his life to a career of teaching at Harvard. One of his notable achievements stemmed from his terrier like determination to advance the theory of interest on invested capital as a cost, despite solid opposition from a majority of fellow accountants. Another important contribution of Cole followed from his interest in perfecting the statement of balance sheet changes. A forerunner of modern fund analysis, this statement (which he called the "where got, where gone" statement) was an adaption of crude railroad cash change reports. Cole's efforts, regardless of their bruntness, probably advanced fund analysis and if nothing else helped to preserve the procedure from atrophying. This in itself is a considerable achievement considering the important place which fund analysis now commands in financial disclosure.

DICKINSON

A father of modern income theory, Dickinson was the epitome of Preclassical professionalism. His 1904 paper suggested the important theory of modified cost valuation, specifying its effect on the indirect approach to profit determination. The income statement format he proposed at an early date remains an essential part of the structure of modern financial reporting.

Trained at Cambridge, in Britain, much of the economic and accounting theory he acquired there was transferred to American thought by virtue of his influence. This is particularly evident in the now traditional treatment of interest on invested capital in the theory of accounting income. His abiding devotion to the public service aspects of accountancy were evident as early as 1902 when he advocated the assumption of a third party attest duty. It seems reasonable to conclude that the ultimate acceptance of this duty by accountants stems in large part from his early and continual efforts in behalf of the attest function.

ESQUERRÉ

A tempermental but intellectual Frenchman, Esquerré immigrated to America before the turn of the century. He acquired his accounting skills in the insurance industry after abandoning a career in bacteriology. Somewhat of a theoretical "gadfly", Esquerré had no inhibitions about challenging traditional approaches -- as in his criticism of the lower of cost or market rule and the suggested bifurcation of depreciation charges. Overall he acquired a wide reputation as a practitioner, teacher and professional. His theory of intangibles remains the principle vestige of his early influence -- his place in the history of accounting thought appearing to have been almost entirely forgotten.

HATFIELD

The chief apostle of Sprague's proprietary based theories, Hatfield was an acknowledge theoretical historian, international accounting authority,

research scholar and academician. Recognized as the first full time professor
of accounting, he worked at developing the pedagogy of accounting, being
among the first to direct attention toward the needs of the executive as
opposed to those of the bookkeeper.

His early work, Modern Accounting, is a groundbreaking digest of
accounting practice which seems to have supported the precedent for basing
the justification of a theory on its correspondence to the customary approaches
of the working accountant -- a tendency which Hatfield was prone to perpetuate
in other works he influenced such as A Statement of Accounting Principles
(1938).

KESTER

As the junior member of this group, Kester can be credited with preaching
the doctrines of Preclassicism to a wide audience by means of his popular
texts which were used for nearly four decades. A representative compendia
of Preclassical theory, these works emphasized net wealth valuation and
the doctrines of depreciation with which the Preclassical writers are
identified. A fitting description of Kester's role would be to say that he
was to Preclassical accountancy what J.S. Mill was to Classical economics;
a belated but essential force in the theory of his school.

MONTGOMERY

Probably the most pragmatic of the Preclassicists, Montgomery was a
self-educated, confident and decided professional. He distinguished himself
by service to the profession as an educator, author, practitioner and servant
of government. Among his most memorable statements was the one included in
the foreword to Peragallo's important study on the origins of the Italian

accounting system. Because of their context and terminal implications, these remarks deserve consideration as a penetrating insight of Montgomery's rationale:

> Accounting methods which have endured are those which have met the test of pragmatists. . . .

> [Accounting] draws upon the resources of many sciences, but remains an art, varying in effectiveness with the knowledge and skills of the practitioner -- this is the lesson of history.

Among the earliest contributors to the distinctly American professional literature, Montgomery also published the first works dealing with the problems of accounting for income taxation. His pragmatic auditor's view of theory was often expressed in terms of a strong conservative bias. He once remarked, for example, that: "In deciding whether an expenditure should be capitalized or charged as an expense it is better to be conservative than accurate." The précis of successful Preclassical practitioners, Montgomery was also a clear prototype of George O. May, whose pragmatic and conservative propensities importantly influenced the development of accountancy in the Classical period.

SPRAGUE

Patriarch of the Preclassical system of accounting, more than any other of his ilk Sprague significantly advanced the theoretical framework of early American accountancy. In the 1880s his deductive system of equations had achieved recognition as a root plan for accounting theory in its period of professionalization. Sprague's achievements are all the more impressive when considered in relation to the surroundings in which they were conceived. As told by Paton, Sprague wrote mostly without the benefit of theoretical precedent -- transforming the incipient notions of some early writers into

a concise and relatively compete system of accounting. His _magnum_ _opi_,
The Accountancy of Investment and The Philosophy of Accounts, are evidence
of his command of inferential logic and a testament to the influence of
Classical economics on early accounting theory.

WILDMAN

A disciple of Sprague, Wildman modified the former's proprietary equation
into a fiduciary expression, recognizing the accountable relationship between
the business executive and absentee owners. A frequent contributor to the
literature, Wildman wrote on nearly every important accounting topic. His
influence in academic circles as a teacher and administrator was pronounced,
as noted by the effect he had on many of his promising students including
Foye and Peloubet.

Respected by his contemporaries, Wildman served as the first President
of the forerunner of the American Accounting Association, having been
instrumental in its formation. Later he headed the unique research
department of Haskins & Sells he was involved in the preparatory activities
for The Statement of Accounting Principles which was released the year of
his death.

Perhaps the least acclaimed amongst the Preclassicists, Wildman's efforts
in behalf of the early profession, his role as professor and research
practitioner, compel those with a sense of equity to accord him much wider
regard.

CONTENTS

Montgomery, Robert H[eister]
THE IMPORTANCE OF UNIFORM PRACTICE IN DETERMINING THE
PROFITS OF PUBLIC SERVICE CORPORATIONS WHERE
MUNICIPALITIES HAVE THE POWER TO REGULATE RATES (Reprinted
from *Official Record of the Proceedings of the Congress of Accountants Held at the
World's Fair, Saint Louis*) New York, September, 1904

Montgomery, Robert H[eister]
THE VALUE AND RECENT DEVELOPMENT OF THEORETICAL
TRAINING FOR THE PUBLIC ACCOUNTANT (Reprinted from *The Business
Man's Magazine & The Book-Keeper*, Vol. XVIII, Number III) September, 1905

Sprague, Charles E[zra]
THE ALGEBRA OF ACCOUNTS (Reprinted from *The Book Keeper*,
Vols. I and II) New York, 1880-81

Sprague, Charles E[zra]
LOGISMOGRAPHY I and LOGISMOGRAPHY II (Reprinted from *Accountics*,
Vol. II, Nos. 4 and 5) New York, January/February, 1898

Wildman, John R.
APPRECIATION FROM THE POINT OF VIEW OF THE CERTIFIED
PUBLIC ACCOUNTANT (Reprinted from *The Accounting Review*, Vol. III,
Number 4) Chicago, December, 1928

Wildman, John R.
DEPRECIATION AND OBSOLESCENCE AS AFFECTED BY APPRAISALS
(Reprinted from *The Accountant*, Vol. LXXXI, No. 2865) London, November, 1929

Wildman, John R.
ADDRESS OF THE PRESIDENT (Reprinted from *The American Association of
University Instructors in Accounting, Papers and Proceedings of the Second
Annual Meeting*, Vol. II, No. 1) Philadelphia, March, 1918

ACCOUNTING METHODS FOR DETERMINING COSTS AND PRICES

William Morse Cole

ACCOUNTING METHODS FOR DETERMINING COSTS AND PRICES

WILLIAM MORSE COLE

Those who are trying to develop the comparatively new science of accounting are placed in a position unlike that of almost any pioneers who have preceded them—if not in ¹ ·d, at least in degree. They are facing in extreme form the sort of thing that economists in general have long suffered. For many years economists were rather laughed at by business men because they were giving strange uses to old words or seeking peculiar visual angles for the observation of common transactions. With this you are all familiar. Only those who are specially engaged in the consideration of accounting, however, realize in what a high degree this is true of the accounting branch of economics. In this branch the professional man (and by this term I mean both the practitioner and the teacher) is using not only the common terms of business but also the detailed paraphernalia of forms of record, and yet he is forced commonly to recommend that they be put to uses that violate the traditions of generations and generations of competent or quasi-competent and altogether respectable bookkeepers. The business man does not object to economic theories as such, nor always to the application of those economic theories in public affairs, but when these theories knock at the door of his own counting room, and bring with them a reputation that leads the bookkeeper to say, "If you let them in, you and I will have to go to school again and learn a new language", he is inclined to shrug his shoulders and say, "Go away, little boy, go away!" His attitude toward the little boy is natural enough—and the epithet "little boy" is not altogether bad. Accounting is a little boy— he is far from maturity; but he is a stalwart youngster, and he has already done a great deal for those who have trusted him with a job. Undoubtedly for many years the so-called practical business man will laugh good-naturedly at much that the professional accountants advocate, and the more conservative accountants will laugh at much of what the more venturesome will practice. The test will lie always in the results—where men can be found bold enough to forget tradition and try results—but it takes a long time to get the community into a frame of mind receptive enough to test the results fairly. One thing is obvious: for an accountant to install for his client a system of accounting that the client does not trust is practically to foredoom the experiment to failure. The client must see the value of what is recommended; and he must see the economic principle underlying the accounting system, or he will not see the value of the system as a whole. To get the accounts of the business of this country put upon a sound basis means the education of the public to something of an appreciation of fundamental economic principles.

We who are here are supposed to be without the prejudice of tradition—we are supposed to be open-minded enough to welcome any new thing that can justify itself both rationally and practically—whether it violates tradition or not. I am going to ask you therefore to forget what has customarily been done with regard to the determination of costs, and to consider the subject independently of tradition. Then when we have considered what is desired, we may see how far the traditional methods may be used to produce the thing desired. If we can get the thing we want without much disturbance of tradition, so much the better.

In the first place, I wish to premise that business is not always profit-making or even intended to be profit-making. Many large and valuable enterprises are concerned solely with product; they not only seek no profit, but they distinctly wish to avoid profit. They are concerned only to get the maximum product at the minimum cost. The number of such enterprises is continually increasing. It is futile to deny that these are business enterprises, for they seek to produce definite results through the employment of paid human agencies; and I conceive that element, bargain and sale relations between human elements, to make the distinction between business and other things, mere handicraft on one hand, and mere physical and mental activity on the other. No accounting is adequate unless it is based on the fundamental fact that costs have in them no element of profit for the enterprise concerned. If profit is in the enterprise, the profit is an amount over and above the cost, and the cost must as clearly exclude any element of profit for the enterprise as if the enterprise were concerned solely with product and sought to avoid profit. We may say, indeed, that accounting is concerned with the economics of consumption quite as much as with those of producton; and no accounting is adequate which tries, figuratively speaking, to treat them both as if they were opposite sides of the same account—and therefore presents what looks like a balance between them as if that were the final figure desired.

My second premise is this: With the determination of how much absolutely is a fair profit, accounting has nothing to do; but the facts upon which the fairness of profit hinges must be shown by the accounts just as far as those facts are capable of expression in figures. Let me illustrate: Whether interest shall be 6 per cent or 4 per cent, whether wages shall be $5 a day or $2, whether rent shall be $5 an acre or $1 a foot, is not a question for accounting to settle; but to discover all the figures that can be known as material for determining the fair rate of interest, of wages, and of rent, is the accountant's particular task. The final decision may involve important considerations of risk, of social desirability, of spiritual progress, that cannot be recorded in accounts. This is so obvious that you may wonder at my mention of it. I do it only because I find often that it is neglected in practice. In other words, the temptation is strong to try to strike a balance between the economics of consumption and those of production, and show a result which is neither—and therefore worthless for the purposes of either. For illustration, if in some municipal activity allowance for social value has been allowed to creep into a figure of cost (let me say a disregard of some fact in distribution of costs because the social value of the service is deemed to offset an actual outgo), the result may be satisfactory for the purposes of that particular calculation, and yet be seriously misleading when the figure is used for purposes of comparison in another connection or as the basis for a new figure where the social value of the service is not a factor of the same weight.

From these two premises that I have made—first, that accounting *is* concerned with *all business*, in the largest sense of the word, and, second, that accounting is *not* concerned with questions of policy but only with questions of fact (facts which justify policy or are the results of policy)—comes my fundamental thesis, that the proper function of accounting is nothing more or less than telling the truth, telling the economic truth, and telling it in such fashion that the known facts shall not be held in solution, so to speak, in a lot of supposed facts, estimated facts, and *quasi* facts. It is obvious that many figures in accounting are bound to be estimates—as allowances for depreciation, debts that will prove uncollectible, valuations of property owned, demands on contingent liability, etc.; but it is equally obvious that these estimated figures may be shown in their true character—as the results of estimates, with the bases on which they were deduced—and that they need not be combined with known items so as to hide the identity of the known items and put the combination into the category of estimated items. In other words, the method of accounting should be the general method of science—expressed in the precept "So far as possible, isolate your causes, and distinguish your results." A physicist who should conduct all his experiments regardless of atmosphere and temperature would learn nothing of natural law. An accountant who constantly and unnecessarily combines known and unknown quantities gets results that tell little about business operations; he certainly is contributing nothing to the advance of economic knowledge.

Let us now examine the application of some fundamental economic principles to accounting, and see what they suggest in the way of accounting facts and methods. It is clear that here, at least, abstruse and somewhat disputed refinements of economic theory can have no place; for, however advantageous it might be to put certain of such theories to the practical test of operations and accounting record, such experiments are available only where a business enterprise is offered as a voluntary laboratory; we could hardly recommend that sort of thing as general accounting policy.

The subject of our discussion this evening, as indicated by the program, is a method of determining costs and of using those costs as criteria for fixing prices. Whether the prices are to yield a profit or not does not concern us here; for even if they are to do so, the amount is to be determined by the application of some ratio or formula to the cost already found. Let us begin our application of these principles with interest on capital invested.

On this matter of what is a fair return for capital invested, all communities are much divided; but if my fundamental thesis is accepted, this does not much concern the accountant. He is not— that is, as an accountant—concerned with policies, but with facts. It is his business to record what has happened, and to do it in such fashion that every one may for himself determine what he thinks ought to happen. If the accountant bases his figures on his own theory of what ought to happen—for example, in the matter of payment of dividends—his figures are of practically no use to anyone who has a different theory; indeed, the accountant's figures are of little use even to the people whose theory is identical with his own, for unless he has informed them as to the theory that underlay his figures, they know nothing as to what those figures really mean. Let us take a concrete case. A company has inaugurated a new business which is slow in development. For the first year it does not pay, for it has not yet developed its following or created a sufficiently large demand for its product. The books show a deficit. At the end of the second year, the condition is improved, but though there is every prospect of success not only ultimately but even in the coming year sufficient to wipe out the deficit, the net result of the two years is still a deficit. The accountant decides that this deficit is really an organization expense; indeed, that the full first year's deficit is an organization expense; and that the real result of the two years' operations is a profit, for the amount sunk in the first year is permanent investment, akin to payment for good will. He even goes so far as to say that interest on that first year's deficit should be met out of the product and should be charged as a cost—exactly like interest on funds locked up in machinery. He will say in future years that no profit is shown until enough has been deducted from product to pay interest on this year's deficit. In other words, he will have capitalized this deficit. There are logical grounds for such a view. When, however, we in later years make a study of dividends of this company, and find that none were paid in this first year, we naturally think that a fair return on the investment has not been made unless the later years have paid enough to offset the loss in that first year. Unless we learn that this deficit was capitalized, and that in later years interest has been paid on this capitalized deficit before net profits were deduced, we never appreciate what has happened. The accounts are figures plus a point of view; and the reader of the figures does not know which is which. The accountant, as an accountant, should have no visual angle. He should always face front. Our real problem is to learn what are the focal points on which the face-front accountant should fix his attention and to which he should relate all the facts.

With regard to interest on capital, which we have just been considering, we are forced to observe, as a practical application of our principle of isolating causes, that ordinary interest is made up largely of return for risk assumed. That, of course, is the really variable element in most interest rates. Accounting that disregards it is by so much failing to tell what it might of business conditions and of the affairs of any particular business. It is easy to say that the gross interest rate is good enough for practical purposes, and that one interested in the risk element can easily deduct a minimum rate, for the true interest rate, and use the residue as the compensation for risk. That would be true if interest were always a final figure, or were always a coefficient. As a matter of fact, however, the interest rate is likely, mathematically speaking, to turn up anywhere in an equation—as a coefficient, as a divisor, as a power, as a root. Every time it turns up anywhere except as a final figure its weight is affected. Let us take as an illustration a case in which profit is sought. In our cost of manufacture we usually consider interest on machinery employed in processes as a part of the cost of the product. This is necessary if we are to distribute costs properly between different articles of product and fix prices accordingly. The selling price is usually determined by adding to the final figure for cost a figure for profit; and this profit must include not only interest at the minimum rate on the investment in the business as a whole, but also an element for risk. If the interest rate used in figuring the manufacturing cost—that is, interest on the cost of machinery—is at a normal market rate, it includes the element of risk; and the element is also included in the allowance for risk to be added, as a final figure, to the manufacturing cost. If the plan is well worked out, this risk element will not get in twice; but precaution must in any case be taken, and the precaution cannot be taken by general principle but must be by constant adjustment, for any change in the conditions—that is, in the place that the normal interest occupies in the equation—necessitates a new adjustment. If most of the property of the business is in a manufacturing plant, it would be true, assuming the normal interest rate to be used for figuring cost on machinery employed, that the return for risk which the company would have to earn on its investment would be practically all provided for in its manufacturing cost, and very little would need to be added, as a final figure, for risk included in profit; but if little of the property were so invested, a good deal must be added for risk. This gives a curious conclusion. If your property is in machinery, your risk is counted as cost, not as an element of profit; if your property is not in machinery, risk is counted as profits and not as cost. Surely there is no adequate accounting when the visual angle turns cost into profit. This illustrates what I mean by sug-

gesting the need of the front-face. What does clearness require to
be shown with regard to one's own property used in one's own
business?

It seems rather foolish to attach certain risks to manufacturing costs and then neglect others, no less connected with manufacturing, until the final figures are sought. No one thinks, for
instance, of charging probable losses from bad debts to the cost
of manufacturing the articles that will be ultimately sold for
the bad debts, or of increasing the recorded cost of goods sold
because of the practically certain loss on some goods remaining
unsold. The fact is that the risk element of interest should be
considered only as a final figure—not a manufacturing cost, but
a return of the business as a whole, to make good in good years
the evil chances of the lean years. When we have any consideration of interest as a factor within the business—that is, as cost
—we are properly concerned only with that which is pure interest—roughly speaking, the lowest rate at which money is ever lent
where the risk is negligible, say 2 per cent. (The exact rate is not
here of consequence. I desire merely a pure interest rate that
eliminates the variable element.) It is true that if your
general risks are provided for in your final figure, the only actual
known cost to you of using money in your business is, roughly,
that 2 per cent; for if you lend it on anything else than the absolute security of a sound government and get more than 2 per
cent you are assuming certain risks. To put this in another way,
we may say that if all your property is invested in manufacturing
plant and you charge in manufacturing costs an interest rate
on machinery high enough to cover the risk on your investment,
you do not need to add a risk element in the profit portion of your
price, for you have already covered the risk in your manufacturing rate; conversely, if you have included in the profit portion
of your price a proper risk element, you need to charge only
pure interest (say 2 per cent) in the cost portion of your price.
Practically, and for any particular case, it makes no difference
where your risk element goes; but the moment you attempt to
make comparisons of cost where conditions are dissimilar the
difference in visual angle makes futile any attempt to make
things coincide. Here is a case, then, in which only the application of a theoretical economic principle gives the front-face that
enables accounts to tell the exact truth. We hear much of the
desirability of uniform accounting. There can be no uniform

accounting without similarity of visual angle—or, better, exact front-face. In this matter of interest costs within the enterprise, the approximate pure interest rate is the only fixed element. The judgment of risk is dependent always on the personal equation; and so it should be a final figure to be floated on top of the known figures, so to speak, and not be lost in a combination, or an aqueous solution which is neither one thing nor another. When interest is charged against a department of a business for machinery or other property used by it, that interest might well be carried to an account by itself; for since it represents pure interest it should not be combined with the commercial interest paid and received in ordinary transactions.

Mr. Dickinson and I, you see, are in perfect agreement as to what we want—namely, isolation of causes; but the line of cleavage between causes we are inclined to draw differently. Mr. Dickinson, conceiving profit to be a certain surplus divisible between all three of the agents of production—labor, land, and capital—wishes to exclude all interest from cost; while I, conceiving profit to be only what is left after rent, pure interest, and wages have been paid—that is, virtually the compensation for risks taken—wish pure interest, and pure interest only, to count as a cost. Many accountants count as cost all interest on investment, including all risk elements.

I am aware, of course, that many persons will deny that there is any such thing as pure interest, or that it is sufficiently uniform to serve the use that I am arguing for. In answer I can only say here that I am satisfied that the variations in interest rate are due either to known actual risk or to supposed risk; and for our purposes—since the rate of interest is fundamentally affected by psychological elements—there is no difference between known risk and imagined risk. We may substitute the term "effective risk" for either. The so-called friction in the flow of capital, allowing higher rates in one locality than in another equally safe for the investment of capital, is nothing but the registration of effective risk.

If in any business enterprise new money must be borrowed to install new machinery, and credit is just now so bad that a high rate must be paid, it is absurd to allow that bad credit to go as a cost (as interest on manufacturing plant used) in the manufacture of particular articles of product; for if that is done, an improvement of credit will apparently lower the cost of production: and yet credit has nothing to do with *manufacturing* processes. Even though high interest is actually paid, the risk element in that payment should be counted not as a cost, but as a deduction from profits; that is, the final figure of profits at the end of the earning period will be reduced because the enterprise has borne only a part of its risks, and has hired others (through a high interest payment) to bear some of those risks for it.

As Mr. Dickinson has well pointed out, if interest is allowed to count as a cost, it counts more largely when material is purchased partly or wholly manufactured than when only raw material is used. This does not seem to me objectionable. We are primarily seeking costs for the enterprise immediately concerned. If what is cost to it includes the profits for another enterprise, its costs will be (other things equal) inevitably greater. The accounts should show them so. We .are, moreover, seeking also comparative costs; then, surely, we wish costs under conditions involving some one's else profits to show greater than under conditions where no profits are involved until the end. We wish causes isolated so far as possible. The plan that I suggest seems to me to provide such isolation.

When we come to consider the rate of return to capital in an enterprise as a whole, we may find an account for pure interest to be worth while for a single proprietorship or for a partnership, but it is hardly likely to be serviceable for a corporation. The income to the business as a whole from pure interest charged to departments should be credited to Profit and Loss in the usual way, and then the final net income will be compared with the amount on which the enterprise should earn profits. Whether these profits are fair is a question not for the accountant but for personal or judicial opinion. It involves the visual angle. What information can the accountant give that will serve for the front-face, so that men with visual angles shall know how to read the figures and allow for their own foreshortenings and perspectives? I conceive that in this matter of capital investments there is but one front-face. Any other point of view at once introduces a matter about which there can be honest difference of opinion. One man says rates should be lower because the people have created the value of what the company is utilizing. Only if the accounts show what the owners have actually put in, or left in of their earnings, can anyone tell whether the public did create the value—and even then it is in large part a matter of judgment; but without the figures the judgment has nothing to work on. Another man says that rates should be higher because they do not yield a proper return on the valuation of the property. Yet if the property is the creation of the public and not of the titular owners, the valuation has nothing to do with the justice of the rates; and only accounting for actual investment or virtual reinvestment can tell anything about the real source of the property. A third man says that rates should be lowered because the property could be duplicated for a sum so small that much less than the present rate would pay a fair return on the investment. Yet most of us believe that the return to an enterprise socially serviceable should be not an equivalent of fair interest on what one could now establish it for, after someone else has taken the risks, conducted the experiments, and learned the way, but on the actual cost of the enterprise with compensation for the risks taken. The point here, however, is not that one or another of these points of view is right, but that no common ground exists on which they can be argued except the ground of what has actually happened. The accountant is the scientist who shows the facts, and the prime fact is the actual history of where the property came from and where its product has gone. Then if the community wishes to take the unearned increment, the accountant, as an accountant, has nothing to say; if it wishes to allow men very high return for risks which they have taken, as an accountant he is not concerned; if it wishes to play the game of "heads I win, tails you lose", he again, as an accountant, is not interested. He should keep his accounts, moreover, with an eye single to the truth and not allow himself as an advocate to color the facts with his theories of social justice. Not until the accountant realizes that he is a scientist, and that his work is the discovery of impartial fact, will the public have at its disposal the facts that will enable it to apply its notions of policy with eyes open. To fear the truth is the depth of cowardice, or knavery.

What is the actual investment in a property? As suggested by the supposititious case that I cited earlier in this paper, from one point of view investments may be deficits as well as original sacrifice—when one realizes that operations which establish future producing power and are paid for out of product are taken from the pockets of the owners. Exactly akin is depreciation suffered and not made good—when the product is not enough to make it good. In both cases the cost or sacrifice has been incurred—and that is usually what we mean by investment. Unless we know what has been the actual cost or sacrifice, including risk, we cannot know whether the compensation is adequate or not. That is why I am arguing for the preservation on the books of actual sacrificial cost (if I may use the word in that sense), as distinguished from any combination of that cost with risk elements, valuation elements, duplication elements. We do not want nondescript combinations of figures. We want isolated causes.

Now allow me to suggest how these sacrificial costs may be preserved free from entanglement. In the first place, though I have suggested that depreciation not made good out of product is a sacrifice and a cost, it should be clearly shown for what it is. Some persons might suggest that as I call it sacrifice, not only when invested but afterwards when worn out, I should neglect to note the depreciation and therefore let my original investment in the plant remain on the books at original cost. It is true that for a going concern I recommend cost rather than valuation as the asset figure; but truth demands that the cost figure shall be the present cost figure and by that I mean the original cost figure revised with regard to the facts that have concerned it. If, for instance, a machine has depreciated one fourth—through either use or obsolescence—with respect to the purpose for which it was originally bought, the purpose of the original sacrifice has so far been served, and its present cost is but three fourths of its original cost. In spite, therefore, of the theory that cost and not valuation is the true basis for the accounts, the asset must be written down. To base the accounting on costs rather than on valuations does not in the least confuse capital and revenue. Any judgment as to the fairness of rates or prices or profits must be based on a recognition of both capital and revenue. The front-face accounting will either show directly or give a basis for both of these; first, the original capital costs, plus new investments and reinvestment of profits, less consumption of capital assets; second, the actual profits and the distributed profits. From these figures every competent judge can see for himself, with his own visual angle, whether the profit derived is fair—taking into account those elements of risk, social service, etc., which apply to the particular case. The moment any elements of risk, capitalized earning capacity, cost of duplication, or selling valuation, get into the accounts of a going concern the front-face view has been lost and no one knows just what the figures mean.

My general principle I have illustrated rather fully with the case of interest on capital. I wish to add just a word on rent, for I am not ready to adopt Mr. Dickinson's point of view. Many accountants say that rent is a profit, not a cost. This seems to me a perversion of the economic doctrine that rent does not add to the cost of production. Laying aside refinements of economic theory and taking things in the rough, the natural cost of an article is the cost at the margin of production—the cost at which it just pays. If rent is paid, however, a countervailing advantage must somewhere exist else the work should not be done. Then the costs exclusive of rent are below the margin, or standard. To fix prices at that point is to transfer the benefit of the advantage to the customer and sell goods at a point so low that it cannot persist. The accounts, in other words, have led to a false conclusion with regard to normal cost. The rent, which merely measures the amount by which the *particular* articles are produced *below* the margin, is in this case an element in the measure of *standard* cost, and so should be included in the cost calculations. If the manufacturers are owners of the real estate, rent to them is an income not as manufacturers but as real estate owners. If they pay rent to others, rent is to them a clear cost and should be so reported. I have been speaking, of course, of economic rent, as distinguished from mere interest on the money invested in improvements. The interest portion of rent is subject to the considerations which we have already made.

You will note that I have not attempted to discuss the detailed application of these matters to particular processes. I have thought it well, at least for the sake of variety, to devote my discussion to some very fundamental matters, upon which, if we can once come to an agreement, anything approaching uniformity of accounting methods must be based. Nothing like standard units of cost can ever be learned while fundamentals are treated differently.

AN OUTLINE OF ACCOUNTING FOR INSTITUTIONS

William Morse Cole

INSTITUTION ACCOUNTING AND RECORDS.

An Outline of Accounting for Institutions.

WILLIAM MORSE COLE.

Professor, Graduate School of Business Administration, Harvard University.

We must recognize at the start that cost accounting attempts to give information that shall guide managers in the solution of three sorts of problems: first, how may prices be adjusted to the service rendered; second, does the utmost economy prevail in production and service, and if that is not found how may one trace the waste; and third, had certain work best be performed in their own establishments.

As an illustration of the first of these, need arises for some scientific method of fixing the prices of rooms in a college dormitory or in a hospital, so that the prices paid shall be adjusted to the comparative value of the rooms furnished. It may be true, of course, that in many cases prices are determined by what in railroading is called "charging what the traffic will bear." Thus, although it would normally seem that in some cases a higher price ought to be fixed, putting the charge on the same basis as the charges for other services such a basis would in reality make the charge prohibitive, and so adjustment must be made to that fact. In such a case the price must be lower than that which ought ordinarily to be charged, and that reduction in price is really of the nature of a rebate. If the accounting is serviceable, however, it will make note of both facts—that is, the fact that the actual cost of rendering the service is high in that case, and the fact that the price charged does not bear the same relation to cost that price bears in other cases. Unless the accounting takes note of both facts, it fails to tell the truth.

It is worth while at this point to note what is the purpose of accounting, for commonly a misapprehension prevails. It should be understood at the outset that accounting has nothing whatever to do with questions of policy. The purpose of accounting is to tell about business transactions the truth as exactly as it can be learned, and the determination of the truth should be without respect to persons, prejudices or policies.

It may happen that for reasons of policy the price charged for service rendered is lower than the normal price. In a certain hospital the prices charged for certain private rooms are really lower than on any basis of cost they ought to be. The managers have made this arrangement with the distinct purpose of encouraging persons of means to come to the hospital for treatment; for they believe that the service rendered will be deemed so valuable, and the interest aroused in the hospital so great, that these persons will become valuable friends of the institution and that their influence will increase subscriptions and endowments. This may or may not be wise policy, but good accounting requires that some note shall be taken of the fact and that its cost for advertising purposes shall be considered.

As an illustration of the second sort of problem which cost accounting should help to solve is the economy of laundry work done on the spot. If it is found in any institution that the cost for laundry is 20 per cent higher than the average of other institutions, the management is not doing its duty unless effort is made at once to learn why this is so and whether it can be prevented. The conditions may be such that there is no escape. Then the question arises whether it would be cheaper to have the laundry work done outside.

As an illustration of the third sort of problem, we may take that which arises in many institutions concerning unused land. Most institutions have a considerable tract of land for air, light, and prospect, and much of this could be utilized for raising at least some summer vegetables. In many cases where this has been done the apparent cost of food has been much reduced. Yet it is impossible to know whether this is worth while unless one can know what is the expense for labor attributable directly to the vegetables raised. If the engineer or other employees have much leisure during the summer and that leisure can be devoted to this use, gardening of this sort is likely to be profitable. Only careful accounting can determine just when it is so under these or any other circumstances.

All three of these purposes of cost accounting demand that costs be known as exactly as possible; and the second of these demands that a manager shall know not only the cost in his own institution but in a great many others, for only then can he make comparisons between his own establishment and others and learn whether his costs are excessive. One encouraging feature in institutional service as compared with commercial service is that the only rivalry that can be acknowledged—at least with a good face—is rivalry in efficiency. Every good institution is interested in institutional progress and is glad to conduct experiments and share results with others. Indeed, institutional progress would have been far slower if there had not been something of a professional spirit at work. Professional ethics demands that each person in charge of an institution shall have not only something of scientific eagerness to learn how things can best be done but also altruism enough to help others to benefit by his experience. In order to make possible comparisons of institutions under somewhat similar conditions a uniform scheme of accounting is essential. This means, moreover, something more than a uniform scheme of accounts; for even institutions with accounts of identical names may have results which are not at all comparable; uniformity must extend to the content of the accounts even more than to their forms and names. Before results can be made at all comparable we must be sure that in all institutions under consideration exactly the same kind of things are charged to each account.

Virtually, every institution manager who is subject to trustees or other superiors is eager for additional funds, for he believes that work can be done more economically or at least more satisfactorily with larger capital. The most efficient instrument for inducing trustees to supply needed funds is a statement of financial results which shows not only exactly the cost of each kind of service rendered but how those costs are related to similar costs in other institutions. Trustees are usually business men who know the value of a dollar. They wish to know definite facts about the yield of the dollars entrusted to them, and they are far more interested in these than in hypotheses and mere managerial ambitions. Every institution has some advantages over other institutions, and every one has some handicaps; but the good manager will attempt to learn by concrete figures exactly what are his handicaps and what they cost, and what are the actual savings from his advantages. He should not allow the handicaps for which circumstances—or the trustees—are responsible to swallow up the gains for which the credit is properly his. Until uniform accounting, or at least something approaching it, becomes common, no manager will be in a position to make clear to his trustees just what are the handicaps under which he is working and just what are the economics that have resulted from his management. As an illustration, I know a hospital turning away paying patients for lack of room, and yet giving its matron private quarters which if let to private-room patients would yield several hundred dollars weekly; total costs in this hospital are high, far above its income; another hospital nearby, practically self-supporting, gives its matron quarters worth not half so much; yet the hospital giving its matron expensive quarters shows a lower administrative cost than the other. The objection is not necessarily to the spacious quarters supplied to the matron but to the fact that the accounts take no cognizance, in the administrative cost, of anything but salary, and therefore the result of this extravagance of space does not appear, and a comparison of the two sets of accounts is sadly misleading. Comparisons of accounts when the method of accounting is different are worse than useless, for they may show an advantage where there is really a handicap.

Let us now turn to the methods of learning costs. First, the accounts for each department having an exclusive function should be as far as possible distinct from those of every other department. The steward's department, for illustration, is concerned with food in a more or less raw state—except, perchance, so far as food is purchased necessarily in a cooked state, as are shredded wheat and numerous other cereals. It may chance that in some institution the purchasing is careless and therefore the costs high, and yet the cooking is extremely economical. In such a case, unless a distinction is made between the steward's department and the kitchen department, the normal gross cost for table board, if only that figure is preserved, may hide the fact that one department is well managed and the other ill. The kitchen should be charged for the cost of cooking food and for that alone; this should include the cost of fuel, labor, repairs, etc. The serving department should also be distinguished from the others, for in some cases there is very great wastefulness in the unfortunate arrangement of the establishment, so that the cost of service brings up the total cost of food in spite of the fact that both the purchasing department and the cooking department are well managed.

The expense of the purely housekeeping items, such as sweeping, dusting, and scrubbing, should not be confused with other expenses. Where some of this work is done by persons employed primarily in other departments, as is often the case in hospitals where the nurses have charge of patients' rooms, an attempt should be made to distinguish between that part of the nurses' wages which is for professional care of patients and that which is for housekeeping. At least it is true that the cost of taking care of the general rooms, such as halls, stairways, reception rooms, assembly rooms, etc., should be carried distinct from the cost of the care of private rooms. Laundry charges should be carried distinct from all others, and should include fuel, soap, starch, labor, etc.

The cost of the care of grounds should be separately determined; this would ordinarily include the care of flower beds, the mowing of lawns, shoveling snow from walks, etc. This appears on the face of it to be a small item, but it is obvious that an institution having large grounds with many walks has a very much heavier charge in this respect than others, and a manager who is judged by his total cost per resident-day is handicapped as compared with a manager who has no expensive grounds to care for; he should be able to point out to the trustees of his institution just what it costs to maintain its external attractiveness. Separate accounts should be kept for maintenance of buildings and for maintenance of equipment. Of course, as in all business operations, separate accounts should be kept for taxes, insurance, water, gas, electric light, legal expenses, etc.

The accounts just mentioned may be called the primary accounts. These require nothing more than simple bookkeeping. We must now pass on to the accounting which involves an analysis of transactions so that the distribution of charges may be properly determined. In order that we may know what are the exact costs for various kinds of service it is necessary to know not only the total per capita cost per day but the per capita cost of each of many separate items per day. We must distribute most of what are commonly called "overhead" costs—that is, costs incurred for several services in common—among the various departments.

To say that we must know the costs of rooms for employees is not to recommend stinginess in provision for them; to say that we must figure the difference in cost between a seven by seven bed-room and a ten by twelve bed-room is not to recommend the seven by seven bed-room; it is only to say that we must know what we are getting for the money spent. All the costs which are indirectly incurred for any department should be ultimately carried to the accounts of that department. It will cost more to do the laundry work in an establishment paying its laundresses such high wages that they can live comfortably in rooms which they must hire in the neighborhood at normal city lodging-house prices than in an institution where the laundresses are boarded on the premises; and if the accounts in both of these cases charge to the laundry department only the actual

money-wages paid, one will show a high labor cost and the other
a cost singularly low.   Before any comparison can be made between
the two cases, therefore, the laundry accounts must be brought to a
common basis and the cost figures for laundry work must include
not only the obvious primary costs like fuel, supplies and wages,
but also a charge for laundry space, for laundresses' rooms, for food
(including cooking and serving), for the laundresses' own laundry work
(if done in the laundry), for lighting, for heating, etc.; and we must
realize that included in the cost of the rooms are necessarily not only
the care of the rooms but a share of insurance, taxes, depreciation,etc.,
on the cost of the building.   In other words, every secondary cost
involves many other secondary costs, and no comparison is possible
between two institutions until a general scheme of distributing such
secondary costs has been applied to them all.

This sounds very complicated.   As a matter of fact, however, when
a system has once been devised it is not a laborious task to make a
proper distribution of secondary costs, and no extensive bookkeeping
is involved.   When the primary accounts have been charged with the
obvious items of cost, we have merely to subdivide the total of those
which stand at the foundation of the whole institution and distribute
them among the various departments on an equitable basis.   For
illustration, insurance on buildings, taxes on buildings, depreciation
of buildings and repairs of buildings, are shared by the various departments in the ratio of the building space occupied.   Usually the square
foot of floor space is a satisfactory unit for distribution—unless,
indeed, it chances that some stories are higher than others or some
buildings are less expensive than others.   It is obvious that if the
first story has a height of twelve feet, the second ten, and the third
eight, it is hardly fair to distribute room costs on the basis of floor
space alone, for the expense of the structure lies in height quite as much
as in horizontal dimension.   Ordinarily, too, an upper floor is less
desirable than a lower.   In the matter of cleaning, window space and
wall space may be quite as important as floor space.   The actual
distribution must be determined in every case by the circumstances
of that case, and when the principle has once been recognized there is
likely to be very little serious discrepancy as between institutions.
Ordinarily, it is enough to say that if the dining room occupies one
thousand square feet and the whole establishment occupies fifty
thousand square feet, the serving department should bear one-fiftieth
of this group of expense—as well, of course, as an additional share

determined by the floor space occupied by waitresses' sleeping rooms. Lighting may well be distributed by the ratio of the number of lights in a room to the total number, although, of course, allowance must be made for rooms which are only occasionally lighted. Heating would ordinarily be distributed on the basis of cubic capacity—for the normal time a room is heated.

The most complicated figure to get is likely to be that for food costs, —at least in an institution supplying several kinds of diet. In a hospital, for instance, there is likely to be a table for house officers, which may or may not be the same as that served ordinarily to patients in private rooms; next in order is likely to come the regular house diet for patients in wards and for nurses; next comes the coarser diet for non-professional employees; and last, the fever or liquid diet. Many institutional managers will say that the attempt to learn just how much food goes to each of these groups of diet is more expensive than the value of the information will warrant. I believe they speak without adequate knowledge, for much of the needed information is— or should be—at hand.

In any accounting worthy of the name careful store records are kept. Everything going into the storeroom is debited, and everything going out is credited. Many things go out of the storeroom for use in all four of the classes of diet mentioned, and many others go out for the use of only one of them; but it is always someone's business to know the destination of everything issued. Three kinds of records of stores going into the kitchen will usually give all necessary information with a minimum of labor. The first of these should show for each meal the foods peculiar to one diet—such, for instance, as high-cost fruits or meats for private patients. The second sort of record should show for each meal the foods common to several diets but peculiar to that meal, such as vegetables and desserts. The third sort of record should show for long periods—e.g., monthly—the consumption of common foods general for all diets. A small amount of additional labor will give the exact cost of food material for each diet.

Lists of the first sort, that is, for foods peculiar to certain diets, must, of course, be made out and figured for each meal; but as a matter of fact the housekeeper must regularly provide such a list as a guide in the preparation of the food, and the only additional labor necessary for learning costs is that of entering the amount consumed, the price, and the product. The calculation may of course be made in the office at convenient intervals.

Exactly the same thing is true of the second sort of lists. The total cost divided by the number of persons served gives the cost per person for each thing served. Food listed on the third sort of record, such as flour, sugar, butter, milk, etc., ordinarily needs to be registered only monthly, for these things are presumably consumed in something approximating a steady proportion for all kinds of diet. It may be known, for instance, that persons on fever diet consume only one-eighth as much flour and sugar as those on house diet. If that is the case, the number of fever-patient meals should be divided by eight before determining the ratio. If account of stock is taken monthly, the figure of cost for foods of this sort may be determined by dividing the cost of the total consumption for the month by the number of meals served, and charging each department on the basis of its own number of meals.

At the end of the month we have in these records the total cost for food for each class of diet, as follows; list 1, total cost of special foods; list 2, total cost of foods common to several diets but not common to all meals; list 3, total cost of foods common to all diets and all meals. The total of each list divided by the number of meals served on that list gives the average cost per meal for that list. For each class of diet, the sum of the averages of those lists which served that diet is the total average food cost per meal.

If to this food cost we add the kitchen cost—which is the sum of the space-cost of the kitchen, cooks' wages, fuel cost, rooms and board of cooks, etc.,—the serving cost, the housekeeping cost, the laundry cost, room cost, etc., we have the total cost per resident day. This is obviously our final figure, the ultimate thing sought,—for all the departments are subservient to the residents. As we go along, however, we determine for each department its own cost, in order that we may know whether it is most economically managed.

Under the method of primary and secondary accounts outlined above any number of subdivisions may be made, and even with uniform accounting an institution desiring to trace any detailed costs may make as many as it likes without destroying the uniformity, if only its subdivisions are based on the uniform plan—that is, are capable of combination to produce a total identical in significance with that of the institutions which have not made subdivisions. The minute subdivisions would ordinarily be kept for purposes of comparison one year with another within the institution, whereas the figures for groups as a whole would ordinarily be kept for comparison with those for other institutions. It is not ordinarily possible to compare detailed figures with those for other institutions, for conditions are widely different. Total laundry costs per resident day, for instance, may well be compared between institutions, but the cost of fuel should be used for comparison mainly within the institution itself; for one laundry may use coal, another wood, another gas, another oil, another electricity, and another steam.

Accounting is something more, however, than determining mere financial facts. Statistics are of great importance in making it possible to learn why differences in costs persist. With regard to food, for instance, it is true that institutions in some places are able to buy meats much more cheaply than others, but suffer a considerable loss in comparison with others in the purchase of groceries. Differences are very great with regard to dairy products. If, then, we are going to compare food costs and get results worth anything, we must know something of the conditions under which each institution operates. We need to know not only what prices it is forced to pay, but also what is the prevailing tendency in that institution with regard to the kind of diet furnished. For this purpose it is well to keep statistical figures for the average price of several groups of food, such, for instance, as beef, mutton, lamb, fowl, butter, milk, eggs, etc. To these may well be added the average price per pound for certain staple articles like flour, sugar, tea, coffee. Lastly, in order that the records may show the relative importance of various classes of food in the total cost of diet, the total expenditure in each of these groups should be reported. These groups may well run as follows: meat, poultry, fish, groceries, fresh vegetables, canned vegetables, fresh fruits, dried fruits, canned fruits, butter, milk, cream, eggs. Such figures would show surprising differences between different institutions. If any establishment shows a conspicuously low purchasing power of money, that fact should stand out so clearly that the reason is sure to be investigated.

Innumerable other statistics not burdensome to compile are valuable as guides in determining comparative costs. For illustration, the number of pieces of laundry work, distinguishing the character—as by separate count for sheets, towels, pillow cases, etc.—is important if per capita costs are to be compared. The area of garden plots, of lawn to be mowed, and of walks to be kept free of snow, are convenient figures. The area of floors swept weekly per capita gives a hint as to the comparative cost of housekeeping labor. Many of these figures, such as areas and ratios of area, are practically unchanging, and calculations once made are good for months or years. When ratios need to be applied to changing monthly totals, calculating devices like the slide-rule and adding machines may be utilized so as almost to eliminate clerical cost.

In closing, let me reiterate the need of uniformity. No man ever progressed far if he relied wholly on what he learned by his own experience. It is absurd to spend time and money learning for yourself what your neighbors learned years ago,—or even what they are now learning. If they are conducting experiments in some lines, you can most profitably conduct experiments in another. Then compare notes and teach one another what each has learned. Only through uniformity, however, can you ever compare notes and profit by one another's experiments.

BUSINESS IDEALS

A[rthur] Lowes Dickinson

INTRODUCTION

BUSINESS IDEALS
By A. Lowes Dickinson

In a country of great wealth and wonderful possibilities for the material well-being of a much larger population than it even now contains, it is a matter for regret that the scramble for wealth has produced a competition quite as fierce and even more relentless than in the thickly populated countries of the Old World where opportunities for the advancement of individuals are far more limited. It would seem that this condition must be attributed largely to the example of the early pioneers in the development of the country, who, while not altogether selfish in their aims, undoubtedly in many cases put their own gain first and the good of the country a somewhat poor second. There is no need now to analyze or discuss the methods by which these men, while admittedly conferring benefits upon their country, were also enabled to acquire enormous personal fortunes, for these methods are now well known and understood, and few could be found to excuse them. They resulted in the adoption of similar and even worse methods by other so-called financiers who accumulated great wealth by questionable methods, without any shadow of excuse or pretense of conferring any benefit upon their country.

This old, and happily obsolete, condition is only now recalled because of the influence which it has had upon the business ideals of a large majority of the community, who have so far imitated the spirit of a former generation as to setting up as the main object of business the acqui-

9

sition of wealth; and while this is coupled with a certain standard of honesty probably far greater than that of the old pioneers, it is only maintained as long and as far as it does not interfere with the main object of acquisition. There is much truth even now in the old quoted saying of a father, "Make money, my son, honestly if you can, but make it," and the prevalence of this principle thus baldly expressed justifies some examination of its results and some consideration of the methods by which it may be combated and gradually replaced by a higher standard, based upon striving all the time toward an ideal conception of what business should be.

Before setting forth any such ideal it will be well to consider the now-existing defects in business ideals which should be condemned by all thinking men. These may well be divided in accordance with their relation to three main subjects, viz:—

THE NATURE OF THE BUSINESS;
THE CONDUCT OF THE PROPRIETOR;
THE CONDUCT OF THE EMPLOYEES;

and these will be considered each in their turn.

Every one is aware that there are classes of business which make no pretense of conforming to any standards of morality and decency, and which have rightly for that reason been forbidden by law; but the fact that many such flourish openly in spite of, and even with the connivance of, the officers of the law shows only too clearly that with a considerable class mere gain without any regard to, and even in open defiance of, the common good is still the ruling motive. At the other end of the scale there are classes of business which are initiated and carried on with the highest regard for the public good and with little or no hope of gain. Their number is regrettably small in proportion to the total, but their existence even in such small numbers is a great force for good, and it may confidently be hoped that their leaven will gradually sink deeper and deeper into the mass, carrying with it an increasingly wholesome influence.

Between these two extremes comes the great mass of the business of the country, shading downward in its ideals to a minimum at some point far too near the lowest level and then again diminishing to that level. The human animal is at bottom a creature of his desires tempered only by generations of effort toward improvement on the part of its moral leaders; and both past history and present conditions show that it is easier on the whole to succeed in an appeal to man's lowest instincts than to the high moral conscience, which, whether developed or undeveloped, germinates in the secret recesses of even the worst specimens. A few instances only, taken from the immediate present, are sufficient to justify this conclusion. The great success gained in recent years by cheap magazines of little or no merit either literary, artistic or educational; the fortunes made by newspaper owners of the class recently so well condemned by a high public official; the mass of new novels put forth by publishing houses, the majority of which are hardly worthy of the meanest intelligence, even if they do not appeal to lower tastes; the poor class of entertainments provided in the majority of the theaters drawing full houses to laugh at their feeble foolery or their risque jokes, while the few providing decent, well-written, and well-acted plays of artistic or educational value frequently perform to half empty houses; the crowds that will flock to a motor race, an aviation meet, or a prize-fight; all these and many more instances that might be given go to show that immense gains can still be made out of those classes of business that pander to the lowest nature of man. Such must and will undoubtedly continue to exist in some form as long as the human race continues, in spite of the efforts toward improvement of the best natures in every generation, and the fair measure of success undoubtedly attained in the forward march.

Whatever the nature of a business, its proprietors incur heavy responsibilities to the community, whether they be actual owners of a purely private concern or stockholders in a corporation. The responsibilities of a stockholder are necessarily more limited as he has no direct voice in the management; but he can at least decline to hold stock in a concern carrying on a business either in itself or by reason of its methods of operation detrimental to moral progress. A believer in strict temperance or prohibition can hardly, with justice to his convictions, hold stock in a brewery or a whisky distillery; a member of a universal peace society should not be a stockholder in a corporation making munitions of war; and, more generally, a man who holds strong views on corruption should decline to remain a stockholder and wink at such corruption where it is known to exist in a corporation in which he is interested. The immediate responsibilities of the owner of a private business are much greater, inasmuch as he determines on the kind of business; directs its policy; and takes the profits of its operations. If the nature of the business is detrimental to the highest interests of the community, he alone can change it; if it is carried on by dishonest methods such as exaggerating the quality of its products, charging exorbitant prices, delivering short value, making promises which can not be performed, or paying secret commissions to induce sales, he alone is responsible to the community and has the power of improvement or remedy.

Salaried employees, in addition to taking their share in the responsibilities of the owner, have the added duty of being faithful to him. Acceptance of secret commissions or secret profits; the use of their positions to further their own rather than their employer's interests; waste or improper employment of the time for which their employer pays; these are only a few of the evils which are prevalent; and from time to time the public are startled into momentary indignation by the few cases in which the offenders, often men in receipt of such large salaries as should put them beyond temptation, are brought to book and figure in the lime-light of the courts of justice. This neglect of the interests of employers extends even to that class of experienced and successful men of affairs who guide the destinies of corporations as

Directors. In such positions they are morally if not legally trustees for the stockholders, by whom they are nominally elected and by whom they are remunerated for their services. Too often this moral obligation is ignored and they use their positions for their own immediate or prospective benefit, justification for such action being often attempted by the claim that they are large stockholders themselves. The principle involved in this attitude is perhaps best expressed in the reputed words of a great financier now dead, who, on joining the board of a certain large corporation, stated that he did so "to look after my interests," those of the stockholders as a whole being completely ignored. The more gross evils resulting from such a claim are found in the use of early information acquired in their positions of trust to buy or sell stock for their own advantage; in the dissemination of false information with the object of benefiting themselves by influencing the stock market, or inducing minority stockholders to sacrifice their holdings; and in molding the policies of one company so as to benefit some other in which they have a larger or more valuable interest.

It would not be fair or just to call attention to the worst evils affecting the business community, without at the same time testifying to the improvement that has taken place during the last decade. The conscience of the country appears at last to have awakened from its long sleep, aroused by the efforts of an able and honest body of men who both in politics and business have given their time and their money to fight for high ideals. The fight has been carried on under difficulties and subject to abuse from many of those whose base money interests have been or may be prejudicially affected; but it has had the assistance of some of the ablest business men, who know from experience as well as conviction that in the long run honesty is the best policy; and that a clean business under clean management will eventually attain the greatest measure of success. The way is long and the fight is hard, but, while a vast amount still remains to be done, real progress has been made.

If some stress has here been laid upon the evils of the

present condition, it has been only to pave the way for
the consideration of a business ideal which, while it can
never be attained in the abstract, may yet serve as a light
to illumine the path of the younger generation and to
point out to them the true road of improvement.

On the moral side it may be stated, without much fear
of contradiction, that the first essential of an ideal business should be, not its money-making capacity, but its
usefulness to the community in the highest sense of the
word. It should be a business which is necessary for
the upward development of the human race; not pander-
ing to the lower tastes of the uneducated masses, but
striving always to give something better and more
elevating, whether it be manufacture, transportation,
art, or amusement. A fair return on the investment is
the secondary but almost equally necessary element, as
this alone will determine the equality of supply and demand. If all business which pandered to or created the
lowest demands of the community were abandoned, a
demand would arise for the next highest to fill the gap
and so continued progress would be possible.

Such a business should be carried on fairly and
honestly; the profits should be equitably and reasonably
commensurate to the capital employed and the risk involved; and should be combined with the best possible
service to the community. Deceitful descriptions: misleading advertisements; shoddy workmanship; secret
commissions; unfair competition and indiscriminate price
cutting to a level below that which would give a fair
remuneration should be unknown. All such methods
are now designed and used merely to get the better of
some one else, while in an ideal condition competition
should be confined solely to the effort to give the best
service to the community at a fair and reasonable
price.

Employees should be well treated and liberally remunerated. Profits should be fairly divided between
capital and labor with due regard to the necessity of a
minimum living wage and to the consequent greater security in the remuneration of labor. As between different

classes of labor a more equitable distribution of profits would result from an increase in the supply of the higher classes, due to the greater efforts for improvement which would be made by the lower classes under an ideal system. The present disproportion between the wages paid for organizing and administrative ability and for other kinds of clerical and manual labor would also be similarly remedied.

Such an ideal is obviously entirely inconsistent with actual conditions, and probably always will be; but as long as progress continues it should be in this direction; and there are, day by day, in every business, opportunities of making some small step in advance, if a real honest intention to strive for an ideal exists.

Concurrently with the moral progress thus outlined, comes the necessity for material progress in order to produce the best results and to show those results in such form as will disclose the inmost secrets of the business to those interested and to the community. For there can be little doubt that the best remedy for abuses is the fullest publicity which will rouse some small grains of moral sense from the depths of the soul of the most callous and hardened offender. Thackeray has well said that it is not his wrongful act that offends a man, but the discovery of that fact; and if no concealment were possible little or no evil could exist.

On the material side, then, there comes first organization; a leader honest and enthusiastic, of great ability and thoroughly familiar with every detail of his business; holding as his guide in all his actions all the best that is known; supported by carefully selected heads of department of equal ability although necessarily of less experience than himself, but animated by all his ideals and determined to follow out his policies honestly and loyally and with a sole idea to the good of the business, and no side glance toward the attainment of private ends. Specializing should be avoided as far as possible, each man looking forward to the time when he may be called upon to fill the highest post, and endeavoring to fit himself for that position by mastering the details of

each department as he passes through it. Even in the
lowest ranks no one should be content to become a mere
machine, but should strive as long as life and health
remain to fit himself always for a higher position; and
all should be assured that if, without fault of their own
and in spite of their earnest endeavors, they fall out by
the way the business will take care of them and assist
their savings with a fair scheme of profit-sharing and a
contributory pension scheme insuring all a comfortable
old age, so that each as he draws to the close of a useful
and honorable life may feel that "From labor there shall
come forth rest."

Equally important with the actual organization and
operation of a business are the methods by which the
results of such operations are recorded and made available in a form easily understood; and ideals are here also
desirable, particularly in view of the lamentable failures
that occur every day. To enable the managers to confine
charges to a reasonable profit they must first know the
costs of production and these costs must be based upon
correct theoretical principles. The absence in the majority
of cases of any sound and proper system of costs is undoubtedly the main cause of the senseless competition
that has existed and still exists, and which has conduced
so much to the formation of the so-called trusts and
pools, both legal and illegal. Ideals in business can never
be attained until accurate costs are known in every business, for only then is it possible to determine what is a
reasonable and fair profit. While therefore there are
many other dangerous pitfalls to avoid and passes to
cross on the road to the ideal beacon, this one of absence
of costs is by no means the least dangerous or the least
important.

A proper analytical summary of all business receipts
and expenses honestly and carefully prepared is another
necessary element. Such a statement available for all
interested and made public would have entirely prevented
even the barefaced cases of graft, whether "honest" or
dishonest, which have recently been exposed; for such
graft lives in secret places and is impossible in the full

light of day; even the worst offender is afraid to be found out.

And lastly come the statements of results submitted to proprietors or stockholders fully available to the community in all their detail; by which the final seal is put upon the usefulness of the business, the honesty and justice of its operations, the reasonableness of its profits and the fairness of their distribution. Where all are animated by the ideals set forth, all are giving equal publicity, all are in fact carrying on the ideal business, no one can suffer by such publicity, and the community is immensely the gainer.

An ideal in business can not be attained without an ideal preparation for those who carry it on. In spite of the strides made in recent years, the average level of ability and education remains regrettably low. In the last decade business has rapidly expanded and the population has grown correspondingly, but everywhere is the same increasing demand for competent men to fill not merely the highest, but the intermediate and lower positions.

It would seem that, however far below the ideal business may be, the method of preparing those who are to carry it on is even lower. This seems due partly to the want of proper education and partly to the absence of any ideal on the part of the masses beyond that of earning their living, which again is due to the neglect to educate them to the necessity of such an ideal. Improvements in education have probably at least kept pace with the moral if not with the material progress of the country, but there are still far too large numbers of the younger generation who have little or no knowledge of anything that will help them on in life and still less desire to work hard and get on. The existence of so many kinds of business which, breaking the first canon of the ideal here set forth, pander to the lowest desires of the people is undoubtedly largely responsible for this condition. An even greater cause experience shows to be defects in education which, while giving an elementary knowledge of certain very necessary matters, does not teach the pupils how to learn for themselves, nor does it set before them any clear idea that they have duties to perform towards the community, even if it be only to remedy the defects which have led to their present environment. They should have an ideal set before them of honesty and industry; of ambition and perseverance, never content to merely do the minimum that is set before them, but always to do better than their predecessors; to keep progress in knowledge, in morals, in industry, ever before them; and so to render themselves ever more and more fit to mount along the rough and dangerous road that leads to the ideal.

Starting out from school with such principles engrained, they would be ready for the more practical training which is equally necessary, and for which the facilities are still far short of what the demand should be. Twenty years ago, hardly any business training was available except that afforded by entering some office at an early age and making a gradual progress upward from the lowest grade. In the present day, books have been written and classes are held on the theories of every kind of business, and while much remains to be done to make those books and classes available for the masses of the people, many more might avail themselves of the facilities that exist if they knew of their existence and cared to do so.

A thoroughly practical and theoretical training in business principles and methods is essential for any business or any profession. The younger the age at which this general knowledge is acquired, the sooner is it possible to determine on the special line to be followed, and to begin a complete practical study of that line from the bottom upward. This should be a life's work; for in an ideal condition there will be no royal road to success. Influence will no longer assist and the only road will be hard work combined with ability, integrity, perseverance, and a determination to succeed in spite of all difficulties. The road is long even in the ideal condition, but surely it is better to attempt it and fall by the way than to settle down to a humdrum life in an inferior position, contented to get through the minimum amount of work in the stipulated time, draw a minimum salary, and perhaps spend it in a maximum of frivolities which, as they can not really benefit, only lead to deterioration.

And yet this is the life led by large numbers in receipt of small or moderate or even large salaries who might, while they have youth and health, be devoting all their time and energy to qualifying themselves to fill some of the many better positions, where the demand exceeds the supply.

At the other end of the scale are the men of great wealth, inherited or acquired, who have had opportunities in education and training denied to the masses; and who yet in far too many cases waste time and money on even more useless frivolities and extravagances, and neglect the golden opportunities they have inherited of devoting their ability, time, and money to advancing along the road to the ideal the many to whom such advantages have been denied.

The hope for the future lies in the gradual disappearance of the drones at both ends of the scale, whether they are so from misfortune or choice; urged by the new cry for honest and intelligent progress, let them take their places in the ranks and move forward along the upward path, helping each other toward the ideal always in sight before them.

TREATMENT OF MAINTENANCE AND DEPRECIATION ACCOUNTS IN THE NEW CLASSIFICATION OF ACCOUNTS BY INTERSTATE COMMERCE COMMISSION

[Arthur Lowes Dickinson]

I.

SOME CONSIDERATIONS AFFECTING RAILROAD MAINTENANCE ACCOUNTS.

(A communication submitted to Professor H. C. Adams March 8, 1907.)

A study of the Annual Reports of the leading Railroads for a number of years past affords evidence of some recognition of the inadequacy of the standard methods of treating Maintenance Accounts and of wide divergencies of practice in regard thereto, as well as in the provision of funds for improvements and betterments which, while to a certain extent of a Capital nature, result in little if any increase in earning capacity.

These expenses and provisions are among the most important items in Railroad Accounts for the reason that, on the one hand, such expenditures may easily be deferred according to the policy or discretion of the Directors and Officials without the evil effect of such a course becoming apparent for a number of years ; or that, on the other hand, excessive charges to Operating can be made ; both methods creating erroneous impressions as to the true earning capacity of a property.

From the earliest days the treatment by Railroad Companies of Renewals, Replacements and Depreciation has differed from the general practice among commercial concerns. In the latter it is customary to make annual reserves for the purpose of providing for Renewals, the necessity for which is accruing from day to day while the actual expenditures may be deferred for many years ; but in the case of Railways the theory has been that the Capital and Revenue Accounts were distinct, and that the only charges to be made to the latter should be for the cost of replacing property as and when Replacements were made. This difference in treatment was fostered in England by Legislative Enactments in regard to Railroads; but from an accounting standpoint it has never been regarded as resting on very solid ground, and from a financial standpoint its results have not, we think, proved satisfactory. Up to the date of the financial panic in 1893, however, the method was closely followed by a great number, if not the majority, of American Railroads.

Under this system there were charged to Capital various items which, though technically improvements, did not add to earnings or reduce expenses, a typical example being the excess weight of rails where, as was usually the case, the requirements of traffic made it necessary to replace the rail in the track with considerably heavier metal. After the reorganizations which took place between 1893 and 1899, it was generally recognized that, whilst possibly legitimate, it was unwise to capitalize such expenditures, and the practice has now been generally discontinued with excellent results to the various properties.

RENEWAL OF EQUIPMENT. The practice of providing for Renewals as and when outlays were made was first modified by the establishment of the Equipment Renewal Fund System, under which there is charged to Operating Expense and credited to a Renewal Fund the cost of replacing locomotives or cars destroyed, immediately they are reported as having gone out of service and not as and when they are replaced.

The theoretically correct amount for such provisions is the cost at the date of destruction of replacing the equipment destroyed with equipment of similar character and capacity, but in practice the methods adopted vary widely in different Companies, some roads adopting as a basis the original cost of the equipment, others the present cost of equipment of the same class but of the present standard, while some reorganized Companies have adopted as a basis the depreciated value of the equipment at the date of the reorganization. The charges to Operating resulting from these different methods are, of course, widely different; thus, where a box car of, say, 30,000 pounds capacity is replaced by a car of 80,000 pounds capacity, the charge to Operating might well vary from $400 to $900. Indeed in certain cases, owing to very low valuations being adopted at the date of the reorganization and to subsequent increase in the value of the scrap, the salvage from cars destroyed has frequently exceeded the reorganization value, and consequently no charge whatever has been made to Operating when the equipment has gone out of service.

Some Roads, while adhering to rules involving small direct charges to Operating for cars destroyed, have recognized in this, as in other instances, the inadequacy from a sound financial standpoint of methods of treating Maintenance Charges which may be techically correct, and have made supplementary provisions for Renewals or Depreciation of Equipment. These provisions have been made in various ways, as, for instance :

1. By direct charges to Operating, either
    Included in general charges for Renewals of Equipment, or
    Stated separately as " Depreciation of Equipment " or " Fund for Acquiring Additional Equipment."

2. By charges against Income, either
    As Depreciation of Equipment,
    As Betterments and Improvements to Equipment, or
    As Payments on Account of Car Trust Obligations.

3. By charge to Profit and Loss.

As a result of all these variations intelligible comparisons of published figures of Renewals are practically impossible.

RENEWALS OF BRIDGES AND STRUCTURES. The original practice of charging to Capital Account improvements to bridges and structures has, as a rule, been adhered to without any change under the new conditions now existing. There have, however, always been, and still are, important variations in practice which render comparisons between different Roads more or less misleading; some basing their charge to Operating Accounts upon the original cost, while others base it on the cost of Replacement at the time of reconstruction. Bridge and Structure Renewal Funds are seldom met with, and, as a general rule, no provision is made for wear and tear or approaching obsolescence until the necessity for reconstruction or renewal has become urgent, either by increase of traffic or decay of the structure.

RECONSTRUCTION OF ROADBED, CUT-OFFS, ETC. The practice of a few of the most conservative Roads is to charge to Operating Accounts an estimated sum to represent the value of the abandoned portion, including both track, roadbed and earthworks, the whole balance of the cost of reconstruction being treated as Capital or Improvement Expenditure. This cost, however, may be either estimated original cost or estimated cost to replace at the present day. In other cases either no provision whatever is made out of operating for the value of the abandoned portion, the whole new cost being charged to Improvements, or provision is made out of operating for the original cost of rails, ties, track fastenings, bridge material, etc., removed, but not for that of embankments, cuttings or roadbeds.

RENEWALS OF RAILS AND TIES. The treatment of these renewals differs from that accorded to either of the foregoing. In order to distribute expenditures evenly over the different months of the fiscal year, it has become the practice to set aside a fixed sum each month sufficient to aggregate the estimated expenditure for the fiscal year. It has frequently happened for one reason or another that the actual expenditures have fallen short of the provision so made, with the result that a balance has remained unexpended. In the few cases in which a greater sum has been expended the balance has usually been written off, but in the contrary case it has frequently been carried forward and has resulted in the accumulation of large balances to the credit of the Renewal Funds. The charges to Operating have in the first instance usually been based on the estimated amount of rail which the Management have thought it well to relay, and not always, or even frequently, upon any definite proportion of the total rail operated ; with the result that the funds provided are quite arbitrary in amount. It is also a usual practice among the leading Railroads to provide for the whole cost of increased weight of rails laid out of charges to Operating Accounts or to the Rail Renewal Funds, although in some cases the excess weight over that replaced has been charged to Income Account as improvements instead of to Operating.

INCONSISTENCY OF ABOVE METHODS.   From the above general relation of observed facts it will appear that the distinguishing characteristic of the present situation is the absence of consistency and uniformity, both as between Roads and as between the treatment of different Assets by the same Roads. It is not at all unusual to find the same Company treating similar items in different ways, as, for instance, providing for renewals of—

Equipment on the basis of the present cost of equipment of the same class and capacity.

Rails on the basis of the present cost of rails of greatly increased weight and capacity.

Bridges and structures on the basis of the original cost of the structure destroyed.

8

It is obviously to be regretted that such different methods should be used to achieve the same result, and that comparisons between Roads should thereby be rendered so much the more difficult and unsatisfactory, and it is worth considering whether some better methods cannot be adopted.

The possible remedies seem to resolve themselves into the following :

SUGGESTIONS FOR IMPROVED METHODS.

(1) To abandon altogether the present methods and to adopt instead those employed to-day by the most progressive industrial Companies, which those who are familiar with the accounts of both must recognize are superior in the information they afford, alike to the Executive, the Directors and the Stockholders, to the best Railroad Accounts.

These methods are to charge to Operating Costs the actual expenditure upon ordinary repairs and maintenance, and to supplement these charges by a more or less arbitrary provision, based, however, on the estimated life of the different classes of wasting property, allowing for obsolescence as well as wear and tear, and calculated to provide the total original cost over the term of that life. All expenditures tending to increase that life, such as replacement or reconstruction of bridges, structures, rails and equipment, are charged not to Operating Accounts but to the Renewal Funds so created. In addition, funds are created by charges to Income Account to provide for improvements which may be necessary from time to time, but which, either by reason of their not creating additional earning capacity, or by reason of their resulting only in a reduction of Operating Expenses over the term of their life, cannot conservatively be considered as permanent additions to property.

The distinction between the two classes of funds is that the former, or Depreciation Fund, is a necessary Operating charge to be provided year in and year out as a matter of necessity to take care of wear and tear, which is continuously taking place, while the latter is in the nature of a voluntary provision which can be increased in times of prosperity and reduced or even temporarily abandoned when the Surplus Income is insufficient.

There should be no greater difficulty in estimating the probable average lives of railroad properties than those of industrial properties where conditions vary at least as greatly, and such a method as that suggested, if supplemented in the Annual Reports as it should be by full particulars of the basis of determination of the various reserves, would at any rate show clearly and with approximate accuracy the actual position of any road, and enable Stockholders and the Public to judge both of the efficiency of the operating organization and of the manner in which the property had been maintained and improved.

(2) To revert to the theoretically correct basis of the standard method and charge to Operating in every case the estimated present cost of replacing the abandoned property, and to supplement this provision by charging to Income Account the whole, or such proportion as may be thought fit by the Management, of the excess cost over and above the actual cost of replacement.

The effect of this treatment would be to show over a series of years the true Operating Expenses and the true amount provided for future renewals or improvements, but it does not meet the objection already urged against the present system, that if a fair proportion of the property subject to renewal is not being renewed, no provision is being made out of Operating for accruing renewals which are each year becoming more necessary and, when they are at last unavoidable, frequently cannot be met out of the Earnings of the Road.

(3) To provide such definitions of terms and such classifications of expenditures as will result in a clear and intelligible statement of the actual outlays and provisions for future outlays.

It appears probable that absolute uniformity of policy and practice is unattainable, and in the opinion of many even undesirable, as tending, by avoiding competition in such directions, to defer the necessary provision for improvements, and to dictate a definite policy for all roads which is suitable only to the poorest and least conservative.

It is generally recognized that there are at least four general subdivisions of the property expenditures of a railroad, namely—Repairs, Renewals, Improvements and Additions. It is also fairly generally, though not universally, recognized that between renewals and improvements there is a class of expenditures which, while not strictly renewals, and possibly in some cases from a technical point of view justifiably chargeable to Capital, cannot safely be so treated. These comprise such items as excess cost of new rails on account of increased weight, minor improvements to the track, and generally such improvements as do not add to the earning capacity of the road, but either are made to relieve future operating expenses or are forced on the road by the demands of progress. For this class of expenditures, intermediate between renewals and improvements, the term "Betterments," already employed in railroad practice, might well be adopted.

Railroads should be required to group their expenditures upon property under these five fundamental captions, distinguishing between each upon definite principles to be prescribed in the Interstate Commerce Commission Classification, each caption containing sub-headings for every kind of expense which experience has proved to be necessary.

The Revenue Accounts should be divided into three sections, as is in fact usually done at present ; the first, known as

"Operating Account," containing gross earnings and the cost of obtaining them and so showing the income from operations; the second, known as "Income Account," showing the income from operations and all other sources and how that income has been expended or appropriated, and so showing the net income for the year available for distribution and the dividends paid thereout; and the third, known as "Profit and Loss Account," which contains the balance from the preceding year and the net surplus for the year, any special appropriations made out of this total, and the balance carried forward to the succeeding year.

"Repairs" and "Renewals" are clearly always properly chargeable against OPERATING, and if provisions are made for future expenses of similar character these also should be charged to OPERATING under the caption of "Repair" or "Renewal" Funds.

Improvements are legitimately chargeable to Capital, but in practice it is frequently deemed desirable to provide for them out of the Income for the year. In such cases, whether actually expended or merely represented by appropriations for future expenditures, the amount should be charged to Income Account.

Additions, including therein the term "Extensions," are clearly a charge to Capital, but if, as is sometimes the case, it is not desired to follow this course, the amount should be charged to Profit and Loss Account as an appropriation of Surplus.

The suggested term "Betterments" covers charges which cannot properly be included as repairs or renewals and yet are recognized in the best railroad accounting practice as being essentially operating charges. It would seem best to follow this practice and charge all items under this caption to Operating, rather than to adopt a less conservative course and allow them to be absorbed in the general classification of "Improvements."

Whether the term " Betterments " is the best that can be adopted as a description of such expenditures is a matter for discussion, but the term is already in general use without any very clear definition, and it is suggested that it might well be retained for this special purpose and applied to such expenditures as are needed to keep the property up to a certain required but progressively higher standard, irrespective of increased traffic ; while Improvements should consist only of expenditures necessitated entirely by the growth of traffic o'r incurred to provide for its increase.

Finally, it would be necessary to require that any expenditures made out of funds provided to take care of future expenditures under any of the fundamental captions, should be confined to the same classification and clearly detailed in the annual report.

If the above suggestions were adopted and made compulsory on all railroads, it would at any rate be possible in future to ascertain the facts as to all these expenditures, and so to form a critical and correct opinion as to the effects of whatever policy may have been adopted.

The three alternative methods here outlined are offered as suggestions worthy of careful consideration and in the belief that there is urgent need of a change in present accounting practices, if the accounts of railroads are to give the necessary information to enable their Stockholders and the public to appreciate their condition as regards the up-keep of their property and the effect upon this condition of any policy that may be adopted.

II.

DEPRECIATION AND RENEWALS OF EQUIPMENT.

(A communication submitted to Professor H. C. Adams, April 30, 1908).

We would like to place before you some considerations in regard to the much discussed question of Depreciation, which in the present classification of Railroad Operating Expenses is not, in our opinion, treated correctly, having regard to the conditions that actually prevail.

As Public Accountants the whole question of Depreciation, from both the practical and theoretical points of view, and in its bearing on all forms of undertakings, has been brought constantly before us, and received a great deal of attention at our hands for many years ; and we trust, therefore, you will not feel that we are trespassing unduly on your patience if we offer in some detail our reasons for the views which we hold.

We would now state briefly what we consider to be the defects of the present classification.

DEFECTS IN CLASSIFICATION. (1) The object of a Depreciation scheme is, we take it, to make provision for the decrease in value from year to year by reason of wear and tear, etc., as it accrues instead of as it is made good, the latter being the practice under the old classification. It seems to us that to such a proposition there is an obvious corollary that renewal expenditures made to arrest Depreciation should be charged against a Fund created in the years when the Depreciation accrues, and not against the Operating Expenses of the year in which the expenditures are made. The new classification requires, on the contrary, that all renewals shall be charged to Operating Expenses.

(2) Any plan for Depreciation of a number of units is necessarily based on the principle of averages, and assumes an average life which some units will not attain but others will exceed, and, consequently, the difference between the depreciated value of a particular unit going out of service and the scrap value should be charged, not to Operating Expenses, but, at least as regards equipment voluntarily abandoned, to the Depreciation Fund provided for this specific purpose.

Before giving our reasons for these views we would say that we realize that the subject is full of difficulty, and that objections can be urged against any plan proposed. We think, however, that the defects above noted can readily be eliminated, and that unless eliminated they will go far to neutralize the advantages of the whole Depreciation plan.

THEORY OF DEPRECIATION. It is essential to a proper consideration of the subject to have a clear realization of the physical side of the question. A further essential is to arrive at a clear meaning of the term "estimated life." One conception of this term assumes that all repairs, renewals and rebuildings will be carried out as the necessity therefor arises, and that the estimated life is simply the period which will elapse before it finally becomes necessary or desirable to abandon the property entirely. A Depreciation Fund created on the basis of distributing the original cost of the property, less the ultimate scrap value, over the term of the life so estimated, without regard to the cost of renewals and rebuildings which are essential to the realization of that life, clearly does not in the slightest degree provide for wear and tear as it accrues, but only for obsolescence. Obsolescence is obviously the one factor in depreciation any estimate of which is at best a conjecture. It is hardly too much to say, therefore, that a fund created on such a basis will be not only inadequate, but little more than a guess.

Another, and in our opinion preferable as being a more practical, conception of the term "estimated life," is that it means the average effective life of the property, which must be determined on a consideration not only of the term which will elapse before the property is abandoned as obsolete, but also of the estimated life and scrap value of the several component parts of the property and the percentages of the original cost represented by such component parts. It is undoubtedly possible to arrive at an estimated life on this basis which will be approximately correct, and when this is done a depreciation scheme which distributes the original cost over the term of such an estimated life will clearly be sufficient to provide for all renewals which restore or extend life, and will result in the distribution of both wear and tear and obsolescence substantially to the periods in which they accrue. In such a calculation the element of obsolescence is relatively a minor consideration, and any error in the rate of depreciation adopted, which may be caused by an incorrect estimate of the period which will elapse before the property is finally abandoned, will be very small as compared with the error which would result from a similar cause in a calculation made on the basis indicated in the preceding paragraph.

It is a very common error to consider Depreciation on the theory that the property, beginning with a maximum value when new, steadily diminishes in value until at the end of its useful life it has only a scrap value, but this theory is, in practice, seldom if ever found to be in accordance with the facts. On the contrary, the changes in the value of a property will usually be found to be represented graphically, not by a steadily falling line, but by one which rises and falls at different points before it reaches that from which it finally declines to scrap value, the rises being, of course, due to expenditures for rebuilding or renewal.

Commencing with a new property, or a new series of units of equipment, for some years, whilst wear and tear will be taking place, it will not be practicable or economical to make good this wear and tear, consequently the renewals will be light while the value of the property will steadily diminish until a point is reached where any further deterioration would mean a loss of efficiency. At this point renewals will begin, and every such renewal will tend to restore or extend the original life of the unit to which it is applied. The point at which such renewals become necessary will vary with each unit, even of the same kind, but taking all kinds of units and averaging the usual conditions of a whole group, it will probably be found to be from 60 per cent. to 75 per cent. of original cost. Beyond this point the group cannot further depreciate if it is properly maintained ; and hence in practice, while single units may and frequently do run down to a point much below this average without becoming absolutely inefficient, a complete property, if properly maintained, arrives at a more or less stationary value, and never reaches the theoretical scrap value. At this point proper maintenance will call for expenditures for renewals and replacements which will approximately equal the Depreciation Charge; Renewals and Replacements, due either to wear and tear or to obsolescence, all the time tending to postpone the date when final replacement takes place.

SUGGESTED BASIS FOR DEPRECIATION FUND.

It seems to us that under these circumstances the best method of caring for Depreciation is to establish, by annual charges to Operating, a Fund which will provide over the whole useful life of the property for the original cost thereof, plus the expenditures for rebuilding, either in whole or in part, and minus the scrap value. The other extreme is the practice which has prevailed in the past of charging renewals to the years in which they are made, and of writing off the original value of the property, less the scrap value, when it finally goes out of service. Under the new classification, seeing that Renewals which arrest Depreciation and tend to lengthen the life of the property, are required to be charged to maintenance, it is clear that the amount which must be provided for Depreciation is only a proportion of the original cost less the ultimate scrap value corresponding to the years of probable life, as extended by subsequent expenditures for rebuilding or renewal. It follows that in every year of the life of the equipment, except those in which substantial expenditures for renewals are made, the resultant charge against maintenance will be less than the proper amount, and that, at least up to the date of the first extensive renewals, the credits in the Depreciation Fund will always be less than the Depreciation actually accrued.

The only objections we can perceive to the course which we have suggested, are, first, that the calculation of the annual charge for Depreciation is possibly somewhat more complicated than that under the rules established by the new classification; and, second, that it is difficult to distinguish between Renewals which should be charged against the Depreciation Fund and Repairs which should be charged against Operating.

COMPARISON OF DIFFICULTIES IN ESTABLISHMENT OF RATES ON THE TWO BASES.

We do not think there is much force in the first objection. There must be, in existence and available, statistics in regard to a large number of units of different classes of equipment as to the original cost, the expenditures for rebuilding, the final scrap value, and the number of years of actual life (as extended by rebuilding) of such equipment, and it should be possible to determine with approximate accuracy the annual rate of Depreciation on the basis we have advocated. It seems to us clear that in this way a rate can be ascertained which will more nearly represent the actual Depreciation on equipment during the early years of its life than one estimated on the basis of the present classification, and it may be pointed out that when the property has "aged" or reached a state of "average efficiency" it will be possible to test, and if necessary modify, the rate originally adopted. It should not be difficult to determine approximately in regard to equipment or any other class of railroad property the percentage of original cost which is represented by a state of average efficiency. If a fund is established on a proper basis for an entirely new property or group of properties, it should steadily grow until it reaches a sum representing the difference between this percentage and one hundred per cent. of the original cost. This sum will represent continuously what may be called the permanent Depreciation of the property, which in practice will never be made good. Any steady increase in the fund beyond this point must mean either that the property is not being efficiently maintained at a point at which it can be economically operated, or that the basis of Depreciation is too high. The former condition can as a rule be ascertained by a careful examination of the property by experts, and if the latter condition is found to exist a revision of rates of Depreciation should be made, based upon the experience gained in the past.

On the other hand, the rule laid down in the present classification appears to us to suffer from the very serious defect that changes in policy, or technical differences in the treatment of facts which are practically identical, may produce widely different results. Thus, after equipment has been in service for a number of years it is often open to a Company either to sell it to a road whose requirements are less exacting and to replace it with new equipment, or to rebuild it. Obviously, if in calculating depreciation the average life is based on the assumption that the first of these policies will be pursued, and subsequently the second is adopted, the rate will be found to be much too high, and *vice versa*. Again, if a car reaches a point where a substantial part of it requires to be renewed and another substantial part has still many years of useful life, the part which has the useful life will doubtless be combined with new materials to form a perfectly efficient car. If this car continues to have the same number as the old car, presumably the expenditures would be treated as rebuilding or renewals and charged to Operating Expenses. On the other hand, the car produced may be treated as a new car and the old one treated as condemned and gone out of service. The result would be practically identical, but the effect on the accounts of the Company might easily be very different. To take one more instance, supposing two cars of the same series and age to be wrecked, one of which is on the way to the shops for rebuilding and the other of which had been entirely rebuilt within one or two years. The operating charge in respect of the wrecks of the two cars would, under the existing system, be identical, though clearly the loss of value resulting therefrom would be materially different. The system which we advocate, by treating substantial renewals as restoring the value of the car, avoids the inconsistencies which would arise under the present rule in all these cases.

DISTINCTION BETWEEN RENEWALS AND REPAIRS.
With regard to the second objection to the rule we have proposed, there would doubtless be some difficulty in distinguishing between expenditures for rebuilding and renewals which should be charged against the Fund, and ordinary repairs which should be charged to Operating Expenses, but it is equally true that all classifications merge one into the other, and that there are always expenditures on the border line which it is difficult to distribute with entire accuracy. It does not seem to us that the difficulties of distinguishing between

renewals and repairs are any greater than those experienced in distinguishing between other classifications.

AVERAGE THEORY INCORRECTLY APPLIED.

The second feature of the classification to which we have referred as defective does not seem to call for much discussion. It is clear that a Depreciation Fund properly constituted is necessarily based on averages; that in assuming, say, 20 years life for a unit it is not expected that every unit will last 20 years, but that some will drop out long before that period is reached, and others will last a good deal longer, quite apart from the question of renewal expenditures already considered. Hence, any unit dropping out before the average life is reached should be charged off, not to Operating under the head of Renewals, but to the Depreciation Fund created for this express purpose; otherwise Operating will be overcharged when such cases arise, unless, of course, the provision for Depreciation is calculated on the basis, not of the average, but of the maximum life of the equipment.

ACCIDENTAL DESTRUCTION.

In any scheme of depreciation the question of accidental destruction of property as a result of wrecks, fires, etc., has to be considered. It would, of course, be possible to take into consideration the losses from such causes in fixing the annual rate of Depreciation; but having in view the varying standards of efficiency on different railroads in the country, and seeing that the losses by wrecks will depend very largely on the degree of efficiency, it would seem to be preferable on the whole to calculate the depreciation charge without reference to involuntary abandonment. In that case it would, of course, be necessary to establish rules covering, first, rebuilding rendered necessary by wrecks, and, secondly, abandonment as a result of wrecks.

Where cars are rebuilt their value when rebuilt is usually materially greater than immediately before the wreck, except, of course, in cases of cars which are new or have been recently rebuilt, and it would be proper to lay down rules under which the increase in value would be treated as a charge to Depreciation Fund, the balance of the expenditures being treated as the loss by wreck. In the case of abandonment, the difference between the depreciated value of the unit and the scrap value would be a proper charge to Operating Expenses.

TENDENCY OF ERRORS IN PRESENT CLASSIFICATION. It may be interesting next to consider in what direction errors in the classification will tend, assuming our views to be correct. This, of course, depends on the rate of Depreciation established by the Commission, or, if no rate is so established, on the the rates adopted by the Railroads. If the rates are such as to write off the cost of equipment over the average life as extended by rebuilding, the effect will clearly be that in the early years of the life of the equipment the charges against operation will be far too small, and the deficiency of the late classification will be removed only in a comparatively small measure. As, however, units reach the point at which they require substantial rebuilding, some will be rebuilt, and others, perhaps, condemned without reaching the average life. At such a time Operating Expenses will be overburdened in two respects : firstly, by the heavy charges for rebuilding those cars which are retained in service, and secondly, by the charge to Operating Expenses of the difference between the depreciated value and the scrap value of those cars which go out of service. Obviously some cars must last longer than the average, and as the whole of the Depreciation thereon will have been provided for when the average life is terminated, Operating will be undercharged for the remaining years that such cars are in the service.

It may be argued that on most railroads there will be at all times equipment in all the different stages above mentioned, and that consequently the annual charges to Operating will be substantially correct under the new classification, but this is equally true of the old classification, and, indeed, of any method of treating Depreciation and Renewals which provides for writing off property when or before it goes out of service, and which is consistently and conservatively followed.

SUGGESTIONS.   In conclusion, we would strongly urge a change in the classification relating to Repairs, Renewals and Depreciation on the following basis, which will conform very closely to that which has been in successful operation in Industrial and other Companies for many years past :

(1) That a distinction be made in the classification between Repairs and Renewals. The former term should be defined as those general expenses of maintenance and up-keep which are practically continuous and involve the renewal, at short intervals of less than one year, of small parts, while Renewals should include only periodical replacement of important parts, such as will on each occasion give a new lease of life to the unit. The exact dividing line between these two classes of expenditure should be defined in some detail, as is done in Manufacturing Plants, and a minimum figure for the expenditures at one time which may be charged as Renewals might be established.

(2) That a Depreciation Fund be established at such a rate upon the original cost of a unit as will, on an estimated basis, suffice to take care of all these renewal expenses, as well as for the replacement of the entire unit when, either from wear and tear or obsolescence, it ceases to be economical to continue it in service.

(3) That all Repairs be charged direct to Operating Expenses, but that all Renewal Expenses, except such as are attributable to involuntary destruction, be charged to the

Depreciation Fund, irrespective of the age of the unit at the time when such Renewals or Replacements become necessary.

(4) That the difference between original cost and scrap value of units abandoned should be charged to the Fund, except in the case of involuntary destruction, in which case the difference between depreciated value of the unit and scrap value or value for rebuilding purposes should be charged to Operating.

UNIFORM RATES OF DEPRECIATION NOT PRACTICABLE.

The rates to be adopted as the basis of depreciation would require very careful consideration, and it will probably be found that they should vary according to the nature of the road ; and for this reason it may be desirable to leave each road to determine its own rates, subject to the establishment of fixed minima, merely requiring it to specify in its published accounts the rates actually adopted. It would also be desirable to allow some latitude in the annual provision in cases where, for reasons of general depression in business or reduction in traffic, the units are not being so fully used, and for this purpose we think that in the case of equipment the locomotive or car mile basis is preferable to the equal monthly or annual installment basis. This principle, that when property is only partially in use the wear and tear is not so heavy and that consequently less Depreciation is required, is already recognized in many cases by Industrial Companies, and, provided that a fixed minimum is established, would appear to be only fair and reasonable.

The whole question of Depreciation is of so much importance, and its proper treatment so essential to a correct statement of accounts of all commercial enterprises, that a failure of any attempt to deal with it, due to a neglect of the experience already gained during many years by purely Industrial Companies, would be much to be regretted.

III.

RECONSTRUCTION OR ABANDONMENT
OF PROPERTY.

(A communication submitted to Professor H. C. Adams, April 6, 1908).

The question with which we wish to deal in this letter has relation to the treatment proposed in the tentative classification for betterment expenditures which we understand will, with some modifications, become effective on July 1st next. In this classification it is provided that if any property be abandoned the original cost or estimated cost of replacement thereof must be charged into Operating Expense Accounts. It appears to us that this treatment is erroneous and tends to distort Operating Expenses out of their true meaning and intent.

The generally accepted definition of Operating Expenses, with which we believe you agree, would confine them to the actual cost of operating and maintaining the property and any abandonment of property resulting from the wear and tear of operation would properly be chargeable thereto. But there is another kind of abandonment—the necessity for which occurs continually in small and occasionally in very large units—which in no sense whatever arises from the operation of the property, but is due entirely to the necessity of improvements carried out to meet increasing traffic or increasing demands of the Public for better accommodation. In our opinion it is entirely misleading to treat such abandonments as an operating charge, or even as a charge against the Income for the year, but they should be charged to Profit and Loss Account. Our views on this question are as follows :

Property when abandoned may either have reached the end of its useful life and have only a residual scrap value, or may have many years of useful life unexpired and be still entirely fit for the purpose for which it was originally constructed. In the former case the whole abandoned value has been used up in the operation of the road and should properly be considered as an operating expense, while in the latter there is a certain value, being the difference between the present value in service and the scrap value (if any), which is lost to the property but has not in any sense been used up in operating it. This loss must obviously be met out of earnings in some form in order to maintain the integrity of the Capital Account, but it is not a charge against the earnings of a particular year, and should therefore be met either out of accumulated earnings specially reserved or remaining unappropriated in Surplus Account, or out of the earnings of future years if no surplus exists.

We know of cases in which the cost of such abandonments, if wholly charged to Operating Expenses, would absorb the entire net earnings for some years in succession, and thereby prevent the Stockholders from receiving any return on their investment ; and while the policy of actually paying dividends in such cases may be doubtful, it cannot be right so to swell Operating Expenses as to induce the belief that the road cannot be operated at a profit, and by depressing the market value of its securities lead stockholders to dispose of their holdings at a price below their intrinsic value. The advantages which the authorization of such methods by the Interstate Commerce Commission would give to unscrupulous men hardly need be mentioned. To remedy this defect in the classification we would propose the following amendment :

That on the abandonment of any property,—

(1) The difference between its actual or estimated original cost and its estimated value in service at time of abandonment should be charged either to Operating Expenses or to funds which have been provided out of Operating Expenses ;

(2) The excess of estimated present value in service over scrap value recovered, being the measure of the useful life abandoned, should be charged to Profit and Loss Account ; and

(3) The excess cost of reconstruction over the sum of these two elements should be charged to Construction or to Betterments at the discretion of the road.

This is in effect carrying out the principles already laid down for the treatment of equipment. An explicit provision might perhaps be added that the suggested treatment is to be applied only to voluntary abandonments and not to abandonments due to accident, although, as a matter of fact, the requirement of a charge to Operating of the difference between original cost and present value at time of abandonment is an implicit provision to the same effect.

One further point remains to be noted, viz. : that in preparing statistics as to the net returns yielded by the property it will be necessary to consider as deductions from gross earnings :

(1) Operating Expenses.

(2) Net charges to Income including Taxes but excluding perhaps Fixed Charges for use of Capital.

(3) Necessary charges to Profit and Loss Account.

While of course voluntary charges to Profit and Loss, or, in other words, items charged thereto which might under the Interstate Commerce Commission classification be charged to Capital Accounts, would be excluded.

SOME ASPECTS OF
PROFESSIONAL ACCOUNTING

Paul-Joseph Esquerré

SOME ASPECTS OF PROFESSIONAL ACCOUNTING

MAVOURNEEN, AWAKE FROM THY SLUMBERS

BY PAUL-JOSEPH ESQUERRÉ*

LESS than two-score years ago, so I am told, the so-called American "Expert Accountant" was considered by a majority of business people as a disappointed bookkeeper out of a job; an individual who combined a capacity for hard drinking and hard swearing with hard work; an individual capable of producing—after considerable checking and proving, and for a fee which while low was always too high—financial statements few people understood and nobody took seriously.

That in the year of our Lord, 1918, accountants had not yet been able entirely to correct this preposterous opinion which laymen had of the profession, is evidenced by the following quotation from an article headed "The Expert Accountant," which appeared in the issue of *Judge*, October 26, 1918.

> The Expert Accountant is an individual with a trained brain which is capable of extracting more meaning and romance from a column of figures than the average stenographer can worry out of a Marie Corelli novel.

The article in question impressed me all the stronger because, only two or three years before, I had become painfully aware of the slight esteem, if not lack of respect, in which efficiency and production engineers held the profession of accountancy. If my memory serves me right, what I am about to relate occurred in the early fall of 1914.

* Head of the Post-Graduate School of Accountancy, New York City.

One evening I was invited to attend a meeting of the Engineering Society of New York. The well-meaning friend who waylaid me and invited me into that Olympus of highbrows maintains to this day that he had no idea whatever that he had invited me to a barbecue where accountants were to be roasted whole. Be that as it may, I was compelled to sit for two long hours, and look as interestedly pleasant as I could, while an efficiency engineer related one of his experiences with accountants.

The orator of the evening had recently taken a Canadian industrial plant under his wing and had reduced operating costs through the, to him, very simple process of increasing production. This commendable thing he had accomplished to his entire satisfaction, and, I am perfectly willing to assume, to the satisfaction of his clients.

It had been for years the policy of the Canadian concern to engage the services of accountants for the purpose of preparing semiannual financial statements. The accountants appeared in due course and attended to their task in the usual manner. Ignorant of the work performed by the efficiency engineer, they gathered the usual figures, arranged them to suit their purpose, compared them with the corresponding figures of previous years, obtained percentages in their good, old harmless way, and reported, in a rather critical vein, that, as between two accounting periods, the percentage of overhead expense to productive labor had increased 30 per cent. To them this spelled factory mismanagement.

One may imagine the confusion created in the minds of the owners of the Canadian plant, when they became aware of the unbridgeable chasm dividing the camp of the Gods. Had they been familiar with the *Dies Irae Dies Illa* of the Roman Catholic service for the dead, they would certainly have expected a day of wrath, and prepared for the violent demise of accountancy. Whether or not they were ever aware of it, the accountants who were the villains of the engineer's story were wrathfully buried as incompetent bookkeepers, and with them in the same grave, the whole accounting profession was laid at rest. The only flowers that decorated their common burial place were the flowers of rhetoric so generously contributed by the indignant efficiency engineer.

After the meeting I begged to be introduced to the speaker, and tried to convince him that ignorance of the relation between factory burden and the number of units which are to absorb it is not one of the prerequisites of our profession. As the engineer was as big and forceful in personality as the traditional mad bull, while I am rather short of stature, the suavest of diplomacy was necessary to present my case. But it was all in vain! As a parting shot, he told me that there was not an accountant in the world who in his opinion was worth as much as a plugging bookkeeper in an East Side sweatshop.

A few months later I was again a guest of the same engineering society. As I entered the hall, a member was delivering a lecture upon his work as efficiency engineer in charge of the municipal asphalt plant of the city of New York. Among other things

he stated that through efficient management the city had saved, in less than 6 months, some fabulous sum on its street repairs. To support his assertions he presented a few figures abstracted from the results of a system of accounts which I had personally installed in the plant.

Before proceeding further, I must state that at the time I installed the system, I asked particularly how it was to be used. I wanted to know whether the city officials intended to use the figures as an administrative instrument, or for political purposes, or again for the purpose of comparison with the results of private industry. My point was that, under the accounting provisions of the charter of the city of New York, it was impossible to consider as cost anything but the encumbered portion of specific appropriations for the asphalt plant, irrespective of the fact that, as a municipal enterprise, it would enjoy, *gratis pro deo*, a thousand and one privileges and accommodations necessary to its existence, and admittedly very costly to private industry. I was assured that all that was wanted was the control of expenditure by means of periodical statements which would guide the administration in forming a judgment as to the desirability of a plant owned by the municipality.

I shall not attempt to depict my dismay when I heard the efficiency engineer of the asphalt plant read, in a voice suggestive of his consciousness of the triumph of efficiency—a science apparently new to him—tables of figures which he compared with corresponding tables submitted by private industry, much to the discredit of the latter. It was my turn to be furious. I was assured by engineers who sat near me that the chairman would extend to me the courtesy of the floor if I wished to take part in the discussion which was to follow, and so I took advantage of the opportunity to "go over the top."

A timely philosophical reflection impelled me to bottle up my wrath, however. Remembering that in this very room, only a short time before, accountants had been obliterated from the realms of the possible, because of the failure of a staff accountant to see a shining light in the industrial firmament, I reflected that, as between accountants who ignore, and engineers who misrepresent, the Kingdom of Heaven belongs to the meek and simple-minded.

So far I have spoken only of the past; and, as in the last few years we have lived very fast, what people thought of accountants 40 years ago or even in 1918, might very well fail to affect us materially. I shall therefore come down to the present.

Recently a business man of high standing told me that he was conscious of voicing the sentiments of a good part of the business world when he made the assertion that accountancy has forfeited the right to be called an independent profession, that it has sacrificed its freedom of action on the altar of financial prosperity, and that it has degenerated into a handmaiden of banking institutions and of firms of lawyers.

Granted that the business man was talking while under the influence of an attack of nervous dyspepsia; granted that the engineer of whom I have previously spoken was suffering from hydrophobia; granted that the many derogatory remarks made about the profession have no *raison d'etre* and can be classified as the superciliousness of ignorance even when malicious: still, it remains true that we should ask ourselves the question: What is the matter with accountancy?

That there is something the matter will probably be admitted by every accountant, with the exception of the few who, having reached the pinnacle of financial success, see the future through a roseate prism. The defects of the edifice we have so laboriously constructed are easily defined. I submit the following:

1. Untimely depreciation through the failure of the builders to protect the structure from exploitation by unskilled laborers, and unprofessional ignoramuses.

2. Obsolescence of the base caused by the indifference of the head.

What brought this about?

Organically, accountants must have a loose vertebra somewhere in their spinal column. This is evidenced by their indifference to their present status. Is accountancy a profession, or is it a business? If it is a business, it is admitted that everybody can be an accountant without the formality of a "by your leave." If it is a profession, why do accountants permit it to be misrepresented and even disgraced as it is today in so many flagrant instances. Why do they not take such steps as will require qualified accountants to register with the state in which they practice, precisely as other professions do?

As matters stand today, anybody and everybody can practice accounting. A member of the staff of a firm of accountants is "retired" for incapacity; he looks around for employment, and, unable to find it, raises the pirate flag, calls himself "auditor, accountant, systematizer, efficiency expert, curator of your earning power," and what not, and proceeds to exploit a gullible public. An ambitious youth, having completed to his satisfaction a course in bookkeeping, and unwilling to try his luck as a junior ledger clerk, rents office room, circularizes, peddles his nerve from door to door, and sells his services on a "monthly basis of once a week, 2 hours, $17.50; twice a week, 2 hours, $27.50; three times a week, 2 hours, $37.50; once a month, ranging from $5.00," and within the year obtains from some accommodating state, the right to append the magic letters C.P.A. to his name and to represent himself as an accounting prodigy. A subaltern officer of a bank, having outlived his usefulness with the institution responsible for his training, is assured of proper financial backing, incorporates an audit company, hires a number of junior and senior accountants, and sails the high seas, raiding as he goes. Accounting schools by the hundreds promise the youth of the land an increase of 250 per cent in their present salary, as soon as they have completed a course in accounting. Advertisements appear in periodicals of high repute, exhibiting the picture of a mechanic who, upon graduation from a school of accounts, became president of an enterprise with a salary of $80,000. Still another advertisement shows a young man presenting a crisp $100 bill to his happy bride, the reader of the advertisement being gently led to the assumption that our interesting young groom gives away extra money obtained as a result of his taking an accounting course.

No one ever attempts to induce young men to join the ranks of accountants by the dignified statement that accountancy is to business what medicine is to the human body, and that the work of the accountant should be as highly appreciated and respected as the work of the physician, or of the lawyer, but that it cannot be expected to be more remunerative. Lecturers on accounting, or highly successful men in the field of accounting, are asked to address students on the prospects of accountancy: what is expected of them is that they shall paint the future with a golden hue. If, perchance, the lecturer advises the palpably unfit students to sell suspenders, shoe laces or other necessary commodities, as I invariably do, he is accused of narrow-mindedness, or selfish motives are ascribed to him; the very best that will be said of him is that he must have his little joke. Few accountants are aware of what is going on, and still fewer care, provided they are left undisturbed in the enjoyment of the harvest.

To fully realize the danger which is threatening accountancy, and to appreciate at its just value the fruits of indifference to the welfare of our profession, take the career of an accountant attached to the staff of one of the innumerable accounting firms, certified audit companies, *et tutti quanti*, which have grown like mushrooms during the last few years, and which have been permitted by the state to incorporate under names purposely misleading and defiant of the state professional laws.

At the age of 18, either because he has friends in the business or because he knows somebody who knows somebody else, our youth attaches himself to the staff of a rising firm of accountants. For a year or so he adds columns of figures, checks vouchers, inventories, car numbers or policy numbers (it is all the same to him) examines a few checks, scrutinizes their endorsements and their signatures, becoming more and more conscious of his inclination toward a profession so genteel, so diversified in scope, and so remunerative to the employers. Upon the advice of a co-worker, he reads a book here and a pamphlet there and thus picks up a perfunctory knowledge of funds and their uses; he gazes at corporation finance, inhales the mysterious perfumes of political economy, scratches the skin of commercial law, and, last

106 ADMINISTRATION Vol. II
No. 1

but not least, dissects very gingerly the outer envelope of the principles of accounting. This education gives him more and more confidence in his mental caliber, and places him in a position to discuss the weighty business questions of the day with his friends and relatives, and to sit complacently in front of the blank wall where, in a short time, his professional diplomas will hang conspicuously.

At the end of a year, the sum of his mistakes not being too formidable, he is advised to go to night school; there he plugs and plugs during the equivalent of from 150 to 300 hours, and warms his mind at the sacred fire of accountancy fed by the dry wood of bookkeeping, history of commerce, advanced accounting problems, accounts of executors, and the "last word" in theory of accounts and of auditing. If he is a man above the average, he even explores the mysterious caverns of cost, salesmanship, sociology, public speaking, after-dinner speaking, and what not, to say nothing of English grammar, his eternal enemy.

Meanwhile, he has become a semi-senior, and, provided he is given a schedule of the work to be done, of the accounts to be analyzed, of the particular weaknesses to be watched, and a detailed statement of the peculiarities of the client, he is perfectly capable of taking charge of small engagements, such as the audit of grocery stores, cigar stores, candy stores, fruit stands, social clubs, etc. Experience brings understanding in its wake, and at the end of 2 years from the date of entry into the firm, even before he has completed his school course, he may, if he is lucky and not too foolish, be made a full-fledged senior, and instal a system of cost finding in a small factory.

He has now reached the danger point; he knows all there is to be known in accounting except, perhaps, bookkeeping: he does not see the use of bothering his head with the things that he has not met in his "practice," of which he speaks with pride. In a short while, he knocks at the door of the State University and asks that the stamp of approval be placed on his brow.

You may say that I exaggerate; and yet the state of New York, whose professional requirements are probably higher than those of any other state, both from the point of view of preliminary education and of professional training, only requires, for the granting of a C.P.A. degree, to men who have successfully passed the examination, the equivalent of a high school diploma and 5 years of general accounting experience, of which 2 shall have been in the employ of a certified public accountant, in a capacity no less than that of junior accountant. Why junior? Why no less than junior? Could anybody be less qualified than the junior of 22 or 23 whom I have described? For, senior though he may be to his firm, to the rest of the accountants who respect their profession, he is still a junior and will not emerge from that state of adolescence for years to come.

Why do the associations of reputable accountants permit this state of affairs? Is it because they are convinced that having climbed to safe heights the tide of discontent cannot reach them? Or is it because they believe "there is plenty of room for all; give everybody a chance, and water will find its level?"

If we accountants really care for the welfare of our profession, can we not find some means of putting an end to a condition which, whether we are willing to admit it or not, is harmful to the profession? Have we not read, a year or so ago, in a publication devoted to the interest of accountancy, a letter in which an accountant of excellent standing threatened to adopt the admittedly successful advertising methods of the younger generation, unless the organization in whose hands protection of the profession lies, found means of preventing the continuance of such practices? It was not, in this case, a question of professional ethics to be lived up to at all costs; it was a question of imitating the pirates unless the pirates could be made to respect ethics. The obvious deduction was: if commercialism pays, by all means, let us be commercial, provided thereby, we achieve financial success.

How can our societies control men who, for obvious reasons, cannot be members of them, or who do not care to belong to them for the simple reason that within such organizations censure is unavoidable, whereas outside of them it is impossible? What is the use of incorporating societies of recognized practitioners, of adopting stringent codes of ethics, of speaking of our love for our profession, and of making speeches at our conventions about what we have done and hope to do for the business world, when we deliberately allow outsiders to set their traps for the capture of the wary and unsuspecting? How can we expect a public, which has neither the time nor the inclination to learn the intricacies of our profession and its fine distinctions be-

tween legitimate and illegitimate, to have more respect for us than we have for ourselves?

If we accept the premise that accountancy is a profession and not a "business," and that the function of the accountant is to advise, guide, and teach others how best to conduct their business affairs, always placing their interests and welfare above his own, it must follow that the standards of practice must be raised to the highest level of service to the business community consistent with self-respect.

Practices smacking of the competitive methods of modern "business" in securing degrees and in building up a clientele have no place in a profession which aims truly to secure and retain the confidence of the business world through the integrity and high ethical standards of its members.

To what extent this can be accomplished by laws, and how far the force of collective professional opinion can make itself felt effectually under the present conditions is the problem confronting the sincere and thoughtful professional accountant today.

The problem is especially vital at this time, when thousands of young men are being guided into accounting work through the promise of rich pecuniary reward made to them by the many schools offering courses of instruction in accountancy.

SOME NEGLECTED PHASES OF ACCOUNTING

Henry Rand Hatfield

Some Neglected Phases of Accounting*

*Fundamental Valuation Principle Is Not Equity But Attraction of Capital,
With Assumption of Risk by Investor Involved—Author Differentiates
Between Capital Expenditures and Revenue Charges, and Analyzes
Depreciation Accounting, Capitalization of Deficits and Franchise Payments*

HENRY RAND HATFIELD

Professor of Accounting, University of California, Berkeley, Cal.

THERE are five matters that call for careful consideration—namely, the fundamental principle of valuation; the differentiation between capital expenditures and charges against revenue; the treatment of depreciation; the capitalization of deficits, and the effect of payments for franchises.

Paramount among these questions is that relating to the valuation to be taken as the basis for rate regulation. In the torrent of discussion it seems strange that any aspect of the question should have been neglected. Nevertheless in most discussions there is a startling lack of any fundamental principle, of what Allison calls an "over-theory," by which the varying methods can be judged. One proposes a cost basis, another a reproduction basis, another a present-value basis, but comparatively little attention has been given to the principle by which these are to be tested.

EQUITY AS FUNDAMENTAL PRINCIPLE OF VALUATION IS NOT ADEQUATELY CONSIDERED

To be sure, it is generally implied that there must be some equity, but the question of what constitutes equity as between the public and the corporation is not adequately considered. Two writers of prominence, Allison and Whitten, have come to closer grips with the subject, but even these fall short of a satisfactory solution. Whitten's idea is that equity consists in an adequate reward for the sacrifice of the investor. Yet this statement is not followed to its logical conclusion and is made to rest on a forced analogy altogether begging the question at issue. In his argument supporting the cost basis, Whitten states: "[The corporation] devoted a certain amount of money to a public use and is equitably as much entitled to a fair return on that investment, provided the business can be made to earn it, as though it had actually loaned that amount to the public. * * * It is the actual investment or sacrifice on the part of the company that is entitled to consideration."

There are several points for criticism in this statement. In the first place, sacrifice is in itself not a basis for remuneration. In the second place, it altogether begs the question to compare the investment to a loan. Conceivably the transaction may resemble rather a lease with revaluations at stated intervals. In such a lease no one questions its equity, even though the rental paid

*Abstract of paper read before San Francisco convention of American Electric Railway Accountants' Association on Oct. 6, 1915.

in the later years is altogether out of proportion to the original value contributed by the landlord. Doubtless, if the investment in a public utility were like a loan the return should be like interest; but the bald assumption that it resembles a loan rather than a lease is purely gratuitous. Finally, in the statement that a fair return is to be paid "provided the business can be made to earn it," the proviso is altogether out of place. No one asserts that San Francisco's obligation to pay interest on the municipal railway bonds is dependent on the road's making a profit.

Many other writers advocate original cost as the proper basis for rates, but all balk at standing consistently by it. The statement is emasculated by saying that the investment must have been a wise one—as if a loan were less valid because unwise. It must be recognized, says one, that competition may arise and destroy the value of the investment; hence it must be a proper investment as well as a wise one. Thus the statement that equity demands a return on the original cost because of the sacrifice involved has been so explained and modified as to lose any consistent character. Furthermore, in discussing equity, consideration has generally been had to past investments rather than to present-day investments reaching onward into the future. The treatment of an early investment, made without any expectation that it would be subject to valuation, is a more difficult but much less interesting and much less important problem than the formulation of rules by which all future investors are to be guided.

OTHER CONSIDERATIONS ARE MORE FUNDAMENTAL THAN EQUITY

Attempts to formulate a principle resting on equity have led to hopeless confusion. It is time to recognize that, as far as the establishment of a settled policy for the future is concerned, equity is not the guiding principle at all. Any contract entered into freely and intelligently is equitable. In regard to public utilities there are other considerations more fundamental than equity. This has, to some extent, been recognized, as when Bemis says: "The problem now is not so much an ethical problem of what a company ought to receive as it is what return, as a matter of fact, will tempt the investor to furnish the money needed for the growth of the business." Bemis here rejects equity and substitutes the incentive to investment of capital. Yet capital can be attracted either by increasing the prize or by guar-

anteeing against risk, two methods quite distinct in their
effect on the public. More fundamental by far is the
problem of how the risks and the profits of new enterprises are to be borne, and particularly whether the
public is to profit by new discoveries and improvements.

Allison has expressed a vain fantasy in saying: "The
true aim of regulation is to bring about eventually a
condition where, as far as possible, all risk and all specu-
lation will be removed from the enterprise." Risks
never can be eliminated from new enterprises—the question is, who shall bear them? In undertaking a public
enterprise there are two distinct kinds of risks. The
first is that of miscalculation as to the value of the
service rendered, or the cost of its production. Error
here may lead to an investment which cannot be profitable. Such a risk cannot be removed by rate regulation.
If charging all that the traffic will bear still leaves a
deficit, it is evident that no regulation of rates will
prevent loss. Such risks may be borne by the investor.
Yet to induce him to do so, he must be tempted by the
prospect of rates high enough to cover the risk. They
may be borne by the public, but only by public ownership or subsidies.

The second class of risks is more important to the
discussion. It is, in the words of Chairman Stevens,
"the competition of a new and superior service produced
at a less cost which will secure all custom." In ordinary
competitive industries such competition means inevitably a loss to the investor and a gain to the public. In
public utilities direct competition is subordinate to
regulation. Yet if a new discovery is made the public
must adopt one of two courses—either it must maintain rates so as to yield adequate returns on the more
costly plant, or it must adjust rates to correspond with
the lower cost of the substitute process. The whole
question turns on the advisability of allowing the investor to take this risk, or, on the other hand, of protecting him against this risk, as is implied in the original cost-loan theory. There seems no escape. Either
the investor takes the risk, or the public foregoes the
advantages to be derived from inventions, at least of
inventions which would substitute a cheaper plant.

It is true that the public may itself be the investor, by
public ownership or by granting subsidies, but the alternative remains. Either the investor, whether private
or public, must bear the risk of competitive improvements, or the public must forego the advantages of
radical improvements in the arts and sciences. A
compromise may be made, but compromises, while allay-
ing disputes, never settle principles.

It is perhaps not difficult to persuade the investor to
undertake the risk. The risk of loss by supersession
may be offset by the allowance of high returns during
the period before the supersession takes place. Capital-
ists as a class will profit by some of the undertakings,
but lose by others. It is, however, manifestly inconsistent to allow high returns as an offset for possible
losses and then to demand that the high rates be reduced in the cases where the enterprise proves successful. It is difficult to determine the point at which a
rate of return, only sufficient to induce the original investment, becomes exorbitant. There is need of considerable caution in applying the following statement
laid down in the Commonwealth Edison Company report: "Capital is doubtless entitled to returns commem-
surate with the risks incident to the business. * * *
But it should not be supposed that the early large returns should be continued when the development of the
business, the elimination of competition, and the neces-
sities of the community have largely reduced the risk
of the investment." It much resembles refusing to pay
a lottery prize, because the gain seems exorbitant as

compared with the price of a single ticket, although
the purchaser may have squandered a fortune in the
purchase of unsuccessful numbers.

What the Real Fundamental Is

The neglected phase of railway accounting first to be
mentioned then is: In the discussion of a basis for valuation the problem of finding an underlying principle
has been neglected. Even those who have attempted it
have generally erred in regarding it as having to do
with equity. Nor is it merely a problem of how to allure
the investor into putting his money into an enterprise.
He can be induced to take any risk if the stakes are
made high enough. Fundamental to all, however, is the
question as to whether the investor is to take risks, or
whether the public is to go at a dead level, foregoing the
economies coming from new inventions. It suffices to
state the problem thus in general terms, although its
many ramifications, such as the incentive to initiative
in one or the other system, furnish room for much
thought.

Difference Between Capital Expenditures and Revenue Charges

The second point to be discussed is the real nature of
the difference between capital expenditures and charges
against revenue, when these terms are used in reference
to the operations of public utilities. In some aspects
capital charges and revenue charges are distinct, almost
contradictory. These differences are strongly emphasized by the United States Supreme Court in the Kan-
sas City case. Yet even in ordinary commercial undertakings the difference between the two is not diametrical.
The machine, the tool, the raw material are all alike
expenses of producing commodities. All are operating
expenses, provided a long enough field of operation is
taken into view. In public utilities the similarity is
even greater than in ordinary business. Where rates are
regulated so as to yield a fair return, there is little
difference between a capital expenditure and a charge
against revenue. The consumer must provide for both.
For what is called an operating expense the consumer
pays promptly. Where the expenditure is capitalized,
he returns the payment more slowly but pays interest
during the time of delay. There is but little difference
whether principal is repaid or not, provided interest is
paid indefinitely. In a few instances, as where the capital is invested in land, it resembles a perpetual annuity.
Yet what is ordinarily called fixed capital is rather like
a sinking-fund bond, in that the consumer pays interest
on the investment, and through the charge for depreciation provides for the ultimate extinction of the principal. As far, then, as the relation between the corporation and the public as a whole is concerned, it is relatively immaterial whether an expenditure is called an
expense or an investment of capital. In either case the
public must provide for the reimbursement of the
amount expended, together with a fair return on the investment while it remains unpaid.

In only one point is the difference significant. The
public, while a permanent body, is made up of changing individuals. In so far as the body of consumers
changes, injustice may be done to the consumers of one
or another period, if an expense, which should properly
be paid by the consumers of one period, is so treated
that the consumers of another period are burdened by it.
An expense, capitalized wrongfully, burdens later consumers to the advantage of present-day consumers. The
position is reversed when what is properly a capital
expenditure is treated as a current expense. The whole
question then reduces to equity, not as between the

public and the corporation, but as between individuals composing the public at two different dates.

Depreciation Represents Intermediate Position

Somewhat analogous is the third point of depreciation. In the discussion of this subject there has been even greater confusion of thought. Depreciation represents a position intermediate between a capital expenditure and a charge against revenue. An absolutely permanent investment of capital demands perpetual interest but no repayment of principal. A pure expense demands immediate return of the amount expended, payment to be made so promptly as to render calculation of interest unnecessary. Depreciation indicates that so-called fixed capital is, as a matter of fact, being repaid through rates, and presumably interest on the unconsumed capital should also be allowed.

Too Much Controversy About Equity of Depreciation Methods

In this matter there has been far too much polemical discussion as to the equity of one or another method of treating the problem. This discussion has become most acute in the conflict as to whether the straight-line or the curved-line method of calculating depreciation is correct. The advocates of either method almost invariably assume that the other method is unfair either to the public or the corporation. Here again there is, in reality, no question of equity as between the corporation and the public. Advocates of the straight-line method generally base the argument on some statement similar to the following, which is taken from the paper of a distinguished engineer: If one buys ten firecrackers and uses one, he has nine-tenths of his purchase still left to him. Similarly a plant costing $100,000, with a life of ten years, is worth just $90,000 at the end of one year. The curved-line method, calling for a smaller annual charge than the straight-line, is therefore only a partial payment of the property destroyed and consequently inequitable. The one thing which is certain, however, is that an investment of $100,000 in a plant with a life of ten years does not represent the purchase of ten annual units each worth $10,000. The sum of $100,000 represents the present value of an annuity of $12,950, interest being at 5 per cent. The decline in the value of such an annuity during the first year is not $10,000 or $12,950, but only $7,949.

This principle can be perfectly illustrated with few figures by assuming a life of only two years and an interest rate of 10 per cent. A payment of $100,000 for a utility lasting two years represents the present value of an annuity of $57,619. This is made up of: Present value of first installment, $52,381; present value of second installment, $47,619; total, $100,000. At the end of the first year there remains a value of $52,381. The reduction in value then has not been $50,000 or $57,619, but only $47,619.

It is apparent that it is incorrect to say that only the straight-line method is equitable. Yet the real error in most of the discussion is not that either side is wrong in claiming its method is correct, but that it fails to see that, where a public utility is concerned, there is no difference between the two methods. This may again be illustrated by taking a utility having an initial cost of $100,000 and a life of two years, with interest reckoned at 10 per cent. An ordinary two-year investment at 10 per cent should bring in a total return, with interest compounded, of $121,000. Yet exactly the same returns come in with a depreciating property, whether the depreciation is figured on a straight-line or on a curved-line basis. This is clearly shown by the following schedules:

STRAIGHT INVESTMENT	
Interest on $100,000 for first year	$10,000
Interest on above sum during second year	1,000
Interest on $100,000 for second year	10,000
Principal returned	100,000
Total	$121,000

INVESTMENT IN DEPRECIATING PROPERTY—STRAIGHT-LINE METHOD	
Interest on amount invested for first year	$10,000
First installment of depreciation	50,000
Interest on above items during second year	6,000
Interest on depreciated value	5,000
Second installment of depreciation	50,000
Total	$121,000

INVESTMENT IN DEPRECIATING PROPERTY—CURVED-LINE METHOD (Amount of sinking fund, $47,619, + interest, $10,000.)	
Amount paid at end of first year	$57,619
Interest on above amount during second year	5,762
Amount paid at end of second year	57,619
Total	$121,000

One may go further. In a public utility a "fair return" is considered necessary. A fair return is an impossible conception unless return of capital in some form is implied. The return of capital may be made at any time, in any sums, without in anyway affecting the equity between the company and the public. If the capital is excessively reduced at one time, the amount on which the public pays a return is correspondingly reduced. Yet just to the extent that interest paid by the public is reduced, the company is compensated by an early return of capital. Actuarially it is immaterial when and how a debt is returned, provided interest is allowed on the unreturned balance.

Excessive Depreciation Allowance, However, May Prove Inequitable

There is an element of equity, however, that is frequently lost to sight. An excessive allowance of depreciation, being a premature repayment of capital, does work a hardship in so far as there is a shifting of the persons purchasing the output of the corporation. One group can easily be benefited at the expense of another group. Thus in the instance given above the consumers of the first and second years would each pay $57,619 under a curved-line system, while under a straight-line system the consumers of the first year would pay $5,000 more than the consumers of the second year. As far as the corporation is concerned there is no difference, and as far as the consumers as a whole are concerned there is no difference between the two methods. Yet as far as there is a difference between the two groups of consumers, the curved-line method is equitable to both bodies, while the straight-line method burdens the earlier users to the advantage of their successors.

Importance of Specific Depreciation Reserve

The point just made carries with it some corollaries often neglected. Much discussion has been raised as to the importance of having a specific depreciation reserve set aside. Thus it is claimed by Hayes that the investors are entitled to a return on the full value of their investment only in case they can show that there is property in hand equivalent to the amount of the depreciation reserve. The real question is not whether the original value has been maintained, but whether the consumers have paid enough to cover ordinary operating expenses and depreciation. If $100,000 is invested for public use and the consumers pay only enough to cover ordinary operating expenses (not including depreciation), evidently there is a decline in the value of the investment. Obviously, if investors are entitled to a fair return on the full cost of the plant they are none the less so entitled because rates have been made so low as not to cover the annual depreciation. The company is entitled to this return even though it does not comply with the requirement made by Hayes.

The question as to whether there is a depreciation reserve fund so placed as to be yielding interest also becomes meaningless, as far as the public and the company are concerned. The annual appropriation to reserve is less where it is calculated on the sinking-fund plan. But that is neither an advantage nor a disadvantage, for just to the extent that the sinking-fund interest lessens the amount annually set aside, to the same extent are the profits kept down by crediting to the sinking-fund reserve the receipts which otherwise would have gone to the general income account.

The problem of depreciation may be summed up by comparing the investment of the company to a loan which the debtor has the privilege of repaying in installments. If it is a loan of $10,000, it might be repaid in ten annual installments of $1,000. Yet neither creditor nor debtor would be harmed if more or less than a proportional amount were paid in each year. It might be repaid by any system, or with a lack of system. As long as interest is allowed on the outstanding balance, perfect equity is secured. The debtor might either pay in installments or merely keep up interest and himself accumulate a sinking fund with which to pay the principal. On the other hand, the creditor might, or might not, retain the installments as received and invest them in a sinking fund, so that he should have his principal intact at the end of the ten years. Any of these schemes would not affect the equities as between debtor and creditor.

DEFICITS SHOULD BE BORNE BY ALL BENEFICIARIES AS PERMANENT CAPITAL CHARGE

Another difficult problem is the fourth, relating to deficits. Where a deficit occurs in the early operations of a public utility, it is generally admitted that rates in subsequent years should make some adjustment. It is said that such deficits may be treated under either of two distinct theories—the first called "capitalization as an investment" and the second "recoupment as a loss." The New York commission says there is a real and substantial distinction between considering a loss as an investment and as an expense to be reimbursed. Despite such high authority, it seems to some that a loss which must be reimbursed is an investment until it is repaid. If an ordinary business concern were in question, the distinction would indeed be valid. Yet in a public utility both investments and losses must be covered in order to secure a fair return. When the commission admits that the loss "must be reimbursed" all differences vanish.

Whether losses are actually repaid or are to be permanently capitalized is relatively unimportant, just as the nature of a government loan is not particularly changed when it is a perpetual annuity. Equity as between different consumers, however, may enter into the problem. If the loss is regarded as an essential to the establishment of the enterprise, it should be borne by all its beneficiaries, and the only way to spread the expense is to make it a permanent capital charge. If paid off by consumers of the next five years, for instance, they are inequitably burdened with an expense which appertains to them no more than it does to the consumers of any other years. From an actuarial viewpoint the granting of a fair annual return on a given sum is neither more nor less advantageous than the actual repayment of the sum, just as it is neither more nor less advantageous to repay in five than in fifty years. This actuarial truth is not affected by other questions of public policy which may seem to make it more desirable to have debts promptly paid, but the equity of the case is not affected by policy.

The United States Supreme Court is doubtless sound in stating that "instrumentalities which are to be used for years should not be paid for by the revenues of a day or year." (206 U. S. 463.) In so far as the deficit was merely a loss in furnishing service to consumers of one year, there is no shadow of equity in claiming that the consumers of any other year should pay the bills of the earlier consumers. The only justification of carrying the loss forward is that it is considered not as a loss of the first year, but as something pertaining to the entire operating life of the company. If this premise is correct, it follows that all subsequent consumers should pay their share of the burden, and that can most effectively be done by treating the deficit as a capital investment.

FRANCHISE FEE NEITHER BENEFITS NOR HARMS EITHER PARTY

Finally, for the fifth point, reference may be made to the effect of charging the corporation a fee for its franchise. Where such a fee is obtained, it is generally assumed by the city that a most successful bargain has been struck, and that the public has been benefited just to the extent that the corporation has been mulcted of the fee. Yet in the midst of the rejoicing over the shrewd bargain, some facts are apparently forgotten. In the subsequent regulation of prices a "fair return" is to be allowed on the entire investment. Hence the public must reimburse the company for the franchise fee paid, and must pay interest at a comparatively high rate while it remains unpaid. The situation is not different if instead of a direct repayment by the public, the fee is capitalized and counted as part of the investment taken over by a successor company. As long as the rule of a fair return is admitted, the entire cost of the franchise is borne by the consumers, whether it is amortized during the life of the franchise or treated as a permanent annuity. Hence the franchise fee neither benefits nor harms either party. All that it amounts to is that the city receives a considerable sum of income in advance, which is subsequently collected, not from taxpayers but from consumers. This indirect and unconscious collection of revenue may be advantageous or may not. Yet the transaction is certainly different from what it is popularly assumed to be.

Professor Hatfield's Fundamental Principle of Valuation

"IN the discussion of a basis for valuation the problem of finding an underlying principle has been neglected. Even those who have attempted it have generally erred in regarding it as having to do with equity. Nor is it merely a problem of how to allure the investor into putting his money into an enterprise. He can be induced to take any risk if the stakes are made high enough. Fundamental to all, however, is the question as to whether the investor is to take risks, or whether the public is to go at a dead level, foregoing the economies coming from new inventions."—HENRY RAND HATFIELD.

MANAGEMENT OF THE
SURPLUS RESERVE-DISCUSSION

Henry Rand Hatfield

HENRY RAND HATFIELD : Five points may be emphasized in discussing Dr. Meade's paper. These are : the purpose of establishing a surplus reserve, its amount, its investment, its treatment in the balance sheet, and its distribution.

The purpose of establishing a surplus reserve, as stated by Dr. Meade, is either to guarantee interest and dividend, or to provide an investment for the stockholders. There are at least two other purposes distinctly recognized in actual business practice. These are (1) to give creditors a general guarantee, in addition to that furnished by the capital stock, and the stockholders liability. This is noticeable in the case of banks, where the establishment of a surplus is customary and, as in the case of our national banks and in the German Reichsbank, sometimes compulsory. (2) To provide ready funds for emergency purposes.

One purpose in creating a surplus, which is mentioned by Dr. Meade, seems incorrect. A surplus reserve is not designed to provide revenue outside of the scope of the business. This does not mean that the surplus may not at times be invested in outside fields, nor that a surplus when invested should not yield a revenue. The object of any corporation is to carry on some definite business. In carrying on that business it may exercise certain implied powers. If a factory can best manufacture, if it can best maintain its integrity, its solvency, its credit, by holding outside property, well and good. But it is out of place for a coal company to derive its main income from New York real estate. The great trusts are not trust companies, and should only hold outside property in so far as their own particular business demands such outside holdings. If the business itself is not profitable, it is better that that fact should appear, rather than it should be concealed by profits from entirely disconnected sources. If the managers of a corporation cannot make a satisfactory profit in their regular business, there is no presupposition in favor of their being more successful in some outside investment, and the stockholders should not be dragooned into entrusting them with additional funds.

In his discussion of the amount of surplus reserve, Dr. Meade states that it should vary with the constancy of demand for the product. This would be better amended to say that it depends on the constancy of profits; for a lessened demand for the product, if accompanied with a decreased cost of production,—a condition by no means impossible,—would leave profits constant. But a much more serious omission is made by the author, both in his paper and in his work on " Trust finance," in that he neglects to show the bearing which the form of capitalization has on the question of the amount of surplus which should be reserved. The industrial corporations for instance have been severely criticised on the ground that the percentage of surplus to dividends is so much less than the percentage of surplus to dividends is in the case of railroads. This ignores the fact that the railroads have a large bonded debt, while the industrials are almost unbonded. It is apparent that of two corporations, one with $100,000,000 in bonds and $100,000,000 in stock, the other with no bonds and $200,000,000 in stock, the former should reserve a larger proportion of its dividends and should, moreover, maintain a larger surplus in proportion to its total capitalization. For this there are two reasons, (1) the evil of defaulting in interest is so much greater than that of passing a dividend, that the protection should be greater ; and (2) the very fact of the fixed interest charges

makes the fluctuation in annual profits more wide. To
illustrate this. If the surplus of income over operating
expenses varies from $9,000,000 to $15,000,000, the
profits on the $200,000,000 stock would vary from 4½
to 7½ per cent ; but if half the capitalization consisted of
first mortgage 5 per cent bonds, fluctuations in profits
would vary from 4 per cent to 10 per cent per annum ;
in the first case a range of 66 per cent, in the second of
250 per cent. Quite aside, then, from the speculative
character of the business undertaking, quite aside also,
from the question of the nature of the business, as to
its quasi-public character, the form of the capitalization
is an important factor in determining the amount of
reserve which should be kept back as a guarantee.

Turning to the question of the investment of the
reserve, this surely can only be answered when we consider the purpose for which it is established. If it is to
afford investment, it should go into the most profitable
investment ; that is, the business itself. If it is to provide for emergencies, it should be in some liquid form,
which can easily be drawn upon. Dr. Meade on this
point falls into contradiction. In the first part of his
paper, he says that the reserve should ordinarily be invested in plant and equipment. Later, while discussing
the question of extensions, he says : " When a large
margin over fixed charges or dividends is immediately
assured on the investment of capital, the amount should
be raised by the sale of securities and not taken out of
earnings." But it may be questioned why there should
be so much discussion of the investment of the surplus
reserve. Why should the surplus have a special corresponding item among the assets ? It almost seems at
times as though the author were misled by the use of
his pet phrase " surplus reserve," and thought because

there is a surplus, there must needs be a specific reserve,
such as is meant when we speak of the bank reserve.
Is a fund of ready cash, or of easily negotiated securities, desirable in the assets of a corporation ? Is it not
equally desirable whether the corporation have a surplus
or not ? Dr. Meade paints a bright picture of the advantages of having available funds and shows how
railroads have been wrecked, trusts demolished and
stockholders ruined because there was no such reserve.
It would therefore seem that at times the most profitable
investment of any corporation may consist of that part
of its assets held as an emergency fund. But what correspondence is there between this fund and the accumulated surplus? In the case of a bank, there is just as
much wisdom and necessity of having some liquid assets
when the bank first starts as when it has a surplus many
times its capital, and I have never seen any claim that
one should depend on the other. Similarly, in the case
of any other corporation. If some percentage of a
corporation's assets ought to be held in cash, or outside
securities, or New York real estate, such investment
should be made out of the proceeds of the original sale
of bonds and stock just as surely as out of the surplus ;
if such holdings are not desirable, why should surplus
reserve, which economically is indistinguishable from
capital stock, be forced into an undesirable channel?

A fourth question is whether the profits reserved from
distribution should so show in the balance sheet. It is
not clear to me whether Dr. Meade's discussion of the
treatment of betterment and of the source of unusual
expenditures clearly faces this problem or not. A
betterment is either an actual increase of fixed capital,
or it is the recognition and restoration of wasted capital.
In the former case, the actual surplus reserve is un-

affected, and Dr. Meade's discussion is in reality merely whether the surplus reserve is best invested in the plant. If the so-called betterment is in fact only a restoration of wasted capital, there is no special pertinence in discussing it in connection with the surplus reserve, for expenses must be paid, and the property must be kept up before we can talk of surplus at all. The surplus exists, as Dr. Meade shows, equally whether the betterments are charged to cost of plant (road and equipment) or treated as an expense. Whether that surplus shall be made manifest in the balance sheet is another question, and not logically connected with that of the advisability of selling securities.

I should myself urge greater accuracy in having the actual condition made manifest. The paying or the retention of profits is important, but showing of profits and losses is much more important, both to individuals, and to the public. Non-dividend paying bank stock frequently sells at a high premium, because it shows dividends earned. Expedience, public policy perhaps, frequently justify the hiding of earnings because the temptation is generally toward exaggeration rather than toward depreciation of profits, but the ideal goal of accounting is exact accuracy, and a hidden surplus is in its very term a confession of an inexact balance sheet.

Dr. Meade's final discussion of the distribution of the surplus reserve is contradictory. He speaks of such a distribution as being secured by raising the rate of dividend, or by privileged sale of stock. A raising of the rate of dividend, provided the new rate does not exceed the current annual profits, is, however, not a distribution of the surplus at all, nor is the privileged sale of stock at par a distribution of surplus. In the latter case the corporation increases its assets to the same amount that its liabilities are increased, and the surplus remains unchanged. It may be a step toward the disbursement of a larger sum in annual dividends, but unless such distribution is more rapid than the making of profits, there is no lessening of the surplus. The surplus still remains on the balance sheet, and in its tangible, material embodiment among the assets. Distribution of profits derived from the investment of the surplus is no more distribution of the surplus than the payment of dividends derived from investment of the original capital is distribution of such capital.

PRINCIPLES OF VALUATION AS RELATED TO THE FUNCTIONS OF THE BALANCE SHEET

Roy B. Kester

PRINCIPLES OF VALUATION AS RELATED TO THE FUNCTIONS OF THE BALANCE SHEET

By Roy B. Kester
Columbia University

The balance sheet is usually defined as a statement of financial condition. Just what is meant by financial condition is oftentimes very much of a puzzle to a student. In a vague way he knows that it has to do with the finances of the concern referred to in the statement. He seldom is able, however, to formulate a clear, sound and comprehensive explanation of the terms. In our efforts to explain to him what is meant by financial condition we try to point out the major uses made of the balance sheet. Of the various statements drawn up for use in connection with a business the balance sheet doubtless is called upon to serve many varying purposes. Some of these purposes it serves well; to others it is very poorly adapted. Inasmuch, however, as it is oftentimes the only readily available source of information, it has to serve many purposes as best it can. The reader of the balance sheet should understand, therefore, the principles on which the balance sheet is made up and should have an appreciation of its limitations.

Before discussing some of the problems growing out of the demands made on the balance sheet, it is desirable to enumerate some of the purposes which it is called upon to serve. For those within the business who have easy access to the records, the balance sheet does not serve so important a purpose as to the outsider. Even for those on the inside, however, it is advantageous at times for them to attempt to secure the outsider's view point concerning the business. The manager of the business is too often inclined to be over-optimistic with regard to the status of affairs, and is not often inclined to subject his own balance sheet to the same critical analysis that he would give that of another concern. To judge his own financial condition from the outsider's viewpoint is, therefore, oftentimes a very enlightening and wholesome undertaking.

It is sometimes said that the balance sheet is well worth the attention of most of the executives within an enterprise, that it serves well the merchandise manager, the executive in charge of finances, including credits and collections, as well as the general manager. I quite agree that it is desirable for all the executives within a business to know and to study the balance sheet of their organization, but except as indicated above, the information on the balance sheet is too condensed and, therefore, wholly inadequate for serving as a guide in the management of the several activities of the business over which these major executives have charge.

As a report in summarized form to the stockholders it is universally used and serves well that purpose. It is chiefly, therefore, in its external relations that the balance sheet is used. Even here we oftentimes find it somewhat inadequate. Most of our states require corporations to submit at least annually a statement of financial condition. In the case of public utilities, however, detailed statements are usually required, including both balance sheet and statement of operations with such supporting data as may seem necessary. Our Federal and State governments in the administration of the various income tax laws, require submission of the balance sheet and profit and loss statements. Here, of course, the balance sheet is serving chiefly as a proof of the accuracy of the profit and loss statement submitted for the purpose. Sometimes the balance sheet is woefully inadequate in its statement of financial condition for purposes of insurance. Similarly the ordinary balance sheet of a public utility is not a fair basis for the determination of equitable rates as the courts have viewed the matter.

The two main purposes which the balance sheet is called upon to serve relate to its uses in connection with the securing of working and fixed capital from the commercial and investment bankers. It is largely these two latter uses that have determined the present form of the balance sheet and the principles of valuation of its content.

Because it has not been the usual practice of bankers to require the submission of the profit and loss statement by a business seeking credit, the balance sheet has been called upon to indicate the operating as well as the financial condition of such businesses. The credit files of most banks contain the annual statement for several years of their many applicants for credit. It is surprising how much information as to the progress of a business can be secured from comparative balance sheets. Comparative ratios of many of the items on such balance sheets give a pretty reliable picture of the trend of conditions within the business, and, therefore, serve as a guide in conjunction with the current balance sheet in judging the present financial condition and the probable future status of the business.

To set forth the facts needed for the determination of the advisability of providing a business with working capital, the present form of balance sheet makes a clear classification between the working-capital assets and the other assets of the business, and between the current and fixed liabilities. The same classification serves also for the determinaton of the fixed capital position of the business.

While the form of a balance sheet is important in that it indicates a separation of the data needed for judging these two conditions, what these two classes on the balance sheet contain and the basis for determination and stating the valuation of the content are obviously of greater importance. From the standpoint, therefore, of a going business, the content of the balance sheet must be so valued as to give a fair basis for judging:

    (1) Its solvency
    (2) Its soundness, and
    (3) In a somewhat lesser degree, its progress.

Another speaker on this program will discuss the subject of valuation for the purpose of determining profits. Here it is purposed to point out the dependence of the valuation principles of the balance sheet upon its two chief uses, viz: the determination of the solvency of the business and its soundness. I should like, however, to examine briefly the conflict which may sometimes exist between the valuation for the purpose of profits determination and that for the purpose of the balance sheet.

In judging the solvency of a business the ability of the business to pay its debts as they come due is the chief consideration. Classification of the balance sheet is based on this. It is to the current assets that creditors must look as the source of the payment of their debts. Cash is the only universally accepted medium of payment of debts. The content of the current asset section of the balance sheet should, therefore, be stated on a cash basis. The several items among the current assets should be valued on the basis of the amount of cash which it is expected they will realize upon conversion. The general principle of valuation, therefore, for the current assets may be stated as a valuation on the basis of cash-realizable values. Since merchandise is one of the current assets the application to it of this valuation principle raises some question as to the propriety of the same basis for the purpose of the profit and loss statement. As a general principle it is not desirable to bring into the records either an unrealized profit or an unrealized loss, although on the grounds of conservatism—a principle very greatly overworked, in my opinion—the latter is less objectionable than the former. A valuation of merchandise at any other figure than cost does bring into the records an unrealized profit and loss. If then the cash realizable value of merchandise differs from cost there is obviously a conflict of value bases between balance sheet and profit and loss statement. How this can be reconciled will be pointed out later.

In judging the soundness of a business a comparison of the fixed assets and fixed liabilities is the usual procedure. The long term creditor, mortgagee, or bond holder desires to know the sufficiency of the values which are the security for his loan. As a usual thing valuation of the fixed assets is, therefore, based on original cost. The valuation basis is oftentimes reduced to the formula, cost less depreciation. In connection with depreciation there may sometimes seem to be a conflict between the requirements for the balance sheet and for profit and loss. Sound valuation is the thing which the balance sheet should set forth. Is it not sometimes possible that an amount of depreciation required for this purpose may sometimes bring about inequitable results from the standpoint of operating costs? In a period of low production, for example, is it quite equitable for the lessened units of production during such period to be compelled to bear a higher unit cost of depreciation than during periods of fuller production? Which should, therefore, be the controlling factor in determining the depreciation policy, the requirements of the profit and loss statement, or the requirements of the balance sheet? There may also thus be a conflict of valuation bases as related to fixed assets.

An application of these general principles of valuation to the items included under the current and fixed classes in the balance sheet may throw some light on this question of conflict of valuation bases. A creditor desires to know the amount of cash which will in regular course of business become available for the payment of his short term loans to the business. In accordance with the use of the balance sheet for this purpose he has a right to expect that the values which have been placed on the current asset items will indicate the fair expectation of the management as to the amount of cash that will be realized from them and so become available for the payment of short term debts. Naturally the cash item in the balance sheet is already realized in cash and in the majority of cases the item, cash, if the term is properly employed, does not present a question of valuation —it being understood, of course, that only cash which is held for working capital purposes is set forth under this title. The notes and accounts receivable are valued not at their book value, but at the amount which it is expected will be realized in cash from their collection. An estimate must be made, therefore, of uncollectible items.

In connection with merchandise, the old formula, cost or market, whichever is the lower, occupies almost the position of an accounting axiom. The formula relies for its authority and potency on what business men, bankers and accountants call the principle of conservatism referred to above. That formula, I am inclined to think, has been adopted chiefly because of the place which merchandise occupies in the determination of profits, rather than its place as one of the current assets. An interesting side light on such valuation basis was seen in the attitude which bankers took, during the recent depression, towards balance sheets submitted as a basis for loans. In their analysis of such balance sheets not only was the valuation on the basis of current market values investigated, but the probable value of the merchandise on the date of the maturity of the loan was the controlling valuation basis for lending purposes. The creditor's attitude, therefore, based on the use which he desires to make of the balance sheet, wholly disregards the profit and loss features of merchandise valuation. What he desires is the probable cash realizable value of the merchandise. By this, of course, is not meant the selling price of the merchandise. The cash realized from the sale of merchandise is in a sense its cash realizable basis, but does not indicate the cash which will probably become available for the payment of current debts. This is, of course, the desired figure. The margin between the cost and selling price of merchandise must, of course, be used first for the payment of the operating expenses of the business. They constitute a first claim against this margin. What is left of the sale price, after the payment of operating expense, will become available for the payment of short term creditors.

My contention, therefore, is that the value of merchandise should be related to its sale price rather than to its cost, or replacement cost.

The so-called retail method of valuing the inventory very closely approximates this principle.

In order to indicate clearly and fully all the facts bearing on the valuation of merchandise, it is desirable also that the cost price be shown on the face of the balance sheet, as well as this cash realizable value. These two may be adjusted by means of the valuation reserve which will become effective, of course, in the profit and loss statement. As to how that may best be worked out in that statement, I am not so much concerned as with the general principle that for the purpose of judging the condition of solvency of a business, merchandise should be valued on what I have called the cash realizable basis.

In passing I may say that in my opinion in the trading section of the profit and loss statement the valuation of merchandise at cost is the desirable basis, inasmuch as any other valuation than cost will inject unrealized profits or losses into that statement. In the final sections of the statement it will be necessary, of course, to adjust the cost valuation basis to the cash realizable basis used in the balance sheet.

In judging the soundness of the values back of long term loans an analysis of the fixed assets is made. These fixed assets may be divided usually into three main groups:

(1)   Those not subject to depreciation
(2)   Those subject to depreciation and depletion
(3)   Those subject to fluctuation

Under the first group land is the usual item. Under the second group one finds buildings, equipment and mining or other similar property. Under the third group the intangible assets, patents, good will, etc., appear. The first and third groups—with the exception of patents—are usually valued at original cost. It is standard practice to value all other items at original cost, less accrued depreciation and depletion.

The first item, land, under this sub-classification of fixed assets may be subject to depreciation because of changes in the market. More often perhaps it is subject to appreciation, in which case a nice point in valuation is sometimes met when a bond issue is floated based chiefly on the present market value of the land which may in some cases be several times its original cost. In such cases it seems best to state the value of the land at a fair appraised value offsetting the increment in value by a suitably earmarked surplus so that the full facts may be shown.

In connection with the second group of items, which are subject to depreciation or depletion, there arises a possible conflict between the bases of valuation for profit and loss purposes and for balance sheet purposes. From the standpoint of the going concern, in my opinion, the requirement of the profit and loss statement for a fairly even per-unit distribution of depreciation should usually govern. As to the values at which such assets appear on the balance sheet, the creditor should be satisfied rather that adequate provision is being made during the life of the asset for its replacement upon the expiration of its service to the company, than that its stated value is its actual current value.   In such cases it is the depreciation policy which should be investigated, rather than the present current value of these assets.

With regard to the third sub-class under the fixed assets, namely, the intangibles, the price at which these are stated should always be the subject of careful investigation.   Their values are highly speculative and depend in most cases on the net profit results of the business rather than on any other factors.   The statement of their value on the basis of original cost is just as apt to serve as well as any other value.

In bringing before you this topic for discussion, I have had in mind not the presentation of any particularly new point of view, but the necessity of requiring that students examine the foundations on which the principles of accounting rest rather than that they acquire a knowledge of those principles.   Students are too often inclined, as perhaps are most of us, to the acceptance of time honored formulas, rather than an investigation of the data out of which those formulas have come.   They much prefer to accept a formula and learn glibly its applications, than to know why the formula is what it is, and, therefore have an appreciation of its application under varying conditions.   If we as teachers can secure a questioning and investigative frame of mind on the part of students, rather than a facility in the application of a few principles, we will have started the student well along the road toward real preparation for after life. The ability to think a thing out to a logical conclusion is, in my opinion, much more desirable than mere adeptness and facility.

STANDARDIZATION OF THE BALANCE SHEET

Roy B. Kester

STANDARDIZATION OF THE BALANCE SHEET

BY

PROFESSOR ROY B. KESTER

Columbia University

New York City

The Chairman of the Committee in charge of the program has indicated that the term *balance sheet,* as used in the title of this paper, is intended to include not only the balance sheet, but also the supplementary statement of profit and loss or the operating statement, as it is variously termed. I have also included in my treatment of this topic the surplus account which is sometimes listed as a separate statement.

The purpose of my paper is not to discuss in detail many of the controversial aspects of the topic but rather to block out its broad divisions with the thought that the controversial phases will serve as the subject matter for discussion from the floor.

The Standardization Movement

Standardization as applied to business, particularly the manufacturing industry, is not new, although the application of the standardization principle to the financial affairs of a business is of comparatively recent origin.

On the physical and mechanical side standardization is one of the elements of the movement for the elimination of waste. It may be looked upon as one of the methods for the securing of a more efficient use of manufacturing facilities. The reduction of variety of product and of method of production has been the outstanding result or achievement of the movement. In this country the various engineering societies have sponsored the movement and at the present time the American Engineering Standards Committee, composed of representatives of the various engineering associations, is the official organization through which the various standardization projects are being worked out. Such projects as the standardization of the threads on screws and screw couplings, the standardization of the size of building materials, such as bricks, window glass, metal sheets and so forth, have received attention, along with many other things of a similar nature.

It is interesting to note that one of the large banks in New York recently issued a pamphlet dealing with the subject of standardization in the use of capital. In this publication emphasis was placed on the fact that there is little or no uniformity or standardization observed by business as to the various purposes for which capital is used. The amount of capital tied up in inventories in one business may differ, as a matter of policy, very materially from that used by another business similarly situated. So also there is little uniformity in the relationship between the capital tied up in fixed plant and the volume of business done by various corporations. It is suggested that due consideration to standardization in the use of capital might well effect unthought-of savings and so make available large supplies of capital for other uses.

The standardization movement has often-times been criticised on the ground that it represents a tendency toward the further mechanization of our civilization. Those students of contemporary life who maintain that individualism should be fostered if the advance of civilization is to be accelerated, are naturally very much concerned and are probably very much over-wrought because of the standardization movement. This attitude arises, I fear, from a misunderstanding of the real purpose of the movement. The end aimed at by the standardization movement is in no sense a complete uniformity of life and its activities but rather the elimination of those many and, oftentimes, senseless variations from the standard, which serve no useful purpose, and are certainly not an expression of the best individualism.

As our civilization grows more complex it becomes more and more difficult to understand and to interpret properly. This is due in very large measure to the varying terminology used in the record and expression of the facts of business and social life. That science is in an extremely fortunate position which has been able to build up for itself a technical terminology whose meaning is clear in all its uses. A great saving will accrue as a result of the further exten-

2

sion of the standardization movement into the field of business records and reports. The use of a standard terminology here will make possible the easy understanding of business and other data and will bring about a confidence in the correctness and accuracy of the comparative statistics based on these data. This will in turn enable us to build up standards by means of which we can measure the results of accomplishment.

One of the outstanding characteristics of the present day administration of business is the development of measuring sticks for the various kinds of business activities, which have in most cases in the past been thought not possible of satisfactory measurement. The standardization movement is closely related to the development of such measuring sticks.

The application of standardization to the construction and interpretation of financial statements is a comparatively recent development, and has concerned itself with the following aspects or phases of the subject:

1. Standardization as to form and classification
2. Standardization as to content and terminology
3. Standardization as to valuation
4. Standardization as to audit and verification procedure

Need for Standardization of Balance Sheets

In connection with the standardization of balance sheets some advantages are immediately apparent. These may be grouped under two headings.

1. External, or those advantages accruing to outsiders.

2. Internal, or those advantages accruing to the executives of the business.

Among those on the outside of business the most interested are the bankers and note brokers whose function it is to furnish short-term commercial credit. To an almost equal extent, the investment banker, who is called upon to furnish capital for the growth and expansion of business, is also an interested party.

An inspection of the credit files of the ordinary commercial bank will indicate the urgency of the need for standardization in order that there may be had a proper understanding and evaluation of the balance sheets presented as the basis for the extension of

3

short term credit. This lack of standardization is chargeable not only to the accounting departments of private business but, in no small measure, to the various public accounting firms whose members are responsible for the form and content of the balance sheets submitted. Much the same situation is faced by investment bankers in the use of balance sheets excepting that because of the greater stake involved they are in a position to demand a special investigation which will bring to their knowledge, as far as possible, the exact state of the applicant's business.

An interesting side light growing out of bond underwritings is seen in the necessity for a careful definition of accounting terms in the bond indenture which provides for a sinking fund. A frequent provision of the indenture is that the corporation must at all times maintain a stated ratio between current assets and current liabilities. Because of the lack of uniformity in the use of the terms, current assets and current liabilities, it has been found necessary to define these terms in the bond indenture in order that there may be a clearer understanding as to whether at a given time the terms of the indenture are being lived up to.

In the management of business today a large measure of dependence is being placed on normal or average standards of operation. These may be made to serve as measuring sticks by means of which the variation of individual businesses from this standard can be determined.

An outstanding development of present day business methods is the trade association movement. There are in existence in the United States of America today several hundred of these associations having a national or state-wide scope. The more progressive of these associations have developed bureaus for the collection of the financial and operating statistics of their members. A careful summarization of these statistics has been made in order to determine what may be looked upon as the average or normal performance of the industry. These summaries have been furnished to members, in most cases without a divulgence of the individual data from which the summaries were made up. A comparison of these normal or average statistics with the performance by an individual member provides that member with an invaluable measuring stick or standard by which to judge the accomplishments of his business.

4

As a prerequisite to the compilation of these financial and operating statistics, it has been necessary for the trade association to develop and adopt a uniform system of accounts so that the statistical data furnished the trade association bureau will be of a strictly comparable character. Otherwise little or no reliance could be placed on the summarized statistics. Thus it is seen that for this purpose, standardization of financial statements is an absolutely necessary prerequisite.

Standardization of Form and Classification

Financial statements are important chiefly for the reliability and accuracy of the information which they contain, rather than because of the structure or form of the statement. However, in the handling of many financial statements a very great saving of time and effort is secured when there has been a due regard to correctness of form. The reading and interpretation of financial statements is greatly facilitated by a proper form and structure.

The more important phases or aspects of the question of form are seen in the following tabulation:

1. Lack of uniformity, as between the so-called English and Continental form of balance sheet
2. The use of the account and report form of statement
3. The main titles or sections of the statement. In some balance sheets the Liability and Proprietorship or Capital sections are merged under the one title, Liabilities. Others designate three separate sections, under the titles, Assets, Liabilities, and Proprietorship or Net Worth.
4. Lack of uniformity in the classification of sub-divisions as seen in the use of the terms: current, fixed, and other assets and liabilities. A notable lack of uniformity is found in the title, "deferred charges."

In viewing individual balance sheets, particularly those drawn up for internal use as distinguished from those drawn up for publication, one is sometimes amazed at the lack of uniformity in the titles of classes and sections.

While the form or structure of the statement is important, of equal or greater importance is the assurance that the individual items

5

of the balance sheet have been placed under the proper classification. The inclusion of any items of fixed or other assets under the classification "Current Assets" is of course misleading and renders the statement impossible of clear interpretation.

Standardization of Content and Terminology

The content of financial statements is, of course, of much greater importance than their form. The way in which the content is expressed is also of great importance. By content of a financial statement is meant the items which are admitted to it. By the way in which the content .is expressed is meant the terminology used for the proper setting forth of the content. The discussion at this point will be limited to the balance sheet.

In a general way it may be said that only those items should be admitted to the balance sheet in which the company has a legal property interest or right. This means that all property owned by the corporation, and all those items which indicate claims of creditors against the company's properties are to be admitted. It would seem that ordinarily there should be little variation of practice in regard to the content of the balance sheet. This, however, is not the case; the variations are quite marked. They are seen particularly in the class of items known as intangibles, under which appear such terms as goodwill, patents, trade marks, franchises, contracts, etc. It is a frequent practice of some of the best manufacturing corporations in the country to eliminate from the balance sheet all intangible items as quickly as possible. Such companies are in most cases the very ones in which these items of goodwill, patents, etc. are particularly valuable. Even with such companies the practice with regard to these items varies; some indicating the existence of such intangibles by means of memorandum or memoriter accounts, usually carried at some nominal valuation such as one dollar; others making absolutely no reference to them on the balance sheet.

Variation of the content of balance sheets is seen also in the manner of handling the class of items known as contingent assets and contingent liabilities. Financial institutions, for the most part, are inclined to give a full expression on the balance sheet of all contingent assets and liabilities. On the other hand, industrial and mercantile concerns seldom show either of these items as integral

6

parts of the balance sheet. The contingent liability items are, as a usual thing, listed as footnotes to the balance sheet and contingent assets are seldom shown.

A great hindrance to the understanding and interpretation of balance sheets is the lack of a technical terminology. This is a condition which prevails among many of the sciences, particularly the social sciences. Accounting, instead of having a technical terminology of its own, has been compelled to use terms which have for centuries been employed in the business world, where unfortunately they have not been as closely defined as is oftentimes desirable and necessary in accounting. Examples of such terms are accounts receivable, accounts payable, reserves, and funds. In any instance where such terms are employed an intimate knowledge of the content is necessary before there can be a proper classification and understanding of them. Under the balance sheet term, accounts receivable, for example, may be included—because of its broad meaning—not only claims against customers arising in the course of trade, but numerous other items such as claims against subsidiaries for advances, claims against officers or employees for loans made them, and almost any other kind of claim.

The term, reserve, has at least three different meanings when used in accounting. It is used as the title of an asset valuation account, such as reserve for depreciation and reserve for doubtful accounts. It is frequently used to express the estimate of a liability whose amount is not determinable at a given time, such, for example, as a reserve for federal income tax. And, finally, it is used to express the appropriation of profits for a given purpose, such, for example, as a reserve for sinking fund. Similarly the term, fund, is used to indicate an asset account, and it is also used to express a capital or proprietorship item. With the term, surplus, are often merged such varying items as capital surplus—that is, surplus originally contributed by the stockholders—surplus arising from revaluation of plant and equipment, and earned surplus. A suitable terminology must be developed to give a proper determination of these various meanings before accounting will be easily interpreted and understood.

On the border line between the subject of content of the balance sheet and its valuation are some items which rest largely on human judgment and corporation policy for their placing on the financial statements. The distinction between capital and revenue expenditures is important here. In some corporations conservative policy dictates the charge against revenue of all possible items and the capitalization of only those items about which there can be no doubt as to the propriety of their inclusion as asset charges. In other companies the reverse policy is pursued. The treatment of advertising expenditure—particularly what has come to be known as expenditures for national advertising—constitutes another instance of items of this kind about which there is variety of practice.

Standardization as to Valuation

While in the interpretation of a balance sheet, form and content are of course important, the valuation basis on which items are admitted to the balance sheet is most important of all. Here one finds a considerable lack of uniformity. The common bases used are (1) cost, (2) reproductive cost, (3) sales valuation, (4) going concern value. In a study of the individual items which are shown in balance sheets, one not infrequently finds several or all of these valuation bases used in the same balance sheet. It is probably for this reason that the term, going concern valuation, has been employed to cover the variety of valuation bases. In the showing of accounts receivable, for example, some concerns carry the item at book value less an allowed amount for doubtful accounts. In the case of other corporations, however, not only is an allowance made for doubtful accounts but also for cash discounts which its customers will probably take in the settlement of their claims.

In connection with the item, merchandise, we often find three or four valuation bases used. Some concerns hold largely to a cost valuation throughout; others to a market valuation; still others to a valuation basis denominated cost or market, whichever is the lower, as applied to each item of the inventory; and still others use a valuation basis which is dependent upon the retail sale value of the commodity. Again variety of use is found in the application of the cost valuation basis. Actual cost, a cost of the most recent purchases, replacement cost, and, in the case of industrial concerns, manufacturing cost to which has been added so called putative interest on investment, and/or with which have also been included

8

elements of value to cover a proper share of the selling and administrative costs.

Permanent investments are valued sometimes at cost and sometimes at cost plus or minus pro-rata share of the profits and losses resulting since the date of purchase and remaining undistributed as dividends.

Great variation is noted in the valuation of fixed properties. Not only is depreciation computed on different bases in different concerns, but also the entire policy with regard to depreciation differs radically. Depreciation is sometimes based on lapse of time, that is the calendar year; again it is based on production output; and sometimes the method for the distribution of periodic depreciation involves the use of compound interest calculations. A recent analysis of financial statements compiled by Mr. Laurence H. Sloan, of the Standard Statistics Company, indicates that in many instances the periodic depreciation charge has been related rather closely to the amount of periodic net profit determined before depreciation or depletion charges have been taken into account. Mr. Sloan says, as a result of his studies, that depreciation "is chiefly a question of practicability. On the average, and over a period of time, what industries can *afford* to charge depreciation has an important bearing upon what is actually so charged."

The variety of practice with regard to the valuation of intangible items in the balance sheet was referred to above.

In connection with the valuation of liabilities and of net worth items, there is not usually seen as great variety of practice as in connection with the asset items, although even here some variations are found.

Before leaving the question of valuation, brief reference should be made to the suggestion, which is particularly pertinent in times of rapidly changing price levels, that balance sheets should use a valuation which will express or reflect the present purchasing power of the dollar or other monetary unit of measure. Thus with prices in the building industry, for example, a little more than double what they were fifteen years ago, a *dollar* of value now has approximately one-half the value that it had in 1913 and 1914. This is a very important question about which, however, there is a great difference of opinion, and only this brief reference will be made to it here.

9

Standardization of Audit and Verification Procedure

Inasmuch as the great majority of financial statements of the leading business corporations of the country carry the signatures and certifications of public accountants, the question as to uniform practice in the verification of content and valuation of financial statements is an exceedingly important one. The banker, the trade creditor, and the general public have a right to expect that there should be a very large degree of standardization in this important matter. I feel, from my contacts with public accounting, that the degree of standardization here is nothing like as great as these outside interested parties should demand.

Standardization of the Profit and Loss Statement

What has been said as to variety of practice with regard to the balance sheet is to an almost equal extent true with regard to the statement of operations, frequently termed the statement of profit and loss. The discussion as to form, content, and valuation given above is applicable with some slight adaptation to the profit and loss statement, and no more detailed discussion will be given here. It is desired, however, to present a few points which are pertinent only to the statement of profit and loss. There is considerable variation in practice as to what the statement of profit and loss is designed to show. A great many such published statements fail to show the volume of business done, these statements usually showing only the so-called gross profit. Most statements show what is termed net profit. Oftentimes, however, this is the item which is usually termed, net operating profit, and not the amount of final net profit carried to surplus account. Some corporations include as a part of the statement of profit and loss a complete surplus statement, showing the surplus at the beginning of the period, together with all changes in it during the period, thus arriving at the amount of surplus shown at the end of the period on the balance sheet. There is noted also a great variety of terminology. This is even more confusing in connection with a proper understanding and interpretation of the profit and loss statement, than is true of the similar situation in connection with the balance sheet. There is little

10

standardization of use in the terms gross and net earnings, income, sales, and profits.

Before leaving this subject of standardization of the profit and loss statement, I desire to call attention to the desirability of including as a foot-note to the statement the amount of unfilled orders at the close of the period under review. While the volume of business done during the period just closed is important, it is equally important in a proper showing of financial condition to have some indication as to the probable condition of business in the near future. Some of our best managed corporations issue as an important item of financial information a statement of unfilled orders at the close of the fiscal period.

Practicality of Standardization

The question of the standardization of financial statements has received a great deal of attention from the outstanding leaders of the accounting profession and also from business analysts and others who are so largely dependent on the information furnished by the accounts. The most recent promulgation with regard to this matter is that of the American Institute of Accountants, recently issued under the title, Verification of Financial Statements, which is a complete revision and recension of an earlier pamphlet, Approved Methods for the Preparation of Balance Sheet Statements. The publication contains a brief history of the work of the committee of the American Institute of Accountants which had charge of the revision. The complete report of the committee is published in the May, 1929, issue of the Journal of Accountancy, which is the official organ of the Institute. The larger portion of the report has to do with the methods and procedures to be followed in the audit and verification of balance sheet and profit and loss statements. Many controversial points are covered, and, for a statement of the conclusions reached you are referred to that issue of the Journal of Accountancy.

For the purpose of comparison with the forms of statements suggested by others, there are here included the forms of balance sheet and profit and loss statement suggested by the committee. These are given below:

FORM OF BALANCE SHEET

Assets

CASH:

    On hand...

    In bank...

NOTES AND ACCOUNTS RECEIVABLE:

    Notes receivable, customers' (not past due)...................

    Accounts receivable, customers' (not past due)................

    Notes receivable, customers' (past due)......................

    Accounts receivable, customers' (past due)....................

LESS:

    Reserve for bad debts.....................................

    Reserve for discounts, freight, allowances, etc.................

INVENTORIES:

    Raw material on hand.....................................

    Goods in process...

    Uncompleted contracts ....

    Less: payment on account................................

    Finished goods on hand....................................

OTHER CURRENT ASSETS:

    Marketable securities......................................

    Indebtedness of officers, stockholders and employees............

    Indebtedness of affiliated companies (current).................

        Total current assets..................................

INVESTMENTS:

    Securities of affiliated companies............................

    Indebtedness of affiliated companies—not current..............

    Other (state important items separately)......................

FIXED ASSETS:

    Land used for plant.......................................

    Buildings used for plant....................................

    Machinery ....

    Tools and plant equipment.................................

    Patterns and drawings.....................................

    Office furniture and fixtures................................

    Other fixed assets (describe fully)..........................

        Total fixed assets....................................

12

LESS:

    Reserve for depreciation, depletion, etc. (describe fully)..........

DEFERRED CHARGES:

    Prepaid expenses, interest, insurance, taxes, etc.................

OTHER ASSETS (describe fully)..................................

        Total ....

Liabilities

NOTES AND ACCOUNTS PAYABLE:

Secured liabilities—

    Obligations secured by:

        Customers' accounts assigned in the amount of...............

        Liens on inventories.......................................

        Securities deposited as collateral...........................

        Other collateral ....

Unsecured notes—

        Acceptances made for merchandise or raw-material purchases

        Notes given for merchandise or raw material purchased........

        Notes given to banks for money borrowed...................

        Notes sold through brokers................................

        Notes given for machinery, additions to plant, etc............

        Notes due to stockholders, officers or employees.............

Unsecured accounts—

        Accounts payable for purchases (not yet due)...............

        Accounts payable for purchases (past due).................

        Accounts payable to stockholders, officers, or employees........

ACCRUED LIABILITIES, (INTEREST, TAXES, WAGES, ETC.)...........

OTHER CURRENT LIABILITIES (describe fully)......................

    ....

    ....

        Total current liabilities..................................

FIXED LIABILITIES:

Obligations secured by:

    Mortgage on plant (due date)..............................

    Mortgage on other real estate (due date)....................

    Chattel mortgage on machinery or equipment (due date).........

Other funded indebtedness (describe fully) . . . .
. . . .
. . . .
. . . .
        Total Liabilities . . . .

NET WORTH:

  If a corporation—
    (a) Preferred stock (less stock in treasury) . . . .
    (b) Common stock (less stock in treasury) . . . .
    (c) Surplus:
          Capital or paid-in
          Arising from revaluation of capital assets (see footnote) . . .
          . . . .
          Earned (or deficit) . . . .
  If a person or partnership—
    (a) Capital
    (b) Undistributed profits or deficit
          Total . . . .
          Contingent liabilities—classify and explain

FORM FOR PROFIT AND LOSS STATEMENT

Gross sales . . . .
Less: outward freight, allowances and returns . . . .
    Net sales . . . .
Inventory beginning of year . . . .
Purchases, net (or cost of goods produced) . . . .
Less: inventory end of year . . . .
    Cost of sales . . . .
    Gross profit on sales . . . .
Selling expenses (itemized to correspond with ledger accounts kept) . .
    Total selling expenses . . . .
General expenses (itemized to correspond with ledger accounts kept).
Administrative expenses (itemized to correspond with ledger accounts
    kept) . . . .
    Total administrative expenses . . . .
    Total expenses . . . .
    Net profit on sales . . . .
OTHER INCOME:
    Income from investments . . . .
    Interest on notes receivable, etc. . . . .
        Gross income . . . .

14

Deductions from Income:
    Interest on bonded debt. . . . .
    Interest on notes payable. . . . .
    Taxes, depreciation, etc. (separately shown) . . . .
        Total deductions. . . . .
Net income for the period. . . . .
Add: special credits to profit and loss (separately shown) . . . .
Deduct: special charges to profit and loss (separately shown) . . . .
    Profit and loss for period. . . . .
Surplus beginning of period. . . . .
Add or deduct items in the surplus account attributable to prior
    periods. . . . .
Dividends paid. . . . .
    Earned surplus at end of period. . . . .

Very great progress has been made in the standardization of accounting methods and statements by the various trade associations to which earlier reference was made. One of the first of these associations to recognize the value of uniformity in accounting methods was the United Typothetae of America. Following their lead a great many other associations recognized that the foundation of the statistical services to their members must be a uniform system of accounts which through summarization could be expressed in uniform or standard financial statements. Some of the most recent developments along this line by associations are the manuals of accounting of the National Association of Ice Cream Manufacturers, the National Association of Machinery Builders, and the Controllers' Congress, which is composed of the accounting officers of the National Retail Dry Goods Association. The Controllers' Congress has developed an accounting manual which takes cognizance of the varying requirements of concerns of different sizes so far as the need for detailed information is concerned. The system of accounting developed is so arranged that, although a much greater classification of accounts is provided for large concerns than for small, the broad classifications are such that the summarization of the accounts as shown in balance sheet and profit and loss statement are uniform regardless of the size of the company.

Among bank credit men, the research work carried on by Alexander Wall at Lansdowne, Pennsylvania, has given impetus to the movement for standardization of financial statements.

In the last few years, characterized by great activity of the various stock markets of the country, a very great deal of attention has been given to the statistical analysis of financial statements. Many business enterprises have been established, the business of which is to provide service and information of this character. One of these, the Standard Statistics Company, was referred to above. Mr. Laurence H. Sloan of that company has recently published a book entitled, "Corporation Profits" in which he points out that one of the great handicaps in the comparative study of corporations is the lack of standardization and uniformity in financial statements. As a result of his studies he and his associates have developed what they consider to be "The Ideal Financial Report for the Average Industrial Corporation." Through his courtesy I am including these forms immediately below.

"IDEAL" FINANCIAL REPORT FOR THE AVERAGE INDUSTRIAL CORPORATION[1]

INCOME ACCOUNT

1. Gross Revenue or Gross Sales

Not unless the security owner has a record of gross can he arrive at an understanding of the meaning of the net income figure. In many cases, not unless he has a long-term record of gross can he determine whether his company is a growing or a decadent one. Gross must be the starting point of every income report; in only a minority of cases is it now the starting point of that portion of the income account which *is made public*.

2. Operating Expenses or Cost of Sales

Should be subdivided under two heads:

a Cost of production;
b General selling and administrative expense; (where taxes other than Federal are a major item, they should be reported separately.)

Such a subdivision makes possible a check and analysis of the most important elements in cost. The ratio between gross revenue and

[1]Compiled by Howard G. Parker and Ivan S. Dobson, of the Standard Statistics Co. Taken from Sloan's Corporation Profits, p. 338, e.s.

16

operating expense over a period of time is a very significant one; detailed information as to costs makes it possible to explain variations in this ratio.

3. *Expenditures for Maintenance, etc.*

Should always be separated from other elements in total costs. The value of the figure lies in the fact that it gives a clue as to whether property is being kept in first-class condition, and as to whether expenditures in a given period are subnormal, normal or supranormal.

4. *Operating Income*

Obtained by deducting Items 2 and 3 from Item 1. Reports the amount of profit derived directly from the operation of the business.

5. *Other Income*

Including all profits other than from operations, such as bank interest, dividends on securities owned, etc. Profit on sale of any current assets, such as securities, should be itemized separately. If "other income" is not reported separately, and in detail, the security owner has no basis for judging what proportion of total income is likely to be nonrecurrent.

6. *Total Income*

The sum of Items 4 and 5.

7. *Depreciation, Depletion, Obsolescence, Reserves, etc.*

This account is one which is much and frequently abused. Refer to special analysis dealing with the item. Details of this reserve should be listed separately in the income account.

8. *Federal Taxes*

This item is computed after allowing for income charges, but it ranks ahead of these charges in payment, after the fiscal year is ended.

9. *Other Deductions*

Such as inventory adjustments, loss on sale of any current assets, and all other deductions which can be classed as legitimate charges against the business for a given year. Reserves for probable losses on inventories and receivables should also be shown here. (Full details should be shown.)

10.   Net Profit
Item 6 minus Items 7, 8, and 9.

11.   Fixed Charges
Including bond interest, other interest, amortization of bond discount, subsidiary preferred dividends, and bond sinking funds. (Details.)

12.   Net Income
Net profit minus fixed charges.

13.   Preferred Dividends
Amount paid in cash.

14.   Common Dividends
Amount paid in cash.

15.   Balance After Dividends

16.   Surplus Credits
Including all items such as profit on sales of capital assets, transfers to surplus from any reserves, credit adjustments of any prior year's items, etc.   (In detail.)

17.   Surplus Debits
Including stock dividends, reduction in stated value of good will, loss on sale of capital assets, etc.   (In detail.)

18.   Net Increase or Decrease in Surplus During Year
Sum of Items 15 and 16, minus Item 17.

19.   Surplus Balance Carried Forward From Previous Year
As shown in previous year's balance sheet.

20.   Balance in Surplus Account at End of Current Year
Sum of Items 18 and 19.

BALANCE SHEET

ASSETS

1. Property Account

Should be stated whether value assigned is at cost or appraised value. Reserves for depreciation, depletion, obsolescence, etc., should be noted separately.

2. Long Term Investments

Statement should specify whether investments are carried at cost or market, and investments in subsidiaries should be reported separately. Full list of investments of this type should be published at least annually. Any major change in holding from one year to the next should be explained.

3. Intangibles

Should be detailed, viz:

   a Good will.
   b Patents.
   c Leasehold value.
   d Unamortized bond discount.
   e Other.

4. Advances or Long Term Accounts Receivable

Should be segregated, so that differentiation can be made between advances to subsidiaries and others. The necessity for such advances should be explained.

5. Prepayments

Such as insurance, taxes, etc.

6. Other Assets

Such as real estate not used in operation, employees' stock subscriptions, etc.

7. Current Assets

Should be subdivided as follows:

   a Cash in banks and on hand.
   b Government securities.
   c Other temporary investments, such as marketable securities, demand, call, and time loans, etc. Should be reported at market value. If marketable securities constitute a large proportion of total assets, details of holdings should be shown.

    d Accounts receivable (trade).

    e Temporary advances to subsidiaries.

    f Inventories: (1) finished goods; (2) goods in process; (3) materials and supplies.

    g Other current assets, such as cash surrender value of insurance policies, etc.

8. *Total Assets*

LIABILITIES

9. *Preferred Stock*

Details should be given if preferred is of more than one class. If it carries no par value, the liquidation value and the number of shares outstanding should be stated.

10. *Common Stock*

Should be reported as an item separate from surplus, regardless of whether the issue carries a par or no par value. Number of shares outstanding should be stated. If common is of more than one class, proper distinction should be made.

11. *Funded Debt*

Complete list, with details as to coupon, maturity dates, etc., should be carried either in the balance sheet or in the annual report accompanying.

12. *Other Long-term Obligations*

Should be segregated as to subsidiaries and other, with full explanation.

13. *Reserves*

This item should report only reserves which are set up against fixed assets and reserves for general contingencies. Reserves set up against current assets should be reported under current liabilities.

14. *Other Obligations*

Such as deposits returnable only under special conditions, etc.

15. *Surplus*

Subdivided as follows:

    a Capital and appreciated surplus.

20

    b Appropriated surplus (for improvements, sinking funds, etc.)

    c Earned surplus.

16. *Current Liabilities*

  Should be subdivided as follows:

    a Loans payable to banks.

    b Notes payable (trade).

    c Accounts payable.

    d Temporary loans from subsidiary companies.

    e Accrued expenses—interest, taxes, dividends, insurance, etc.

    f Tax reserves (Federal and other).

    g Current reserves—against receivables, inventories, etc. Details should appear.

    h Dividends payable.

    i Other current liabilities.

17. *Total Liabilities*

18. *Contingent Liabilities*

Any guarantee or endorsement to which the company is committed should be reported in detail.

THE ANNUAL REPORT

"A number of corporations have already adopted the practice of appending to their annual income accounts and balance sheets a statement giving further information to stockholders. When this report is complete, it is of inestimable value in analyzing the statistical statements. It becomes particularly illuminating when it explains important *changes* that have occured as compared with the year preceding the current one—changes in the tempo of production, in market prices for the goods that are produced or sold, in the amount of gross and net income (especially in nonrecurrent income), in dividends, fixed charges, and special adjustments, in the property and investment accounts, in capital structure and in cash, inventories, and receivables.

"It is especially important to explain changes in the surplus account. Without such an explanation, it is often virtually impossible to analyze a financial statement. The surplus account is a

21

catch-all, offering the opportunity for many abuses.   An explanation of year-to-year adjustments is essential."

It is, of course, recognized that the development of uniform and standard accounting methods must take cognizance of the legal requirements and restrictions in the various countries.   In the United States, there are not many such requirements and restrictions.   Most of these relate to public utilities rather than to industrial and mercantile establishments.   It may be interesting to note in connection with the standardization movement that the United States Treasury through its Income Tax Bureau is attempting to lay the foundation for a uniform practice so far as the various industries are concerned, with regard to the valuation of fixed properties, or rather, with regard to the depreciation practice and policy relating to fixed properties.

Conclusion

In a paper of this kind the conclusion is concerned chiefly with a restatement and summarization of the advantages to be gained through the thesis developed in the paper.   Briefly stated these advantages are:

1. An elimination of considerable waste of time and effort on the part of those compelled to use financial statements.   It is an interesting commentary on the present status of public accounting that the importance attached by bankers to certified financial statements presented to them for credit or other purposes depends very largely on the professional ability and reputation of the public accountant certifying the statement.   To provide accessible information on this point many banks maintain a rating file for public accountants in which an attempt is made to separate the good from the bad.

2. Sounder accounting methods will be developed and made of general acceptance.

3. This will bring about more trustworthy and reliable data in published financial statements.

4. A better understanding and interpretation of such statements will result.   Here it should be pointed out, however, that

22

for a proper understanding of financial statements not only must the statement itself contain an explanation of facts of generally recognized meaning and intent. but also the reader of such statements must have a fairly intimate knowledge of the methods of accounting in accordance with which the summarized material in the statements has been built up.

5. A better and more intelligent administration of the work of the various governmental supervisory boards and agencies will result.

6. Sounder business policies and practices will be developed and employed by business in general because the analysis of business undertakings will be based on more accurate data.

These several advantages so far outweigh any possible disadadvantages that greater uniformity of accounting methods and standardization of financial statements will undoubtedly be developed in the not distant future.

THE PUBLIC ACCOUNTANT

THE PUBLIC ACCOUNTANT.

In our January issue we began to publish a series of "definitions" of a "Public Accountant." The publication of these definitions is continued in this number, wherein we take pleasure in presenting contributions from Buffalo, Philadelphia, Pittsburg and Chicago.

Definitions.

"A Public Accountant is a person who renders to others a degree of temporary service so valuable that they could not afford to engage his entire time. His report should be so comprehensive that it will be a retrospective view, a present exposition, and a basis for all future operations."

W. G. Mowatt, C. P. A.,
Buffalo, N. Y.

"A Public Accountant is a man fearless and unprejudiced, with the ability to look at both sides of a question; one who will not allow his honest opinions to be changed by client or adverse party; who dictates and is never dictated to; who places his devotion to his profession above the opportunities of gain by questionable means."

R. H. Montgomery, C. P. A.,
Stephen Girard Bldg., Philadelphia,
Member of the Pennsylvania Association of Public Accountants.

"A Public Accountant is one who professionally practices the career of an accountant to the general community. He is one who holds himself ready to accept special engagements from the people, in which his advice, discretion, experience, knowledge in the science and skill in the art of accountancy may be deemed desirable and necessary."

Equity (of Pittsburg, Pa.).

("Equity" is one of the most prominent accountants of the State, but, being over modest, he prefers a nom de plume.—Ed.)

"A person whose training enables him to understand and examine into all classes of accounts and books subsidiary thereto, with the object of presenting to his client, without fear or favor, report and statements accurately setting forth the past workings for a given period, present financial condition and future prospects."

Ernest Reckitt,
Royal Insurance Bldg., Chicago,
Fellow of the Illinois Association of Public Accountants.

A Public Accountant should be a thorough figure-man and organizer, having an analytical mind, a knowledge of all laws effecting commerce and of the best business methods, able to apply them to any business. In other words, should be a thorough business expert, able to practically apply his knowledge.

Walton, Joplin & Co.,
Fellows of the Illinois Association of Public Accountants.

A man's books are the written history of his business. In them are recorded the experience of years. It is important that these records be correct. A public accountant is a specialist in accounts and in the varied and complex interests of our present business life he is a necessity.

Robert Nelson, Chartered Accountant,
1201 Mallers' Building, Chicago.

THE IMPORTANCE OF UNIFORM PRACTICE IN DETERMINING THE PROFITS OF PUBLIC SERVICE CORPORATIONS WHERE MUNICIPALITIES HAVE THE POWER TO REGULATE RATES

Robert H. Montgomery

The Importance of Uniform Practice in Determining the Profits of Public Service Corporations Where Municipalities Have the Power to Regulate Rates.

By ROBERT H. MONTGOMERY, C. P. A.

Attorney-at-Law, New York City,

Of Lybrand, Ross Bros. & Montgomery, Certified Public Accountants.

There is a growing tendency in the United States toward municipal ownership of all public utilities, and, while this desire on the part of certain zealous advocates extends to almost every industry which might by any stretch of imagination be called public, the more general aim embraces only those utilities which affect most vitally public health and comfort.

In a recent editorial of *The Commoner,* Hon. William Jennings Bryan said:

> "Private contracts for water, lighting and street car facilities have been the fruitful source of municipal corruption, and there is no solution of these municipal problems that does not involve municipal ownership. The progress made in this direction in European cities shows what can be done, and it is only a question of time when in each city in the United States the people acting through the municipal government will do for themselves, without the intervention of corporations, that which is now done at greater expense by private corporations."

This is not quoted as being authoritative, but as a good illustration of one kind of popular agitation which is bound to affect public sentiment.

Politicians usually consider it unsafe to array themselves against municipal ownership, and in many local campaigns it is the most popular issue.

In numerous cities where private corporations have been specifically invited by the authorities to build plants, perhaps during early and struggling days before credit had been established, later generations frequently attempt to secure possession or control of the enterprises. Natural growth has changed conditions; the uncertainties and hazards of the early venture have been forgotten, and the only thing now apparent is the prosperity of the Company which arouses a feeling of envy in the minds of those who believe that its acquisition by the city would result in personal benefit, or political advancement.

If the credit of the municipality be strong enough perhaps they wish to build plants of their own and crush out the existing Company rather than purchase it at a valuation considered fair by the private corporation; but the desire to build or purchase is not always sufficient to carry out the

143

HUNT LIBRARY
CARNEGIE-MELLON UNIVERSITY
PITTSBURGH, PENNSYLVANIA 15213

project, or, no matter how strong, financial resources may not permit, and consequently there is called into play the power of regulation, which may be a more valuable asset to a municipality than the physical ownership of the utilities.

This right is called the police power and is inherent in all sovereign bodies; some legal writers say that it is undefinable, but it is sufficient for us to know that under it plenary powers exist to regulate all affairs relating to public health and comfort.

The Supreme Court of the United States has decided that

> "Where a business is impressed with a public interest the legislature has the right to fix the maximum charge,"

and the legislature can, in order to meet local conditions, delegate this right to municipalities.

Several of the States have expressly delegated this power, and in others the power of regulation seems to exist without any specific legislation.

Certain advocates of municipal control have, through the proper authorities, availed themselves of this right, and as the results of their success in reducing rates are usually published broadcast, others are encouraged to follow their example, and in the near future we may expect a still larger increase in the number of cases.

The procedure is generally the same and the following recent clipping illustrates the method adopted:

> "Among the last of the important measures adopted by the City of Houston, Texas, during the past year was the passage of several ordinances fixing the rates for public utilities, such as street railway fares, gas, electric light and telephone rates, hack and dray charges, etc."

The authorities, however, are sometimes blinded by their seeming right to compel reductions and pass sweeping ordinances, but the Company which is, of course, under the Constitution of the United States and their own State protected to an extent, and guaranteed certain rights, may secure an injunction against the immediate enforcement of the ordinances, and if it can be shown that the reduction amounts to a confiscation of property, the injunction will be made permanent.

A recent decision of the Illinois Courts held that the Peoples' Gas Company of Chicago could not prevent a reduction by Council in the rate of gas from $1 to 75 cents per 1,000 feet, but the Company at once secured an injunction which has prevented the action of Council going into effect until the matter has been passed upon by the Courts.

This is one of many cases now pending, and, while some of them will be decided wholly on points of law, the great majority will require accurate statements of the corporations' accounts, and the most important statement will be that of profits.

It was because the whole question so intimately concerns professional accountants, whose services in these cases are invariably needed, that the title of this paper suggested itself to me, and if it serves, through awakening discussion, to settle some of the accountancy questions involved, just as the trial of the cases will tend to settle the law, my object will have been reached.

So far the cases have been widely scattered and not enough have gone to the Supreme Court of the United States to settle the general law applicable to them, and we shall not, therefore, discuss their legal aspect.

Profits are the real basis of the litigation; but there are some peculiar features about the profits of these privately formed corporations that differentiate them from the profits of a Company whose finances concern stockholders only.

Taking into consideration all the foregoing features of the case I feel that more attention should be paid towards securing uniformity and the establishment of good practice in keeping and stating the accounts of such a corporation.

Of course, no one denies that it is important to have uniformity of practice wherever the question of determining profits is an issue, but no such uniformity now exists, and we can make better progress and reach the desired end far sooner by taking up definite questions than to attempt a general reform at first.

Even in England, where the affairs of Public Companies are frequently regulated directly by act of Parliament, and where one might think that uniformity would exist, in their cases at least, accountants differ as to what constitutes net profits.

We shall, therefore, confine ourselves to a discussion of the accounts of public service corporations operating in communities or States where some sort of supervision or regulation is or may be exercised by the public authorities, and as nearly all the litigation in the past has concerned water and gas companies, we shall confine ourselves to the consideration of their accounts only. It is of equal importance, of course, that the books of *all* public service corporations should be kept correctly, but the accounts of companies other than water and gas are not so likely to be reviewed by the Courts, and by narrowing our subject and the discussions which may follow we may more readily secure a definite expression of opinion.

There are enough accountants here to revolutionize the account-keeping of public service corporations, provided we can agree on the proper principles. It is unquestionably of the utmost importance that the Company likely to be so regulated should prepare its current accounts not only for its stockholders, but for those to whom some day may be delegated the power of regulation.

Truly " a stitch in time saves nine," and it might be comparatively easy for a Company whose books show proper Depreciation and Reserve Funds, to establish their correctness in Court, whereas on the other hand it is difficult, and, as some recently decided cases have proved, fruitless for a Company whose books show no such accounts to claim that they should have appeared in their books in the past, although no mention was made of them either in the books or in the published reports to the stockholders.

A Company, forgetting the inevitable day of reckoning, may publish statements year after year exhibiting large earnings; these on their face may appear so large that inquiry is pertinent as to whether the rates producing them are not unreasonable; then if this inquiry leads to a more definite charge and the Company is confronted with an ordinance reducing rates, it naturally seems inconsistent for the Company to base its defense on the ground that its books are incorrect, that the earnings were really not so large, because, forsooth, they had forgotten or overlooked certain charges against the earnings. The Court and the lawyers naturally believe that these claims are made for a particular purpose, and do not represent scientific bookkeeping, or else why should the books themselves be so far at variance with the claims now presented?

This plea has been presented more than once to my knowledge, and when it occurs it is not a desirable thing to have the burden of proof thrown on us. The task is particularly undesirable if the accounts under review have been made up under the orders of one of our modern commercial promoter-lawyers, who knows nothing and cares less about bookkeeping, but who knows full well how great the profits should be to send up the market price of a particular stock.

As accountants it is not our intention to advocate the preparation of accounts designed to fit a particular purpose. A reputable member of our profession would show the same net profits no matter which side he represented. We can, therefore, reassure ourselves that there is no prospect of our profession paralleling the performances of the experts of another profession whose testimony always fits in exactly with their side of the case, irrespective of the fact that other experts representing another side find diametrically opposite results from precisely the same array of evidence.

We can, however, deal better with the future when we have had some experience in the past; and, therefore, for the purpose of discussion let us assume that we have been requested to ascertain for a term of years the exact net profits of a water or gas company operating in a city whose authorities are clothed with power to regulate rates, and that the Company is operating under a limited franchise. (I understand that no municipality has the power to grant perpetual franchises.) The object of the inquiry is to determine whether the net profits have been so large that the rates producing them are unreasonable. The latter part of the inquiry would naturally be hard of solution and honest differences of opinion, even among accountants, could readily occur, the question largely being a geographical one requiring the testimony of bankers and business men familiar with local conditions and the usual rates of income from investments, taking into account, of course, the hazards and problems of the particular enterprise.

However, professional accountants should not differ radically on the question as to what constitutes net profits, and we may therefore profitably inquire as to whether or not we can agree on the proper procedure to comply with our engagement. And we shall, of course, proceed with a firm determination that our results may be used with confidence either by the Company which attempts to show that their profits are reasonable, or by the city government which is trying to show up unconscionable profits.

GROSS EARNINGS.

Probably no difficulty will arise in determining the gross earnings, for the books will, no doubt, show them properly apportioned to the fiscal periods.

The question of bad debts should be considered, but in public service corporations it is not usually a serious factor, and can readily be adjusted.

146

EXPENSES.

I. *Operating Expenses.* Very little difficulty arises in connection with ordinary operating expenses, as practically all companies, despite their shortcomings in other directions, place great importance on their accuracy.

The use of any proper system of stock accounts will enable the actual expenses to be easily ascertained; if stock accounts have not been kept and inventories are not available, some difficulty may be experienced in allocating the various expenses to their proper period; but if the investigation cover a term of years, the discrepancies would probably be slight and make no appreciable difference in the result.

For comparative purposes the usual ordinary operating expenses should be grouped together and their aggregate shown separately.

The propriety of including certain extraordinary expenses among ordinary operating expenses has been questioned, and the controversies resulting have not always been settled the same way; a further question in connection with them is to place them in the proper period.

These extraordinary items include legal expenses, personal injuries to employees, damages to plant, etc.

The legal expenses may have been unusually large during the period under review, and occasioned perhaps by the very litigation which resulted in the investigation, or probably the litigation has been brought about by the municipality, whose representatives will claim that had the rates been reasonable the action would not have occurred, and the inclusion of the legal fees among the current expenses would therefore become unjustifiable.

This view, however, can hardly be sustained, for the fact remains that the Company must defend itself on all occasions, whether the action is just or not, and irrespective of the result. Most public service corporations are engaged in constant litigation, and, if it be not the municipality against them, it may be some aggrieved citizen. These charges having been incurred certainly cannot be *capitalized,* and should be included among the expenses.

As to the period which should bear them, I think that they belong to the fiscal year in which the bills are presented, provided, of course, that the bills are sent in in regular course, and that good faith exists in regard to this and other points. Items which are not legitimate in every sense of the word do not belong in such a statement.

This ruling also applies to the payment of damages for personal injuries to persons and accidents to property. If the Company carry liability insurance, the premiums will, of course, be charged in the proper period; if none be carried, good practice requires the creation of an insurance fund. But even these precautions do not always cover large losses, which should be charged at the time the liability is fixed.

In other words, *all* expenditures made in good faith to preserve the property, no matter how unusual, belong to the period in which they occur.

It is not likely that the investigation would cover one year only, and by ascertaining averages extraordinary expenses could be distributed over several years, which method would not materially alter the above suggestion.

Ordinary operating expenses include those current repairs, occasioned by ordinary wear and tear, which are necessary to the up-keep of the plant.

There may be extraordinary repairs, however, occurring only at long intervals, which may more properly be classed with renewals.

II. *Depreciation.* To estimate the proper allowance for renewals and extraordinary repairs noted above will probably be the most difficult task.

An accountant cannot usually rely entirely on his own knowledge in fixing the rates of depreciation, and he should decline to act except in conjunction with a competent engineer upon whose experience he can rely to supplement his own knowledge, and whose technical knowledge can be applied to the various questions that will arise.

The expenditures for renewals during the period should be carefully analyzed, and the exact cost of the various parts of the plant ascertained. In almost all cases he will be compelled to work this out from the beginning, but if he is dealing with a corporation which succeeds another, or which has bought out several others, and he finds it impossible to analyze the construction account, he may have to rely almost entirely on the engineer to give him the cost of construction. The cost of duplication or reproduction is, of course, not the question before him; the present plant may have cost more or less than it would cost to reproduce it, but in the very nature of things we must deal with conditions which exist, and which have existed, rather than with an imaginary plant the depreciation of which must necessarily be imaginary too. This point is brought up because it has been urged in several cases that in arriving at depreciation an estimated cost of duplicating the plant should be used as a basis rather than the cost as shown by the books.

Obviously a going concern which has required years to create cannot be duplicated without considering the vital elements of time and constantly changing conditions.

If the Company built its own plant, there can hardly be any difference of opinion as to the proper charges to construction. These include all costs and expenses, including interest on the capital furnished up to the time the plant commenced to operate.

If the accounts have been kept carelessly, or, as is frequently the case, made up to show large profits, it is likely that certain renewals and repairs will be found charged to Plant, which must, of course, be eliminated and transferred to the proper accounts.

After the actual cost of the plant is ascertained and properly grouped, the accountant will take up the question of depreciation, bringing to bear his previous experience and that of the engineer's. If the renewals do not equal a fair annual charge for depreciation, he must increase and adjust the charge by the creation of an account which is usually called " Reserve for Depreciation."

In certain cases lawyers have argued that depreciation *as such* is not properly an operating expense, and the accountant, in order to win his point, may have to carry on a campaign of education. It might be suggested that the word " depreciation " does not always carry the desired meaning to a layman, and that the term " renewals," or " reserve for renewals and repairs," while not technically correct as covering depreciation in its broad sense, nevertheless is more easily understood, and, if we gain our point by so calling it, we can comfort ourselves by reflecting that "a rose by any other name smells as sweet."

The argument may be urged that there is a certain appreciation of values which offsets the depreciation. Such a claim as applied to a statement of current operations is, of course, absurd and will hardly be considered seriously by an accountant.

If the annual charge for depreciation amounts to more than the actual expenditures for renewals and extraordinary repairs, as it will wherever the plant is comparatively new, the part unexpended should be carried in "Reserve for Depreciation" until the necessity for the renewals arises.

In water works plants instances are known where pipe which has been in the ground fifty years will, in all probability, be good for fifty more. In this case the annual allowance will be added and carried in the reserve for many years, but some day that pipe will have to be replaced; if there were no reserve, you could hardly find a manager strong-minded enough to keep the new pipe out of construction.

Therefore, at the end of any given period the plant should be worth its cost, or else the deficiency must be provided from this account, "Reserve for Depreciation."

This annual charge must allow for more than the *ordinary* wearing out which inevitably occurs according to the well-known laws of nature, for the owner of a perishable plant, such as water or gas, is entitled to reserve out of his earnings such a further sum as will enable him to be prepared for events which cannot be foreseen, and the prudent man will always include this allowance with his annual charge for depreciation. These contingencies include electrolysis in gas and water pipes; accidents to plant and other effects from the "acts of God." Testifying along these lines in a Southern State, I stated that this provision was a proper one and so included it, but counsel for the City interjected the remark, "We do not have any acts of God down here," so the effect of the claim was partially lost. Another contingency in the case of water companies is the possible failure of the supply of wholesome water, or the possible obligation of filtering.

In all plants using machinery the question of obsolescence is an important item, and must be considered, for, in this day of keen competition, when new devices and processes are succeeding each other with bewildering rapidity, provision must be made for keeping up with modern improvements, and it may involve the abandonment of comparatively new machinery or processes. All these do occur, though not regularly, nor can they be guarded against. The only safe plan is to have a sufficient reserve to meet conditions which arise, and not to place dependence upon any past freedom from unexpected occurrences.

Mr. J. W. Best, speaking at a meeting of the Sheffield Society of Chartered Accountants not long ago, on the subject of tramway depreciation, said that an undertaking belonging to a limited company managed by commercial men would not be regarded as soundly financed unless the directors "not only kept up the revenue-producing character of the undertaking by necessary or desirable repairs or renewals, but *out of revenue* accumulated a fund equal to the difference between cost and residual value."

III. As we are dealing with a Company whose life may be terminated

149

upon a certain date, surely we must prepare for the impending event, and, as we know the day, we can provide for it with some degree of accuracy.

In the absence of an agreement with the municipality to purchase the plant at cost, and if there be no provision for a renewal nor certainty thereof, the Company is entitled to charge annually against the earnings, in addition to all other charges, such a sum or annuity as will upon the termination of the franchise amount to the difference between the cost of the plant and its break-up or scrap value.

The cost of the plant here includes all payments for the franchise itself in the way of bonuses and similar items.

It cannot seriously be questioned that the owners of a plant are either entitled to the use of their property at all times with a reasonable earning power or else, if the plant is to be worked out like a mine or quarry, they are entitled to provide out of the current earnings for its compulsory abandonment. The provision should be made during the term, by a series of annual charges, and a Sinking Fund created therefor; otherwise the dividends or returns have been an actual return of capital; in any event the net profits cannot be stated without allowing for this item.

Good practice, in my opinion, demands that all the above deductions be made before arriving at or stating for any purpose the net profits of a business, and it is here that the necessity for a uniform standard will be emphasized, for, unless we can agree in some measure as to what constitutes net profits, there will constantly be the danger of having to express disagreement with the results arrived at by other accountants, and this is not pleasant nor profitable for any of us. We have a duty to each other and to the profession in general which we should not disregard.

Surely the certification by one reputable accountant to a statement of profits should be ample notice to any other accountant that the results as stated are accurate, and no re-examination should be necessary in case the other accountant desires to use those results.

How long would it take to bring the profession into contempt were it realized by business men that many accountants are so far apart in their ideas of good practice that very few of them, while acting for one side of a case, will accept the statements of the accountant representing the other?

Until we direct our attention to individual cases we are prone to believe that we all have very nearly identical ideas, and that no material difference exists in our practice so far as it applies to the foregoing proposition, but an actual instance of recent occurrence will illustrate my point that we are *not* agreed on important principles.

A short time ago a representative of one of the largest bond houses in New York called upon me and with the object of selling bonds displayed a statement of earnings of a gas company operating in one of the Western States. Noticing that the item "Repairs" was extremely small, and that there was no allowance at all for depreciation or any other fund of similar nature, the salesman was asked what they would do in case any renewals were required. He answered, "Oh, we can sell more bonds!"

In commenting further upon the statement which showed a small surplus above interest charges, he stated that it was to go to the preferred stockholders, and that the following year they hoped to have something for the common stock!

That statement of earnings was certified to by an audit company of standing, which may or may not have been aware of the fact that in that very State municipalities have the power to regulate rates; some day the Company may be charged by the municipal authorities with earning excessive profits, basing their claim upon statements similar to those mentioned. Will it be edifying to us to know that, in all probability, any fair re-statement of those profits, setting aside proper allowances for depreciation, etc., would result in a very material reduction?

Probably the bond house paid for the examination, and naturally wanted the profits to be as large as possible, but surely accountancy theories and principles do not vary automatically with clients' wishes, and, if the same accountants should subsequently represent the Company in stating the case for court, and attempt to reduce the profits as much as possible to show that they were not excessive, thereby producing a net result different from their former effort, they could, and no doubt would, be severely censured. I do not claim that any of us might not have fallen into the same sort of error in the past, but I do urge the immediate importance of establishing a general standard which will be firm enough for all of us to rest upon in the future.

In some cases like the above, letters have accompanied the certificates of profits, qualifying them, and calling attention to the absence of depreciation charges, etc., but unfortunately for us the letters and the qualifications do not go to the investor—who sees only the certificate, and who has no time nor inclination to analyze that; moreover, he has a perfect right to rely on the certificate itself, and if subsequent unsatisfactory results impel him to take up the matter anew and ascertain all the facts he will probably be added to the number of men who express themselves as being afraid to rely on an accountant's certificate of profits.

In direct connection with our subject is the question of the reasonableness of the profits, and, as stated previously, opinion may differ here without fear of criticism. In my opinion, where this is an issue, additional allowances should be provided from the earnings. Although we have arrived at what we call the net profits of the undertaking we cannot safely rely on the entire amount being available for dividends, nor have we yet reached a net result upon which can be based arguments concerning reasonableness of rates.

In other words, "net profits" may not in these cases represent a final result from which no further deductions should be made.

One of these allowances is for what is usually known as the good-will of the concern, representing the difference between the cash cost of the plant and its value as a going concern, and which is usually reflected by the market price of its stocks and bonds. Possibly this good-will has been more than covered by an injection of "water" into the original stock issues, but in any event, if the venture has been very successful, or particularly if it has been worked up from an unprofitable to a very profitable basis, the Company is certainly entitled to some return from this increment and is justified in ear-marking part of the net profits as an income or return on this increase. This amount would hardly find its way into the books or statements, but if there *is* litigation and the issue is raised an accountant is bound to take this point into consideration.

Where the Company has been worked up to such a profitable basis, the municipality should not expect it to reap no return beyond the usual or legal rate of interest upon its cash outlay in former years. For this reason, before the rates in force could be considered unreasonable, this further reserve or annual charge should be provided out of the earnings, not as a deduction before showing net profits, but as a special return which might form part of the dividend.

In support of this contention the following extracts from decisions by the Supreme Court of the United States are pertinent. The cases were along the lines of the question we have been considering:

"What the Company is entitled to demand in order that it may have just compensation is a fair return upon the reasonable value of the property at the time it is being used by the public."

"That is decided and is decided as against the contention that you are to take the actual cost of the plant, annual depreciation, etc., and to allow a fair profit on that footing, over and above expenses."

"Nor would the mere cost of reproducing the water works plant be a fair test because that does not take into account the value which flows from the established connections between the pipes and the buildings in the city. It is obvious that the mere cost of purchasing the land, constructing the buildings, putting in the machinery and laying the pipes in the street—in other words, the cost of reproduction does not give the value of the property as it is to-day."

"Being a system in operation, not only with a capacity to earn, but actually earning, makes it true that the fair and equitable value is something in excess of the cost of reproduction."

Of course, arriving at the proper capital sum to be so returned would be difficult, for the entire capital stock might be "water." Nevertheless, many holders may have been purchasers for value, and they would have certain rights. In such a case it would not be legitimate to provide a Sinking Fund out of earnings large enough to retire the whole issue at the end of the concession, but only the actual value should be considered.

Another point requiring attention is that all public service corporations furnishing gas and water are under the obligation of making extensions to their lines upon being instructed so to do by the authorities, arbitrarily perhaps, and without regard to the fact that the income from a certain extension may be insignificant when compared with its cost, and if these extensions were called for near the end of the franchise no return at all might be received.

Therefore, it would seem that a Company might deem it desirable to set aside certain of the profits to provide for this contingency, and it would undoubtedly be prudent to do so. If the extensions were made near the expiration of the franchise, it would be simply impossible to provide for them out of earnings, and in this case the Company would be in an unfortunate position. It emphasizes the importance, however, of setting aside sufficient Reserves or Sinking Fund to take care of the outlay during the earlier period.

It might be urged that a strict following out of these theories would result at the end of the term in the Company's not only having a Sinking Fund sufficient to cover the deficit between the cost and the break-up value, but that there might be a balance in the Depreciation Fund which would be equivalent to a further and additional return of capital. It is true that this *might* happen, but the chances are against it, for in nearly all cases we would be dealing with a Company having a long term franchise, and it might easily happen that just before the expiration of the term the necessary renewals of plant had exhausted the fund. It is likely that the depreciation reserves would be too low rather than excessive, so that in a long term the depreciation fund could never be counted upon to show constant large credit balances.

In any event, an accountant is not justified in assuming in special cases that contingencies will *not* occur, and he has a responsiblity to future stockholders which he should consider. Failure to insist on proper reserves at the present time based upon the representation or excuse that the future will take care of itself is not excusable on the part of anyone, and least of all to the accountant.

Summarized briefly my contention is that it is more important for professional accountants to agree on uniform practice in determining the profits of public service corporations *where* municipalities have the power to regulate rates than in any other class of cases, and the following outline representing my personal views is submitted as an equitable basis:

Earnings: The basis being actual earnings as distinguished from receipts can hardly be questioned, and, therefore, needs no comment.

Expenses: Before stating the net profits there should be deducted from the Earnings:

I. Ordinary Operating Expenses, including ordinary Repairs and certain extraordinary expenses actually incurred during the period, such as legal expenses, etc.

II. Depreciation. Allowing enough to cover all renewals known to be necessary and also a reasonable reserve for unknown but probable causes, such as electrolysis in the case of iron pipe, obsolescence in the case of special machinery and processes, etc.

III. In the case of a Company operating under a limited franchise, where there is no agreement to purchase, a sufficient annual sum, or annuity, to return at the end of the concession the actual loss of capital which will be the difference between cost and the break-up value.

The above deductions to be made annually from earnings before bringing down the net profits available for dividends provided extensions, etc., have been allowed for, and then before stating these net profits for the purpose of computing the rate of income upon the investment, also setting aside an allowance to provide for the return of the good-will to the stockholders by the expiration of the franchise.

The remainder can then be used with confidence as a basis for argument as to whether the rates producing this net result are or are not reasonable.

CHAIRMAN.—The paper of Mr. Montgomery is now open for discussion.

MR. DICKINSON.—Mr. Chairman and Gentlemen: Mr. Montgomery asked me to say a few words about the subject of this paper. I am sorry to say that what I ought to have done beforehand I have not done: that is, to read the paper before this meeting, but time has not permitted. I think we ought to thank Mr. Montgomery very much indeed for the care and thoroughness with which he has treated the subject, which is one of considerable difficulty. The importance of it is perhaps only beginning to be appreciated, because it is only in recent years that these franchises are beginning to run out, and the question of renewing them has come up for consideration. The general idea Mr. Montgomery has laid down is that there are certain definite classes of expenses which must be taken into account in ascertaining what is really the earning capacity of a business. In any business there are certain losses which arise out of and are incident to the operation. *i. e.,* the operation cannot go on without them. On the other hand there are other losses which are quite independent of the operations. Now, if a City gives a franchise to a Public Service Corporation and specifies that the profits are not to exceed a certain rate, I think it is reasonable to assume that the charges against earnings before arriving at profits should be those only which are incident to the operations. In ascertaining the amount available for dividend it would not be reasonable for the Company to take into account losses not arising out of or incident to the operations, such as loss of good will, or of fixed capital assets due to fall in values of property generally. One of the most important of such items is Good Will, which may consist of the actual amount paid for the franchise itself. either to the City or to the Intermediary who acquired it from the City, or it may include a large amount of water. While it is true that Loss of Capital must be recouped out of earnings over the life of the franchise, it certainly would not be fair if it were obliged to pay, either directly as part of the purchase money of the property, or indirectly in the rates paid by the citizens, for a large amount added by the Company to the value of the franchise in excess of the amount the City received therefor.

I think, following out that principle, that losses of Fixed Capital should not be taken into account. but that all losses of Wasting or Floating Capital should be a charge against earnings.

I will move a cordial vote of thanks to Mr. Montgomery for the paper he has given us, and the great care and thought he has devoted to it.

(Motion seconded, put to vote and carried.)

MR. CHASE.—I might say that the importance of this matter is brought very forcibly to the attention of the accountants in Massachusetts, where we have special laws relating particularly to gas and electric and other public service corporations, which are controlled by means of a Board of Commissioners under the State laws. These Commissioners practically regulate the price throughout Massachusetts. When a City desires to go into the business of supplying gas or water or electricity it is compelled by law to first purchase the existing Company, if such there be, at a fair market value. The question then to be determined is what is a fair market value for a given plant. I have been on three or four of the important cases in Massachusetts, and it can be easily appreciated that the difference of opinion between the two sides may run from half a million to a million and a half dollars, and the question of depreciation is exceedingly important.

I agree with Mr. Montgomery that action should be taken by the Accountants on lines which could be uniformly followed, and if a Committee in some practical way could come together and decide what could be done and if we could follow that course hereafter it would add another important feature to the results of this Congress.

JOHN ALEX. COOPER, C. P. A. (Chicago).—I took in with a great deal of interest the remarks of Mr. Chase coinciding with Mr. Montgomery's views, that a line of conduct should be laid down in regard to such questions. I cannot help remarking that the position as relating to Massachusetts is so much in advance of many other States, and the conditions are so entirely under control in different ways, unlike they are in the West. I think that things of a corporate nature, not only of utilities, but also manufacturing companies, are much more in control in Massachusetts than they are anywhere else. As to the effect of the difference in the corporation law of Massachusetts, it being so much in advance of that of any other State in regard to the control of corporations, etc., and also in support of his statement this morning that his Society is practically as strong to-day in his own State as if he had the C. P. A. degree, which I know to be the case, I have been called upon to certify to foreign corporations working in

Massachusetts where it is part of the law that foreign corporations of over $100,000 shall require a certificate of the election of their auditor, and also the certificate from the auditor that the returns made on that form are in accordance with facts.

MR. CHASE.—I would like to say that if in Massachusetts we were only handling corporations under Massachusetts law it would be a very simple matter, but we are handling corporations under the laws of other States whose requirements are entirely different from those of Massachusetts, and therefore we appreciate the very marked necessity for some uniform method of treating the matter of depreciation.

CHAIRMAN.—Would Mr. Montgomery like to say anything in closing the discussion?

MR. MONTGOMERY.—No—except this: I would like to have some little expression of opinion from this Congress as to the propriety and desirability of taking these three classes of expenses from the earnings before bringing down the profits. If anyone does not believe in deducting all three of them I think we should have that expression of opinion.

Mr. Pixley's paper covered the question of whether depreciation should be included among the operating expenses, because he said it was just as important to deduct that as wages. If a workman is using a machine and is paid one dollar a day for his labor, and if he is wearing the machine out at the rate of one dollar a day, there is two dollars expense before you can get the profit.

CHAIRMAN.—As it is oftentimes advisable to get a long distance view of things, perhaps Mr. Pixley would just say a word on this subject.

MR. PIXLEY.—I am afraid I don't know very much about what you call " public service corporations." The public service corporations in England are usually restricted and are not allowed to pay above a certain amount of dividend, and there is a government auditor who looks after that and does not allow too much to go to the pockets of the shareholders. Payment for wages and salaries, etc., should be cash payments, but the actual wear and tear, I think, should go into a separate schedule. I should think you would divide them under two heads.

CHAIRMAN.—The point raised by Mr. Montgomery, as I understand it, was simply to bring out that before *net* profits shall be stated all this shall either together or in separate schedules be deducted.

Mr. Pixley.—I agree that no net profit shall be paid until everything has been deducted—interest on loans, all expenses, the percentage of depreciation, estimated losses that may arise on realization of debts, etc. We do not like the words " net profit " ever to be made use of until all these have been deducted. That is our aim in England.

Mr. Chase.—There is a way to bring about some action on Mr. Montgomery's paper. I would like to suggest that a Committee of six be appointed (with Mr. Montgomery as Chairman) by the Chair to-morrow, to report on Mr. Montgomery's paper, their report to be printed together with Mr. Montgomery's paper in the proceedings.

(Motion seconded, put to vote and carried.)

Chairman.—The Committee will be appointed to-morrow. If there is no further business before the Congress we will stand adjourned until ten o'clock to-morrow morning.

THE VALUE AND RECENT DEVELOPMENT OF THEORETICAL TRAINING FOR THE PUBLIC ACCOUNTANT

Robert H. Montgomery

The Value and Recent Development of Theoretical Training for the Public Accountant

By ROBERT H. MONTGOMERY, C. P. A.

Editor of the American Edition of Dicksee's Auditing

The firm of Lybrand, Ross Bros. & Montgomery, Certified Public Accountants, is of the progressive sort that wins recognition through ability and steady application. Throughout Pennsylvania, where their clients mostly do business, they enjoy a very large practice. From offices in the Stephen Girard Building of Philadelphia the firm has branched out to Baltimore and to New York. The individual members of the firm, Wm. H. Lybrand, T. Edward Ross, Adam A. Ross, Jr., and Robert H. Montgomery, are all practitioners of experience, and men who have done much in furthering the cause of accountancy in the United States.

Mr. Robert H. Montgomery, the author of this article, was born in 1872 and in 1889 obtained a position in the office of Mr. John Heins, who was then president of the American Association of Public Accountants.

Mr. Montgomery took an active part in the formation of the Pennsylvania public accountants in 1897 and was a delegate to the organization meeting of the Federation of Societies of Public Accountants. He was elected secretary of the Federation, October, 1904, and was placed in charge of the amalgamation of the Federation with the American Association of Public Accountants.

THE general recognition of accountancy as a profession has made greater strides in the United States within the last 12 months than during the entire previous history of our country. Many proofs of this advance might be cited, but it is, happily, no longer necessary to argue that the public accountant is following a profession, and since this fact has been acknowledged by several universities of the highest standard it is hardly to be expected that any of the readers of this article will be disposed to dissent.

UNIVERSITY RECOGNITION.

The whole subject of accountancy, with its possibilities, has been most exhaustively studied for several years by Dr. James T. Young, director of the Wharton School of Finance and Economy of the University of Pennsylvania, and, as his school is recognized all over the world as being a model of its kind, it is interesting to read what Dr. Young said recently in connection with the introduction of a course in accountancy as a part of their regular work:

"Accountancy is a proper subject for a university course be-

ROBERT H. MONTGOMERY.

cause the subjects required for the accountant can be systematized and taught just as can the principles of the law or of mathematics required for engineering or those of medicine. Every calling which becomes a profession of an advanced character, must rest on definite, fixed principles, rather than upon 'the rule of the thumb.' When these principles reach a certain high point of development they constitute a body of knowledge or a science which can be imparted by scientific teaching methods more quickly and to greater advantage than by compelling each individual to begin at the beginning and learn all those principles through the long process of experience.

"Furthermore, by insisting upon a thorough and well planned scheme of university instruction the calling receives a more adequate recognition as an advanced profession. This has been the experience of all those occupations which are now termed 'professions,' the most striking recent instance being that of the civil, mechanical, electrical or chemical engineer."

It is interesting to note the reference to engineering, for its recognition as a profession has also been quite recent; in fact, engineering evidently has not quite come to its own, for no later than March 26, 1905, Professor Burr, head of Columbia College's civil engineering department, said:

"I believe that civil engineering will never reach the truly professional character which ought to belong to it until the profession is based on a college training—until it is placed on the same high plane with law and medicine—and Columbia is the first university in the country to give full expression to that idea.

"I hope that it will not be many years before the engineering student is fitted out with the same culture studies which now are obligatory for those who wish to pursue the study of law and medicine."

CULTURE ALWAYS NECESSARY.

Even in former days when accountancy was essentially "practical" and a knowledge of its principles was gained only by experience, it was universally admitted that an accountant's education should be of a broad cultural character. The difficulties, however, in the way of an ordinary junior assistant becoming broad-minded and cultured, when his whole time during the day and frequently far into the night was occupied with routine work, were almost too many to overcome; and this probably accounts for the comparatively few accountants of today who can be said to be in the front rank. By this I mean those men who combine with their complete mastery of the practical part of their work the ability to write a clear and concise report, using good English throughout; the ability to consider questions of account in their broadest sense—for instance, an accountant whose practice might touch upon city, state or national finances should be acquainted with city government and public administration; this ability to grasp the scientific principles of the various subjects which arise; and most important of all, the ability to make his influence of value to the community, which must be measured not only by his special services but by his breadth of view and his standing as a man.

FUTURE REQUIREMENTS—UNIVERSITY DAY AND NIGHT SCHOOLS.

We may, therefore, reasonably expect that in the near future a junior assistant, whose intention it is to make accountancy

his life profession, will seek every means to avail himself of the opportunity to secure such a preliminary training as will furnish him with a comprehensive and intelligent starting point. I refer to such a place as the Wharton School, already referred to, or the New York School of Commerce, Accounts and Finance, where for several years Professor Johnson has been carrying on thoroughly first class work, or the recently organized department of the University of California, where Professor Hatfield has introduced an accountancy course into their College of Commerce and which is entering upon an enlarged field of influence, or, as we hope he will soon find, a fully developed accountancy course in any of the higher educational institutions to which he may apply.

Of course there will remain a greater number of young men who desire to study for the profession, but who lack the means to enter day classes. Fortunately the doors are not barred to them, but they will have to bring to bear their full energies to secure by night study all that they otherwise miss. It will probably be the case for some years that all accountancy schools will have night courses as is now the case in Philadelphia and New York, and this enables a young man to secure employment during the day; an accountant's office is, of course, the most preferable place for him to work and if he can secure a position with a reputable firm his day experience will be of inestimable advantage in working out theoretical problems. An untrained junior does not—naturally, command a large salary, but there is practically no limit to the advancement which is sure to follow a good record

POSSIBILITIES FOR HOME STUDY.

If he cannot attend a night school his next best plan is to secure all of the standard text books on the various subjects and master them. The chief difficulty with this is that he loses the advantage of coming into contact with the practicing accountants who lecture in the various accountancy schools. As the profession becomes better known, however, and its influence grows, the literature will expand and in time will certainly furnish the means to the student of securing a comprehensive ground-work. To claim that accountancy cannot be expressed in, and its essentials learned from, books, is to admit that it is neither a science nor a profession, and the day has gone by for any such foolish idea.

THE ACCOUNTANT OF THE FUTURE.

The professional accountant of the future must be educated and developed in the broadest possible sense or he cannot hope to succeed. Experience is quite as necessary and just as valuable as ever, but it is not enough, and in the not far distant future the purely "practical" man will be doomed to failure when he comes into competition with men who have had in their junior days thorough theoretical training supplemented later by practical experience.

The profession of accountancy has in store greater opportunities for the right sort of young men than ever before, but with increased chances for success have come new responsibilities, the most important of which is the necessity for theoretical training.

THE ALGEBRA OF ACCOUNTS

Charles E. Sprague

(Written expressly for The Book-keeper.)

THE ALGEBRA OF ACCOUNTS.

By Charles E. Sprague.

Introductory.

Scarcely any art or science can be presented to the mind in more phases than book-keeping. Not only does its application to different kinds of transactions and different branches of trade give rise to an almost infinite variety of forms, all governed by the same fundamental laws, but those laws themselves appear to different minds in altogether different lights. The laws of debit and credit, by which all book-keeping is carried on, have been stated from a different point of view by almost every writer who has treated upon them. In the practical application of these laws there is not the slightest variation in principle; but in formulating them and stating them to others, we find the utmost diversity. And this is not a hindrance, as might be supposed. The most perfect idea of a statue can be formed by looking at it from all sides, and there is a like benefit in shifting our stand-point in regard to a principle or law in science.

I propose, then, to work out still another way of looking at the principle of debit and credit. Treating the science of accounts as a branch of mathematics (which it is), I reduce it to an algebraic notation: I constantly interpret the algebraic results into common language, and also into the technical, conventional, but often convenient notation used by book-keepers. I show this last to be as truly algebraic as the first; and I teach that no matter what particular form is employed in the presentation of facts, if the equation is preserved, implicitly or explicitly, it is true book-keeping.

But a very limited knowledge of algebra will be needed to follow this explanation. The theory of simple equations is more than enough.

I will now state and demonstrate my proposition.

Thesis.—All the operations of double-entry book-keeping are transformations of the following equation:

What I **have** + what I **trust** = what I **owe** + what I am **worth** or symbolically written.

$$H + T = O + X.$$

1. Book-keeping is a history of values.

2. The mathematical side of this history consists in certain equations, in which addition and cancellation are the only operations employed.

3. **History and Annals.**—Annals or chronicles merely relate facts which have occurred; but true history groups together facts of the same tendency, in order to discover, if possible, the cause of happiness and misery, prosperity and ruin; so true book-keeping, being a history, should group together similar values in its equations to discover the causes and effects of Loss and Gain.

4. **What is Sought.**—In the equations of accounts the answer sought or "unknown quantity" is

"What I am worth."

We will represent it by the letter "X."

5. **Simple Proprietorship.**—If I, the subject of the history, trust no one and owe no one; then I **am worth** all that I **have,** no more, no less; or

(Equation 1.) $H = X.$

what I have is the measure of what I am worth; the property actually in my possession is all mine and I claim nothing more. These readings all convey the same idea: but none

of them express it as definitely and precisely as the algebraic formula

$$H = X.$$

6. The state of things denoted by Equation 1 seldom exists. Usually, or at least frequently, a value-transaction, or exchange of values, is not all completed at the same instant. We buy to-day and pay to-morrow; we sell to-day and receive payment hereafter; we make profits and losses but do not immediately realize them; we "trust" (**Credimus**) other people, and are "owed;" we "owe" others (**Debemus**), or "get trusted." But we believe that we shall receive our dues from others, and know that we must pay those whom we owe; hence, these debts and credits, these postponed receipts and payments, are all elements in our status and cannot be disregarded. What we trust others with, as well as what we have, is part of our worth, a positive element; what we owe is a deduction from our worth.

7. **Proprietorship with Credit.**—If I trust others with part of my wealth but owe no one, Equation 1 becomes

(2.) $H + T = X.$

That is, what I have, added to what is owing me, equals what I am worth; my wealth is composed of the valuables in my possession, together with what I claim and expect to receive from others, my *debtors.*

But I may also owe other people, my *creditors.* Then $H + T$ is not all really mine; I am holding part of it as a *trustee* (in the literal sense) for those who trust me; this part must be subtracted from $H + T$ to give the true value of X. Let O represent the amount of my debts to others; then we have a third equation.

(3.) $H + T - O = X.$

Here we have introduced a negative or *minus* quantity.

It has been found by experience that it is more convenient to avoid subtraction, whenever it is possible, in book-keeping. It is plainer always to add; when we see two numbers together, we know they are to be added together, and can make no error by choosing the wrong operation. But how shall we get rid of the negative quantity? The answer is, by transposing or removing it to the opposite *side.* For instance, if this equation is true: $5 - 3 = 2$, then it will also be true that: $5 = 2 + 3.$ That is, we may transpose a minus quantity from either side of the equation to the other, if we make it a plus; or we may transpose a plus, changing it to minus.

Returning to equation 3, let us transpose the "— O" from the left to the right side of the equation, changing its sign to +. We then have.

(4.) $H + T = X + O,$

which is the fundamental equation,

"What I have + what I trust = what I owe + what I am worth."

8. This fundamental equation gives a mode of representing the financial status of any individual or concern at any fixed time. The mode of representing changes will be considered later.

9. **Balance-Sheets.**—A statement to the effect

"$H + T = O + X,$"

is called in book-keeping a balance-sheet, or exhibit. It is made in various practical shapes to suit different cases. We will illustrate this with numerical examples. Suppose

H = 10,000 (the dollar being unity) ; T = 5,000 ; O = 6,000. Then solving the equation by the rule of algebra, we find

$$X = 10,000 + 5,000 - 6,000 = 9,000.$$

The practical way of writing the equation as a balance-sheet would be

H	10,000	O	6,000
T	5,000	X	9,000
	15,000		15,000

That is: We write the specifications of the values in two columns, corresponding to the two sides of the equation ; opposite the specification, write the numerical value ; add each side. A single line below the items indicates that the amounts above, added together, make the sum below ; a double line below the two sums indicates their equality and may be considered as the sign =. We might omit the formality of writing "15,000" under each side and simply write

H	10,000	O	6,000
T	5,000	X	9,000

10. Debit and Credit.—We apply these two terms to the side of the equation or balance-sheet. Literally speaking, only T can be called a debtor amount and only O a creditor to us ; but by analogy the terms are extended to all values of the same side : H and T are spoken of as debtors, debits, or "Dr.;" O and X are spoken of as creditors, credits, or "Cr."

11. Other Forms of Balance-Sheet.

a.	I have	10,000	I owe	6,000
	I trust	5,000	**I am worth**	9,000
		15,000		15,000

b.	Dr.		Cr.	
	10,000	I have		
	5,000	I trust		
		I owe	6,000	
		I am worth	9,000	
	15,000		15,000	

c.		I have	10,000	
		I trust	5,000	
		I owe		6,000
		I am worth		9,000
			15,000	15,000

d. (This form of expressing the equation is called a Journal Entry.)

Sundries Dr. to Sundries :

Property Dr.	10,000	
Debtors "	5,000	
To Creditors		6,000
" Capital		9,000
	15,000	15,000

The word "to" before a word has the same meaning as "Cr." after it, implying a term on the credit-side. "Sundries" mean more than one item. "Sundries Dr. to Sundries" therefore means "more than one item is to be placed

on the left hand side, and more than one on the right hand." This preface, which some find convenient, is, however, frequently omitted, and is unessential.

11. Detailed Balance-Sheets.—The above examples give a broad view of the essential character of a balance-sheet. It is the equation of value at rest written out in the book-keeper's style of algebra. If books have not previously been kept, or have been so kept as not to *preserve the equation* ("by single entry," as it is called), then we must find the value of H, T and O, by actual examination ; by count, by weight, by inspection, or by such imperfect records as have been kept. In this case X is really an unknown quantity, and can only be found by solving the equation ; i. e. by adding together H and T, and subtracting O. But as we shall see hereafter, the peculiarity of double-entry is to keep a constant record of the changes of X, so that at any instant we know its value without taking off the balance-sheet. In practice, balance-sheets, though constructed on the principles above stated, contain much more detail. Instead of grouping the values of all *property* into one sum, they give the amount of each *kind* of property ; instead of grouping all debtors together, they give the amount due from each debtor ; instead of grouping all the creditors together, they state how much is due each creditor ; if the concern has more than one proprietor, as a partnership or company, each one's share of the worth is (sometimes) stated. That is to say, H, T, O, and X may be subdivided into their component parts.

12. Suppose that H is composed of Cash (I), Merchandise (K) and landed property (L) ; that the debtors who owe the amount T are U, V and W ; that the creditors are P, Q and R (bills payable) ; and that the concern is a partnership, the members of which are Y and Z. Then representing the *values* by these same letters we have

$$(5) \quad H = I + K + L$$
$$(6) \quad T = U + V + W$$
$$(7) \quad O = P + Q + R$$
$$(8) \quad X = Y + Z.$$

Then equation (4) becomes

$$(9) \quad I + K + L + U + V + W = P + Q + R + Y + Z,$$

which still means

$$\left. \begin{array}{l} \text{what we have} \\ + \text{ what we trust} \end{array} \right\} = \left\{ \begin{array}{l} \text{what we owe,} \\ + \text{ what we are worth.} \end{array} \right.$$

13. Let us assign numerical values to the terms denoting known quantities, for instance :

I = 2344.25	P = 2374.64
K = 5655.75	Q = 3273.29
L = 2000	R = 352.07
U = 3999.23	
V = 109.32	
W = 891.45	

Substituting these in equation (9) try to work out the values of Y and Z. You see at once that Y + Z = 9000, but that is impossible without further information to find the separate values of Y and of Z.

The algebraic reason is that the equation is *indeterminate*, there being only one equation and two unknown quantities. Assume that the proprietorship is divided in the ratio of 3 to 4, or that

$$Y : Z :: 3 : 4.$$

then it follows that the value of Y and Z are

$$Y = 3857.14 \quad Z = 5142.86$$

(Continued.)

(Written expressly for THE BOOK-KEEPER.*)*

THE ALGEBRA OF ACCOUNTS.

BY CHARLES E. SPRAGUE.

(Continued.)

Now, as we have all the numerical equivalents necessary, we can write out the equation in the accountant's manner of notation. This we will do with all the traditional forms.

Balance-sheet of the firm of Y—— & Z——.

NEW YORK, Jan. 1, 1880.

Dr.   Cr.

Cash, balance on hand...	2,344	25	P—, amount due him...	2,374	64
Merchandise "	5,655	75	Q—, " "	3,273	29
Real Estate, value........	2,000		Bills payable, outstand'g	352	07
U—, amount due from him	3,999	23	Y—, his capital........	3,857	14
V—, " " "	109	32	Z—, his capital..........	5,142	86
W—, " " "	891	45			
	15,000			15,000	

14. By adding two other columns we can unite the detail of equation 9 to the comprehensiveness of equation 4.

Balance-sheet of Y—— & Z——.

NEW YORK, Jan. 1, 1880.

Dr.   Cr.

Cash............. 2,344.25			P—,.............. 2,374.64		
Merchandise 5,655.75			Q—,.............. 3,273.29		
Real estate 2,000.00			Bills payable,........ 352.07		
Total property..		10,000	**Total due creditors,......**		6,000
U—,.............. 3,999.23					
V—,.............. 109.32					
W—,.............. 891.45			Y—,.............. 3,857.14		
Total due debtors,......		5,000	Z—,.............. 5,142.86		
			Total capital,..		9,000
	15,000	15,000		15,000	15,000

Compare this with equations 9 and 4.

15. In Hopkins' "Exhibit Book-keeping" a different arrangement and a different use of terms are found. We give the above balance-sheet after Mr. Hopkins' plan, which is ingenious and effective. It will be seen that this too is a form of writing our fundamental equation. No arrangement for exhibiting the condition of financial affairs at any time can possibly be made which is not reducible to

$$H + T = X + O.$$

Mr. Hopkins subdivides H into "Actual Resources" and "Speculative Resources." This distinction we omit here as unessential in an exhibit taken at a time when all resources have been actually valued.

Financial Exhibit made July 6, 1879, from the books of Y—— & Z——.

RESOURCES.		BALANCES FROM EXHIBIT REGISTER.	LIABILITIES.	
10,000		Actual (and speculative) resources, [H]........		
5,000		Anticipated resources, [T].....................		
		Contracted liabilities, [O]....................	6,000	
		Proprietary liabilities, [X]...................	9,000	
15,000		............Totals......................	15,000	

RESOURCES.		STATEMENT IN DETAIL.	LIABILITIES.	
2,344	25	Cash, on hand and in bank.		
2,000		Real estate, valuation.		
4,344	25	[Total actual resources].		
5,655	75	Merchandise.		
10,000		**Total actual and speculative resources.**		
3,999	23	U—, due us on account.		
109	32	V—, " " "		
891	45	W—, " " "		
5,000		**Total anticipated resources.**		
		P—, due him on account, ...	2,374	64
		Q—, " " "	2,273	29
		Bills payable,...............................	352	07
		Total contracted liabilities,..........	6,000	
		Y—, his 3-7 of capital,......................	3,857	14
		Z—, his 4-7 of capital,......................	5,142	86
		Total proprietary liabilities,.........	9,000	

16. We will now place this equation (No. 9) in the form known as the "Journal entry."

                                      Dr.   Cr.

	SUNDRIES DR. TO SUNDRIES.				
1880.					
Jan. 1.	to open the accounts of the firm of Y— & Z—, showing its assets, liabilities, and capital :				
	Cash, Dr. for amount on hand and in bank, ...	2,344	25		
	Merchandise, Dr. for amount in store,......	5,655	75		
	Real estate, Dr. for property 266 3d Ave., ...	2,000			
	U—, for amount due from him,........	3,999	23		
	V—, " " " "	109	32		
	W—, " " " "	891	45		
	To P—, for amount due him,....			2,374	64
	To Q—, " " " "			3,273	29
	To **Bills payable,** for amount outstanding, ...			352	07
	To Y—, for his 3-7 of capital,....			3,857	14
	To Z—, for his 4-7 of capital.....			5,142	86

In this form of the equation (the Journal entry) we have purposely retained the traditional forms in full. Many of these are entirely unnecessary, or so considered by bookkeepers, who discard them. In fact, the Journal as a full record of business annals is becoming obsolete ; its place is taken by special books into which its contents are divided so as to put each class of entries by themselves ; or else, by using a number of columns it is made to perform some of the work of classification. But we use the Journal as a type of all books of original entry, arranged in order of dates.

17. Assets, or Resources, and Liabilities.—What I *have* is in my possession *now ;* what I *trust,* is *to be* in my possession. But many things (such as bank notes, mortgages, promissory notes), which are really only promises, are spoken of as if they had intrinsic value ; we call them not dues receivable, but property. Hence the categories H and T shade into each other. This makes no difference, as both equally tend to increase the amount of X. The names "Resources" or "Assets" are applied to H + T. Let H + T or the "Resources" [assets] be represented by A ; then substituting this value in equation (4).

$$(10.)\quad A = O + X.$$

My assets = what I owe + what I am worth.

The word "Liabilities" is sometimes applied to O alone, sometimes to O + X together. But generally there is a sharp distinction between O, the outside liabilities and X, the difference of A — O, the net proprietorship. X participates in the profits and losses ; X can only be paid off after O is fully satisfied. **It is the losing sight of this distinction between O and X which causes most of the misunderstanding respecting the processes of double entry book-keeping.**

18. So much for the equation of the property *at rest ;* now we must provide for recording its changes.

19. There are only two kinds of change ; *increase* and *decrease, more* and *less,* + and —.

20. *More* gives four modes of increase.

1. I have more.
2. I trust more.
3.　　　I owe more.
4.　　　I am *worth more.*

21. *Less* gives four modes of decrease.

1.　　　I have less.
2.　　　I trust less.
3. I owe less.
4. I am *worth less.*

22. In section 7 we illustrated the transposition of a negative term to the opposite side of the equation. The same principle is applied to the four terms in section 21.

I have more is added to the debit :
But *I have less* instead of being subtracted from the debit, is added to the credit.

I trust more is added to the debit :
But *I trust less* is added to the credit, not subtracted from the debit.

I owe more is added to the credit :
But *I owe less* instead of being subtracted from the credit, is added to the debit.

I am worth more is added to the credit :
But *I am worth less* is added to the debit.

23. Hence the list of debits and credits, while the equation is undergoing change, is extended from 4 to 8.

a.　　　*Elements of the Equation of Value at Rest.*

Debits.	Credits.
Have.	Owe.
Trust.	Worth.

(*b.*)　　　*Elements of the Equation of Value in Motion.*

Debits.	Credits.
1. Have more.	2. Have less.
3. Trust more.	4. Trust less.
5. Owe less.	6. Owe more,
7. Worth less.	8. Worth more.

These tables are :

a. A complete rule for balance-sheets or statements of financial condition.

b. A complete rule for "journalizing," that is, for ascertaining the debit and credit in any transaction or shifting of values ; in other words, directions for placing the values on the left and right side of the equation respectively. As list *b* contains all the possible changes in the elements of the equation, it must suffice to represent any transaction or business occurrence.

24. **Tendency of the Eight Elements.**—Consider the last pair of elements in *b,* Nos 7 and 8. In these two, the credit side is what is to the benefit of the proprietor, and the debit is what is against him. On the other hand, in the other three pairs, debit is in favor of the proprietor, and credit is against him. The tendency of *worth* is directly contrary to that of *having, trusting* and *owing.* Bear in mind this characteristic of the term X or the worth, as it gives a new phase of meaning to "debit" and "credit."

25. **Representation of Change.**—Every change or interchange of values is represented by an equation. Otherwise unequal amounts would be added to the two sides, and the result would be an inequality ; but this is impossible, as the fundamental equation always holds true.

26. **Forming Equations of Change.**—Illustrations.

1st. Let the transaction be : I buy Merchandise worth k, and pay cash, i, getting trusted by P—— for the remainder, p. Then we must ask—

Which of the 8 elements of change is true of Cash ?

Which of them is true of Merchandise ?

Which of them is true of indebtedness to P—— ?

Answers : I *have less* Cash, a credit ;
I *have more* Merchandise, a debit ;
I *owe more* to P——, a credit.

Therefore, k is a debit, i and p are credits ; the **equation is**
$$k = i + p.$$

Assuming the numerical values,

$$k = 1,000, \quad i = 500, \quad p = 500,$$

we can put this equation into the form of a journal entry.

Merchandise Dr. to Sundries,	1,000	
For purchase from P——.		
To **Cash,** for amount paid,		500
To **P——**, for balance unpaid,		500

2d Example. I sell for $2,630 ($i_2$) the Real Estate which is valued in my balance-sheet at $2.000 (L), and receive my pay in Cash.

In Cash, I *have more*, therefore the change of 2,630 is a debit.

In Real Estate I *have less*, therefore the change of 2,000 is a credit.

As the result of the transaction, I am *worth more*, having gained $630 (x).

We denote the changes in any department by small letters corresponding to the capitals in the balance-sheet.

$$\text{Equation} \quad i_2 = L + X.$$
$$\text{or } 2,630 = 2,000 + 630.$$

Journal entry.

Cash Dr. to Sundries,	2,630	
For sale of property, No. 266 3d Ave.		
To **Real Estate,**		2,000
For valuation of same.		
To **Profit and Loss,**		630
For gain on the sale.		

(*Continued.*)

(Written expressly for THE BOOK-KEEPER.*)*

THE ALGEBRA OF ACCOUNTS.

BY CHARLES E. SPRAGUE.

(Continued.)

3d Example. U—— pays in cash the amount due me, $3,999.23.

Cash is debited because I *have more.*
U—— is credited because I *trust less.*

$$i_3 = U.$$

Journal entry.

Cash Dr.	3,999.23	
To **U——,**		3,999.23

For payment of his debt in full.

4th Example. I sell to V——, Merchandise to the amount of $3,204, and trust him for it.

As to V—— I *trust more,* therefore he is debited with $3,204 (v).

But as to merchandise, I surely *have less;* yet I do not know how much less, for I do not know what the wholesale price of these particular goods was. Most merchants have no system of keeping account of their profit on merchandise which they sell, or of keeping account of how much merchandise they ought to have on hand. This is an imperfection, and in the book-keeping of the future the merchant will know every morning what he made or lost the day before, and how much merchandise ought to be on his shelves. But we are speaking now of the now prevailing methods. We credit merchandise with the *whole proceeds,* disregarding the profits. Then at certain periods we ascertain the profits.

On this plan, the equation is

$$v_1 = k_2 \text{ or } 3,204 = 3,204.$$

Journalized :

V—— Dr.,	3,204	
To **Merchandise,**		3,204

For amount sold him on credit.

5th Example. I pay P—— in cash all I owe him, $2,874.64
P—— is debtor, for I *owe* him *less,*   2,874.64 (P).
Cash is creditor, for I *have less.*   2,874.64 (i$_4$).
Equation : p = i$_4$

Journal entry.

P—— Dr.,	2,374.64	
To **Cash,**		2,374.64

6th Example. I pay Expense in Cash, $250.
Cash is creditor, for I *have less.*
Profit and Loss is debtor, for I *am worth less.*

$$X_2 = i_5.$$

Profit and Loss Dr.,	250	
To **Cash,**		250

From examples 2 and 6 it will be seen that gains and losses are not usually credited and debited directly to "Capital" account, which department represents the present worth, but to "profit and loss." This is done, in order not to disturb the "Worth," except periodically in a gross amount, which amount shows the extent of our business success. "Profit and Loss" is a sort of reservoir into which all gains and losses are poured merely to be held until a convenient season, when the net result is transferred in one sum to the "Worth" account, called "Capital" or "Stock." As "Profit and

Loss" is tributary to "Worth," of which it is a subdivision, so there are other accounts tributary to "Profit and Loss" itself. Instead of making "Profit and Loss" the debtor, we may temporarily consider "Expense" as debtor, understanding that at the time of balancing the books (reducing the equation) we transfer its net result to "Profit and Loss." Gains from Interest and losses by Interest may be grouped into an "interest" account or department ; commissions paid and received may be grouped into "commission" account. Such accounts subordinate to Profit and Loss may be multiplied to any extent desirable.

27. **The Journal.**—We have now given six examples of transactions, and have made each one of them into an equation expressed in two ways, first by letters and then as a journal entry. We will now unite the balance-sheet entry in section 16, and these six entries of change into a journal, placing the literal expression of each entry opposite.

JOURNAL. [PAGE 1.]

Date.		Dr.	Cr.	
18—.	SUNDRIES DR. TO SUNDRIES,			I + K $\cdot$ L + U + V + W
Jan. 1.	to open the accounts of the firm of Y—— & Z—, showing their assets, liabilities, and capital :			(Balance sheet.)
	Cash, Dr. for amount on hand,.......	2,344.25		= P + Q + R + Y . Z.
	Merchandise, Dr. for am't in store,..	5,655.75		
	Real estate, Dr. for property No. 266 3d Ave.,............................	2,000.		
	U—, Dr. for amount due from him,....	3 999.23		
	V—, " " " "	109.32		
	W—, " " " "	891.45		
	To **P—,** for amount due *to* him,..		2,374.64	
	To **Q—,** " " "		3,273.29	
	To **Bills payable,** for amount outstanding, ...		352 07	
	To **Y—,** for his 3-7 of capital,....		3,857.14	
	To **Z—,** for his 4-7 of capital,....		5,142.86	
2.	**Merchandise,** Dr. to Sundries,.... .. For purchase from P—.	1,000.		k = i + p
	To **Cash,** for amount paid,......		500.	
	To **P—,** for balance unpaid,......		500.	
2.	**Cash,** Dr. to Sundries,.............. For sale of property No. 266 3d Ave.	2,630.		i$_2$ = l + x
	To **Real estate,**................ For cost of same.		2,000.	
	To **Profit and Loss,** .... For gain on the sale.		630.	
3.	**Cash,** Dr............................	3,999.23		i$_3$ = U
	To **U—,**......................... For payment of his debt received in full.		3,999.23	
4.	**V—,** Dr.......................... ..	3,204.		v$_1$ = k$_1$
	To **Merchandise,**............. For am't sold him on credit.		3,204.	
5.	**P—,** Dr...........................	2,874.64		p = i$_4$
	To **Cash,**...................... For amount paid him in full.		2,874.64	
6.	**Profit and Loss,** Dr............	250		x$_2$ = i$_5$
	To **Cash,**...................... For amount of expense paid.		250.	
	Total,..........................	28,957.87	28,957.87	

Eq. 1. / Eq. 2. / Eq. 3. / Eq. 4. / Eq. 5. / Eq. 6.

28. Hopkins' Method.—The foregoing is a journal in the traditional form. It was formerly customary to rewrite the whole contents of the other books of original entry (cash-book, sales-book, invoice-book, etc.) into the journal, making double work, for the other books can just as well be arranged so as to exhibit the equations of values. In Hopkins' Exhibit Book-keeping, the book nearest corresponding to the journal is the Exhibit Register. The work of making up a journal, which, in the old form, is believed by many to be mostly wasted, is utilized by Hopkins in two ways: first, by eliminating the element "Cash," and saving the labor of many half-entries and of an account ; second, by the use of six debit columns and six credit columns, classifying the elements into three classes of "Resources" and three classes of "Liabilities." The effect of this is to enable the proprie-

tor to form from the Exhibit Register every day, or as often as desirable, the equation

$$H + T = O + X,$$

without the laborious process of gathering together the items of which each term, H, T and O, is composed. The following is an explanation of Mr. Hopkins' titles of columns :

H responds to "Actual and Speculative Resources," the distinction not being made by us in the equations, although it might readily be made.

T corresponds to "Anticipated Resources."

O corresponds to "Contracted Liabilities."

X corresponds to "Operative and Proprietary Liabilities."

For "Operative Liabilities" as distinguished from "Proprietary Liabilites" see section 26, Ex. 6, explaining Profit and Loss.

EXHIBIT REGISTER. [Left hand page.]

Specula-tive.	Anticipa-ted.	Actual.	Vou-cher	Resources Increased.	Ledger Folio.	Resources Diminished.	Vou-cher	Actual.	Anticipa-ted.	Specula-tive.
5,655 75			B	Merchandise.		Real estate.	2	2,000		
	3,999 23	2,000	B	Real estate.		W—.	3		3,999 23	
	109 32		B	U—.		Merchandise.	4			3,204
	891 45		B	V—.		Balances.		5,348 84	4,204 77	3,451 75
1,000			1	W—.						
	3,204		3	Merchandise.						
		5,348 84		V—.						
				Cash on hand.						
3,451 75	4,204 77	5,348 84		Balances.		Cash.		5,348 84		

EXHIBIT REGISTER. [Right hand page.]

Opera-tive.	Contract-ed.	Proprie-tary.	Vou-cher	Liabilities Diminished.	Ledger Folio.	Liabilities Increased.	Vou-cher	Proprie-tary.	Contract-ed.	Opera-tive.
	2,874 64		5	P—.		P—.	B		2,374 64	
250			6	Profit and loss.		Q—.	B		3,273 29	
380	3,625 36	9,000		Balances.		Bills payable.	B		352 07	
						Y—.	B	3,857 14		
						Z—.	B	5,142 86		
						P—.	1		500	
						Profit and loss.	2			630
						Balances.		9,000	3,625 36	380

We give no opinion here as to the advantages or disadvantages of this method of presentation, our object being merely to show the algebraic nature of all proper systems of accounts. It will be seen that the two lines of "Balance" under "Resources Increased" and "Liabilities Increased," are an equation : our old one,

$$H + T = O + X.$$

29. Classification.—The journal, as we have given it, is a chronicle of the business. It contains a record of whatever has happened, but unclassified. It records changes in each item, but those of the same item need to be grouped together before we can ascertain what the final result is. The method described in Section 28 serves to give values at any time to all the terms in the equation

$$H + T = O + X,$$

but we need something more than this, we want to be able to know, after all the changes have been made, the values of all the terms

$$1 + K + L + \cdots + U + V + W + \cdots$$
$$= P + Q + R + \cdots + Y + Z + \cdots$$

We will now show how this grouping is done, first algebraically, then in the method of practical book-keeping. Our equations are :

(10.) $1 + K + L + U + V + W = P + Q + R + Y + Z$

(11.) $k = i + p$

(12.) $i_2 = L + x$

(13.) $i_3 = U$

(14.) $r = k$

(15.) $p = i_4$

(16.) $x_2 = i_5$

The large letters denote elements of the original balance-sheet, and the small letters *more* or *less* of the same kind, the different increments and decrements of the same kind being distinguished by small figures below.

Let us add all these equations together into one, grouping those of the same letter.

$$
(17.)\quad
\left.
\begin{aligned}
&(I + i_2 + i_3)\\
+\;&(K + k)\\
+\;&L\\
+\;&U\\
+\;&(V + v)\\
+\;&W\\
+\;&P\\
\\
+\;&x_2
\end{aligned}
\right\}
=
\left\{
\begin{aligned}
&(i + i_4 + i_5)\\
+\;&k\\
+\;&L\\
+\;&U\\
\\
\\
+\;&P\\
+\;&Q\\
+\;&x\\
+\;&R\\
+\;&Y\\
+\;&Z
\end{aligned}
\right.
$$

30. **Chronicles Transformed to History.**—Examination will show that this grouping process has given us the materials for a history of each department of the business.

All the increase and decrease of cash, for example, is denoted by the terms $i_2 + i_3$ on one side, and $i + i_4 + i_5$ on the other.

31. **Posting.**—The grouping process is called in book-keeping "posting." The matter of the journal is re-written in a form known as the **"Ledger."**

32. **The Ledger.**—This form of the equation differs from the journal in this: it allots a page or space, called an **account,** to each department of the business, just as in the above equation we alloted a line to each letter. The account must have two sides (just as the equation has,) one for the "debits" and one for the "credits." The journal is gone through line by line and dissected; each amount in the Dr. column is transferred to the Dr. side of the account named on the same line of the journal; each amount in the Cr. column is transferred to the Cr. side.

(Continued.)

(*Written expressly for* The Book-keeper.)

THE ALGEBRA OF ACCOUNTS.

By Charles E. Sprague.

(*Concluded.*)

33. It is unnecessary to give here the full Ledger corresponding to the equation in Section 29. It will be sufficient to show the manner of posting by giving the Cash account representing the terms—

$$I + i_2 + i_3 \cdots \text{ and } i + i_4 + 5.$$

Dr.	CASH.				*Cr.*		
18—				18—			
Jan. 1	To **Sundries,** for amount on hand..	2,344	25	Jan. 2	By **Merchandise** for purchase from P—..............		500
	2 To **Sundries,** for sale of property 266 3d Ave.,......	2,630			5 By **P—,** for amount paid him in full..	2 874	64
	3 To **U—,** for payment of his debt, received in full..	3,999	23		6 By **Profit & loss,** for amount of expense paid,......		250

34. This page or **account** is a history of that class of values known as Cash. The left hand side represents how much we *have had* in all since, and including the date of the balance-sheet ; the right hand side, exactly the opposite, what we have *un-had* or parted with. Each account represents some department of values (as I, K, L, P or Y), and shows its becoming *more* or *less* by its two sides, as in the following scheme : We use the Italic capital letters to represent in general both balances and increments ; for instance, I includes I and i, i_1, i_2, etc.

—— 1. ——

In accounts representing **Property,** or *having :*

　The **debit** shows all we *have had ;*　　　$(+H)$.
　The **credit** shows all we *have parted with ;*　$(-H)$.
　The difference shows what we *now have*.

—— 2. ——

In accounts representing **Debtors,** or *trusting :*

　The **debit** shows how much we *have trusted them ;* $(+T)$.
　The **credit** shows how much they *have paid ;* $(-T)$.
　The difference shows how much *they now owe*.

—— 3. ——

In accounts representing **Creditors,** or *owing :*

　The **credit** shows all we have gone into *debt* for ; $(+O)$.
　The **debit** shows all we *have paid off ;*　　$(-O)$.
　The difference shows how much *we now owe*.

—— 4. ——

In accounts representing **Proprietorship,** or *worth :*

　The **credit** shows all we *have been worth ;*　$(+X)$.
　The **debit** shows all we *have lost ;*　　　$(-X)$.
　The difference shows how much we are now worth.

This is the interpretation of all accounts. Any account can be referred to one of these classes and read accordingly.

But accounts may be on the border line between two of these classes, and may represent at the same time　a, Property and Debtors ; b, Debtors or Creditors ; c, Property and Worth ; or even other combinations. We will prove our principles correct by applying them to these difficult cases.

a. You have a man's note, perfectly good, for $100. Is this an asset of the property-class or the debtor-class ? I should say decidedly, of the latter ; but many would prefer to treat the note itself as property in actual possession. Then we may combine interpretations No. 1 and No. 2—

"The debit shows our *having* the note or *trusting* its maker, as you choose to view it."

"The credit shows our *parting* with the note or being paid the debt represented by it, as you choose to view it."

b. You have dealings with a correspondent at a distance, and your account is a running one. He trusts you with values to dispose of for him, and you likewise trust him. He draws on you perhaps for proceeds, and you draw on him, or you allow each other's dealings to offset each other. This may properly be put into two accounts, technically called "his account" and "our account." But suppose we put all together in one account. Then our correspondent belongs both to the debtor and creditor class,—sometimes one, sometimes the other. Then combining interpretations 2 and 3—

"The debit means, we have trusted him or have paid him off, as the case may be."

"The credit means we have gone into his debt, or he has got out of ours, as the case may be."

Or, more simply :
　Debits are *either* "trust more " or " owe less."
　Credits are *either* "owe more " or "trust less."

c. Some property may be parted with, and although we know how much we get, we do *not* know how much is profit and how much is original cost returned (wholesale price). We *ought* to know (as has been said in example 6, Section 26), but such a mass of petty articles have been sold, that we think it too much labor to ascertain the cost price. Then if we credit the whole amount to the account of the property, this account ceases to be a pure property account, and becomes partly a worth or profit-and-loss account. See example 6, which will now be better understood. Combination of interpretations 1 and 4—

　The debit shows how much we have had, at cost.

　　The credit shows partly how much we have parted with, and partly what is the profit (more worth) on it.

　The difference is what remains on hand—less the profit on what has been sold.

Therefore we must add the profit to the difference of the account to give what remains on hand at cost. Or, to find the profit, subtract the difference of the account from the amount on hand, found by actual appraisal.

We will make this last principle a little clearer by algebra. Let C equal the original cost of the whole, C_1 the value of the unsold remainder at cost price, c = the entire proceeds of the sale, p = the profit.

　Then $C - C_1 =$ cost of what has been sold.

　　　$c - p, =$ the same.

　or (1) $C - C_1 = c - p$.

(Things which are equal to the same thing are equal to each other.)

Transposing — C, = — C + c — p.

Changing all the signs (2) C, = C .— c + p.

But (C — c) is the difference of the sides, therefore—

To find the value of the unsold remainder, add the profit to the difference of the sides.

Transposing again and changing sides

$$(3)\ p = (C - c) - C.$$

That is, to find the profit when the unsold property has been inventoried, subtract the inventory from the difference of the sides.

Transposing Eq. (1) so as to make all terms positive,

$$(4)\ C + p = c + C_1.$$

which is the form from which to pass to the book-keeping form of a **Speculative** account. For example :

| *Dr.* | SPECULATIVE PROPERTY. | *Cr.* |

C { Cost at first inventory,....5.655.75 { Subseq't cost of purchase,..1.000.	c. Proceeds at retail,............3,204. C₁. Final inventory at wholesale, 3,739.20	
p. Profit on sales,............. 287.45		
6.943.20	6.943.20	

The above account is in substance the "Merchandise" account from the journal in Section 27, except the entries p and C₁. We will pass to the journal an additional entry, changing the above speculative account to a pure property account.

JOURNAL.	*Dr.*	*Cr.*
Brought forward.................................	28,957.87	28,957.87
Merchandise, Dr., ...	287.45	
To **Profit and loss,**...........		287.45
for gain on sales since the last inventory, ascertained as follows :		
Former inventory, ...5,655.75		
Cost since " ....1.000.		
Total cost,..............................6.655.75		
Proceeds of sales, ...3.204.		
Apparent balance on hand, provided there were no gain,...............................3.451.65		
But there is really on hand, ...3.739.20		
Difference or gain,........................ 287.45		
	29,245.32	29,245.32

35. Trial Balance.—The cash account in Section 3 B has not equal amounts on both sides, nor have the other accounts generally. Still, taking the aggregate of all the accounts there must be an equal amount of debit and of credit. The ledger is nothing but the journal rearranged ; hence it must preserve the same equation. The process of adding all the totals of the accounts together to see if this equality is preserved, and thereby possibly detecting errors, is called "taking a **Trial Balance.**" It is equivalent to substituting numerical values in the equation and reducing.

36. There remain three processes to be algebraically explained, called "transferring accounts," "balancing an account," and "taking a balance-sheet."

37. **Transferring.**—As an example, we will take the Profit and Loss account as made up from the journal already given, including the entry in Section 34.

| *Dr.* | PROFIT AND LOSS. | | *Cr.* |

Jan. 6	To **Cash,** for am't of expense paid,.	250	Jan. 2	By **Cash,** for gain on real estate sold	630
			6	By **Merchandise** for gain on sale,.	287	45

To interpret this account, we refer to Section 34, No. 4. This being a "Worth" account, the rule is—

The credit means worth more,

The debit means worth less.

The difference (if the credit is greater) means net gain ; 917.45 — 250 = 667.45.

The question now is, to transfer this amount to the account of the partners by an entry or equation. Suppose they are to share the profits in proportion to their capital, or as 3 to 4, then the shares are, Y's, 286.05, Z's 381.40. The account as it stands is an inequality $x_2 < x + x_3$. Let X_1 = the net gain, or difference between debit and credit ; then

$$X_1 = x + x_3 - x_2 = \$667.45.$$

Transposing $x_2 + X_1 = x + x_3$. That is, by adding the net result to the smaller side, we make the inequality into an equation. An account which is equated is said to be *closed*, and may be disregarded, because equals may be subtracted from equals, and the remainders will be equal. But in equating this account, we have destroyed the general equality of the ledger, for we have added to the debit and not to the credit. We must add the same amount to the credit ; as we have canceled the temporary account "Profit and Loss " we restore the equation by crediting the partners each his share. The journal entry would be—

Profit and loss, Dr. to Sundries,   667.45

to transfer the net profits to the partners'
capital accounts,

To Y——, for his ⅜,   286.05

To Z——, for his ⅘,   381.40

After posting this entry the Profit and Loss account may be ruled off like the balance sheet and closed.

To transfer the balance from one account to another one, or to others, add to the less side of the first account enough to make both sides equal ; rule off and close ; add to the opposite side of the second account the same amount.

38. **Balancing an Account** is reducing it to a single term ; it is the same as transferring, except that the balance is carried, not to another account, but to the opposite column of the same account below the double lines of equality. The algebraic operation would be to add the net result to that side of the equation which would make the terms of that letter equal on the two sides ; then cancel that line ; and finally add the same result to the other side.

39. As an example we give the cash account, balanced.

Dr.				CASH.				Cr.

	Jan. 1	To **Sundries**, for amount on hand.	2,344	25		Jan. 2	By **Merchandise** for purchase from P—, ...		500	
	2	To **Sundries**, for sale of property 266 3d Ave., ...	2,630			5	By **P—**, for amount paid him in full,.	2,874	64	
	3	To **U—**, for payment of his debt, received in full,.	3,999	23		6	By **Profit & loss,** for amount of expense paid,......		250	
						7	By *Balance* for am't on hand, carried down,...........	5,348	84	
			8,973	48				8,973	48	
	Jan. 8	To *Balance* for am't on hand, brought down,...........	5,348	84						

The process in the equation is : add I_1, the amount of cash on hand to both sides ; in the credit side group it with the I's already there ; in the debit side place it by itself.

$$(I + i_2 + i_3.) \qquad (i + i_4 + i_5 + I_1.)$$
$$+ I_1$$
$$\text{etc.,} \qquad\qquad \text{etc.}$$

The first line cancels out, leaving only the net result to represent the account.

40. **Balancing the Ledger.**—This process, which is also called " taking a balance-sheet," is as follows :

1st. Transfer to capital account (Section 37) all subordinate accounts, as Profit and Loss.

2d. Balance each account (Section 38).

3d. Make a list of the Dr. and Cr. balances as in Section 15, omitting those accounts which close without a balance.

Algebraically :

Resume equation 17, Section 29, adding in the entries in Section 34 and 36.

$$(18.) \quad
\left.
\begin{array}{l}
(I + i_2 + i_3.) \\
+ K + k + x_3 \\
* + L \\
* + U \\
+ (V + v) \\
+ W \\
* + P \\
\\
* + (x_3 + X_1)
\end{array}
\right\}
=
\left\{
\begin{array}{l}
(i + i_4 + i_5) \\
+ k_1 \\
+ L \\
+ U \\
\\
\\
+ P \\
+ Q \\
+ R \\
(+ x + x_3) \\
+ Y + y_1 \\
+ Z + z_1
\end{array}
\right.
$$

x_3 is the profit on merchandise ; Section 34. X_1 is the net result of Profit and Loss account ; y_1 and z_1 are partners' shares : $X_1 = y_1 + z_1$. The lines [accounts] marked * might have been disregarded, because they are equated.

Process 1st has been performed by adding $X_1 = y_1 + z_1$.

Process 2d consists in balancing. When it is done we

have more accounts marked *. Capital letters marked $(_1,)$ as K_1, Y_1, represent net results at the close.

$$(19.) \quad
\left.
\begin{array}{l}
* \quad (I + i_2 + i_3) \\
\quad + I_1 \\
* + (K + k + x_3) \\
\quad + K_1 \\
* + L \\
* + U \\
* + (V + v) \\
\quad + V_1 \\
\quad + W \\
* + P \\
\\
\\
* + (x_2 + X_1) \\
* + Y_1 \\
\\
* + Z_1
\end{array}
\right\}
=
\left\{
\begin{array}{ll}
(i + i_4 + i_5 + I_1) & * \\
\\
+ (k_1 + K_1) & * \\
\\
+ L & * \\
+ U & * \\
+ V_1 & * \\
\\
\\
+ P & * \\
+ Q \\
+ R \\
+ (x + x_3) & * \\
+ (Y + y_1) & * \\
+ Y_1 \\
+ (Z + z_1) & * \\
+ Z_1
\end{array}
\right.
$$

Canceling the lines marked * we have

$$(20.) \quad I_1 + K_1 + V_1 + W = Q + R + Y_1 + Z_1.$$

The balance-sheet form is (Process 3).

Cash,....................	5,348.84	Q—,....................	3,273.29
Merchandise,...........	3,739.20	Bills payable,.........	352.07
V—,....................	3.313.32	Y—'s capital,..........	4,143.19
W—,....................	891.45	Z—'s capital,..........	5,524.26
	13,292.81		13,292.81

This is still the equation,
　What I have + what I trust,
　　　= what I owe + what I am worth.

41. In our example of ledger accounts we have again followed old precedents without recommending the retention of all the features. For example, in the first credit entry of cash :

　　" By Merchandise, for purchase from P.,"

many write merely

　　" By Merchandise ;"

others write "Merchandise," or " Mdse,"

others again "Purchase from P. ;"

and still others omit all words and give only a *number* referring to the original voucher or document of the transactions, or to the page of the original entry. Some place the dates in the middle ; some make the ledger in the same form as the journal ; and others add a third column for the balance after each entry.

42. **Deductions.**—We give the following as results of the foregoing discussion.

I. All the statements of book-keeping are equations.

II. All *minus* (negative or subtractive) terms are transposed to the opposite side where they become *plus* (positive or additive.)

III. Debit and credit mean simply "left hand side " and " right hand side " of the equation. To him who understands the equation, no other definition of debit and credit is necessary. To him who has never grasped the idea of the equation, no definition of debit and credit can make them clear.

LOGISMOGRAPHY I AND II

Charles E[zra] Sprague

Logismography I

By CHARLES E. SPRAGUE.*

This word has been for some time familiar to students in the countries of the Latin race, in its French form of logismographie, and the Italian, Spanish and Portuguese, logismografia. It is not specially descriptive of the system to which it is applied; in fact, etymologically, it would naturally mean a scientific description of accounts. But the sense in which it is accepted is that of a system of keeping accounts on the principle of sub-division, subordination and co-ordination, the primary accounts being divided into groups, and these subdivided and re-subdivided to any desired extent. This is not a thorough definition, but will answer for the present. What it is can only be known by examining it in all its parts.

I do not profess to be entirely satisfied that logismography is the universal remedy which some of its supporters think it; but I think it proper for American students to examine it thoroughly and take advantage of everything good which it suggests. It is only fair to remember that every system in practice differs somewhat from a' book description of the same. There is something unreal and make-believe in the sets of double entry accounts given as illustrations by even the best of text-books, and we should make the same allowances in the case of logismography. Furthermore, logismography appears to be firmly established in Italy, the birth-place of bookkeeping, after a long struggle for existence, and it is fair to presume that it would not have remained in use for twenty years if it had not some solid merits.

What I now propose to do, is to give to those readers of ACCOUNTICS who have not the opportunity of studying the subject in the original, a faithful reproduction of what I find in the Italian works. Where I have occasion to comment and to suggest changes, I will do so only after I have given the method as stated by the Italian authors, using as far as possible an exact equivalent of their language. This may sometimes lead me into the use of strange and unaccus-

*Col. Charles E. Sprague is President of the Institute of Accounts, President of the Union Dime Savings Institution, and one of the Examiners of Public Accountants, State of New York.

tomed English expressions, but this cannot be avoided in the presentation of a new subject, and doubtless Signor Cerboni's terms were also strange to those who first read his exposition.

Logismography is a system for the ordination of accounts, devised by Giuseppe Cerboni, Accountant-General of Italy. Its fundamental character is that of showing at any moment in the most summary form the situation of any concern by means of two accounts, one entitled Proprietor, the other Agents and Correspondents, or, more briefly, Agency. By agents are meant those subordinates of the proprietor, who are responsible to him for values entrusted to them, that is, the keepers of property (cashier, stock-clerk, note-clerk, etc.). By correspondents are meant his customers and all persons with whom he has dealings on credit, (not necessarily by letter). The Proprietor's Account exhibits all the claims or rights of the proprietor, (his resources, his credits, his "active") and all his obligations; (his liabilities, his debts, his "passive"). The Agency Account exhibits the claims of others against the proprietor, and their obligations toward him.

The proprietor does not always figure in doube entry but he always does in logismography. Thus, we say in double entry:

Cash Dr. to Merchandise.

This is expressed in logismography thus:

1	2
Proprietor Dr.	Proprietor Cr.
(as to merchandise)	(as to money)

3	4
(Cashier)	(Stock-keeper)
Agency Dr.	Agency Cr.

In an entry like this, ordinary bookkeeping would suppress 1 and 2. The full meaning of the logismographic form is:

1. The proprietor is poorer in goods, but
2. Richer in money.
3. The cashier owes more to the proprietor, but
4. The stock-keeper owes him less.

The fundamental accounts of logismography give in the highest synthesis the situation of the concern at any moment; but this is not enough to satisfy the needs of administration. Therefore each of the two main accounts is decomposed into other accounts, forming two distinct series, integral and differential. The integral accounts represent in their entirety the claims and duties of the proprietor and those of the agency. The differential accounts deal only with the differences, increase and diminution, in the total net amount or patrimony.

Hence there are four series of derived accounts:

1. Integral accounts of the proprietor, representing claims and obligations, or credits and debits, or the various kinds of values constituting his patrimony, and hence giving the specific status of the business.

tains the chronological registration of the transactions, and the two fundamental accounts of the proprietor and of the agency (parties to the transactions). The credit balance of the Proprietor account shows the amount of his net patrimony and is proved by the debit balance of the other account. The column of Permutations contains sums which, not affecting the net balance of accounts A and B, are omitted from both sides thereof. The account of the Proprietor is headed A and that of the Agency B.

To develop an account is to subdivide it into other accounts, the sum of which is equal to the original. The form of the developments is shown in Fig. 2.

To facilitate reference, each account in the Journal is provided with a capital letter, as A and B. The development of

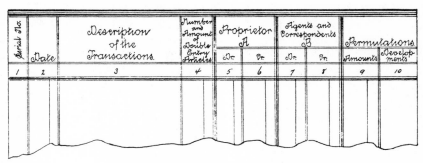

FIG. 1. THE LOGISMOGRAPHIC JOURNAL.

2. Integral accounts of the Agency, giving the amount of claim or obligation of each property-keeper toward the business, and the debit or credit of each correspondent; hence showing the legal status.

3. Differential accounts of the proprietor, giving under various classifications the differences, increase or decrease, of the net patrimony, and showing the economic status, direct.

4. Differential accounts of the agency, giving increase and decrease of the debits and credits of the agents and correspondents, and showing the economic status, inverse.

More briefly: 1. Specific accounts; 2, Juridical accounts; 3. Economic Accounts; 4. Inverse Economic accounts.

The Logismographic Journal, Fig. 1, con-

these are called Development A and Development B. The sub-accounts of Development A are, A1, A2, A3, etc., and correspondingly for B. These are developments of the first grade. If we develop one of these sub-accounts, we have a development of the second grade, and here we use small (lower case) letters. Thus, Development A2, would contain the sub-accounts, A2a, A2b, A2c, etc. For developments of the third grade and beyond, we use numbers again, alternating with letters. B3d5f would be the sixth sub-account, of the fifth sub-account, of the 4th sub-account, of the third sub-account of the Agency account. Developments beyond the second grade are seldom used. Some accountants number or letter all sub-accounts as above; others only mark those which are to be further developed.

But we may develop either of the two principal accounts in more than one way, and then we distinguish them either by accounts or by the Latin words bis, ter, (twice, thrice.) Thus we often have two developments of A, known as A and A' (read A prime) or A and A bis. We might have A, A and A", or A, A bis and A ter. We shall hereafter use the accent.

The four normal developments already referred to are usually designated as follows in complete logismography:

1. Integral development of proprietors' account (specific) by A.

2. Differential development of proprietor's account (economic) by A'.

3. Integral development of agency account (juridical) by B.

4. Differential development of agency account (economic inverse) by B'.

is a guide for the entry of a transaction, indicating the amounts to be written in the Journal and in the successive Developments, and in exactly what columns each amount is to go. By the use of loose Minutes several bookkeepers can be employed at once and the entries in the Developments may be made at once, in any order desired. Various plans will readily suggest themselves for facilitating the compilation of the minutes; they may be in printed form for the most frequently occurring transactions; they may be on the back of vouchers, and they may be in duplicate, for different departments, by the use of carbon paper.

———————————

—If a man look sharply and attentively he shall see Fortune; for, although she is blind, yet she is not invisible.—Bacon.

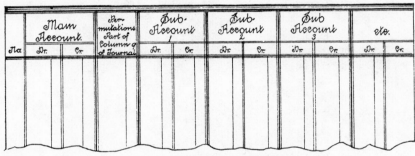

FIG. 2. FORM OF DEVELOPMENTS.

We will illustrate the forms of development hereafter.

The Journal, being the book which contains the two fundamental accounts, and the Developments, being each a statement in greater detail of the elements composing one of those fundamental accounts or some portion of it, it would be possible to make the entries in the Journal with all necessary information, and thence carry them to the proper Developments. But for convenience the entries are prepared for the Journal and Developments by means of the Minutes and the Scheme of Accounts.

The Scheme of Accounts is an analytical List or Index of all the accounts and sub-accounts, describing under each book the contents of every column in the book, referring to them by numbers. The Minute is either a loose sheet or it is contained in the Minute Book. Each minute

The Use of Local Checks

The subject assigned by the National officers to the local associations of credit men, for discussion at the January meetings, is "The Use of Local Checks by Out-of-Town Merchants: Its Abuse and the Remedy." This is by no means a new subject, for in the past it has received informal discussion, in various directions, and numerous articles bearing upon it have appeared in trade and financial papers. In an effort to reform this method of making remittances frequently employed by country merchants, it is probable that the National organization will issue a letter in the near future calling attention to the injustice that results from the practice. There is also in contemplation a pamphlet, wherein will be presented in considerable detail reasons why the custom is wrong.

Logismography II

By CHARLES E. SPRAGUE

(Continued from page 75, January Number)

We will now give a few entries taken from Marchesini's work in the form of the logismographic journal, to illustrate the principle on which the two fundamental accounts and the permutation column are kept, (Fig. 3). We will then illustrate how the same material appears

$15,000, there will be two articles (entries) in double entry.

Agents and Correspondents, Dr.

Proprietor, Cr............................ 140,000
for total resources.

Proprietor, Dr.

Agents and Correspondents, Cr......... 15,000
for total liabilities.
                            155,000

We will now place this in the columns of the journal, and for convenience will omit the number, date and description of the transaction, commencing with the col-

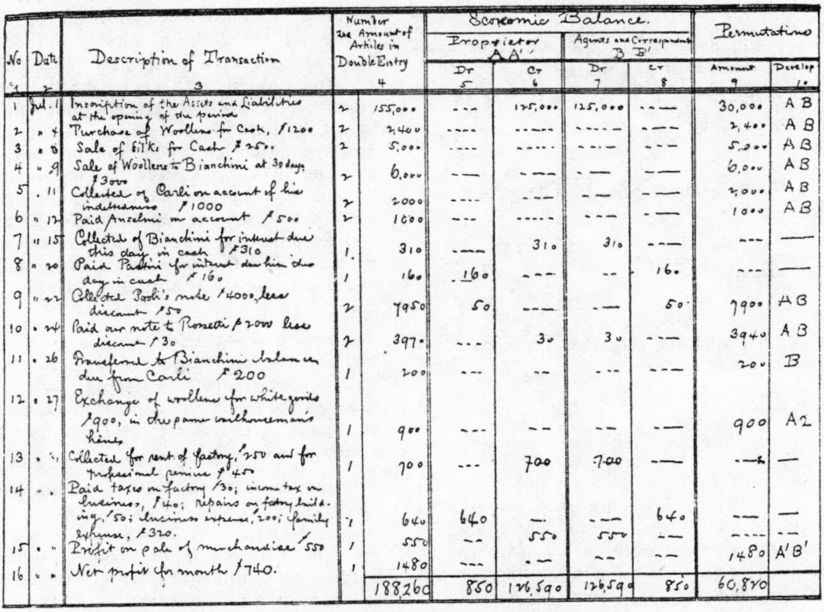

FIG. 3. ENTRIES IN THE LOGISMOGRAPHIC JOURNAL.

when it is distributed into various developments. In the illustration we use the dollar, whereas in the Italian original the lira was employed.

Having ascertained the active and passive (resources and liabilities) from the inventory, the results are entered in the journal and in the successive developments. It must be stated in the journal that the proprietor is creditor for the active and debtor for the passive of the inventory; also that the agency (agents, consignatories and correspondents) is debtor for the active and creditor for the passive. Supposing that the active amounts to $140,000 and the passive to

umn headed "Number and amount of Articles in Double Entry," to which column we will hereafter give the briefer name of "Total." The two entries just cited will appear in the several columns as shown in Fig. 4.

This will give the integral view. There is, however, an amount of $15,000 in each side of the proprietor's account, which may be cancelled by subtraction and placed in the permutation column, as shown in Fig. 5. This is the final logismographic form. The amount under permutations is required in Developments A and B, but not in A' and B'.

Hence this formula for opening the

journal with a statement of resources and liabilities: In column 4, resources plus liabilities; in column 6, (Proprietor Cr.) resources minus liabilities; in column 7 the same; in column 9, twice liabilities.

We assume that the assets and liabilities consist of the following, for which appropriate sub-accounts will hereafter be provided:

Cash	6,000	Bills Payable	5,000
Merchandise	60,000	Accounts Payable	10,000
Real Estate	40,000		
Furniture, etc	5,000		
Bills Receivable	12,000		
Accounts "	17,000		
	140,000		15,000

We will assume further that Merchandise is composed as follows:

Woolens	30,000
Silks	20,000
White Goods	10,000
	60,000

We will assume also that the Accounts Receivable are as follows:

Bianchina	12,400
Carli	1,200
Fabretti	3,400
	17,000

We will assume that the Accounts Payable are as follows:

Anselmi	3,200
Pastori	6,800
	10,000

We now proceed to entry No. 2, which is a Permutative, not a Modificative transaction. Transactions which merely transform or permute the assets and liabilities, without any change in the net patrimony—that is, mere exchanges of equal values, are called permutative. Those which show a modification, either increase or decrease, are called Modificative. Some transactions are mixed, being partly permutative and partly modificative.

In ordinary double entry bookkeeping the purchase of merchandise for cash would be expressed thus:

Merchandise, Dr	1,200	
To Cash		1,200

Using the logismographic terms we have the following:

Agency (Warehouseman, Woolen Dept.) Dr.	1,200	
Agency (Cashier) Cr		1,200

This would be the only entry, the proprietor not appearing as a factor. But in logismography the proprietor intervenes. It is he to whom the warehouseman is debtor for the increased stock of woolens, and it is he from whom the cashier receives credit for the payment made in his behalf. Therefore there are two articles from the logismographic point of view, as follows:

1. Agency (Warehouseman, Woolens Dept.)				
Dr			1,200	
Proprietor, (Merchandise)		Cr		1,200
for woolens purchased.				
2. Proprietor, (Cash)			Dr.	1,200
Agency (Cashier)		Cr		1,200
for disbursements made			2,400	2,400

Thus there are two articles and a total value of $2,400. We are now prepared to make an entry on a single line of the journal as shown in Fig. 6. But this is not the final form. As we have seen in entry No. 1, we cancel an equal amount in each pair of columns, placing the amount so cancelled in the permutation column. We then have the form shown in Fig. 7. This means that there are no amounts to be carried into the differential accounts A' and B', but in Developments A and B respectively there will be $1,200 to place in column 4. Hence this rule:

Permutative transactions give rise to two double entry articles, and are journalized by merely entering twice the amount in the total column and also in the permutations, referring to Developments A and B.

Transaction 3 is a sale. Presumably it involves a profit or a loss. As the original cost of the silk, however, is not given we cannot ascertain the exact amount of modification, and hence treat the sale for the present as permutative, applying the same rule as in 2.

Transactions 4, 5 and 6 are also permutative. No. 7 is modificative, being the increase of patrimony in the department of cash, without diminution in any other direction. It gives only the entry, but this is to be considered in two ways, integrally and differentially. Agents and correspondents are debited and the proprietor is credited. Specifically (A), the proprietor's credit is in the department of money; economically (A'), it is in the department of interest, which is a sub-account of Profit and Loss. The juridical relation (B) is that the Cashier becomes indebted to the proprietor, and the inverse economic (B') would be according to what form of development has been chosen. If we have established a classification B'1 Commercial Results, B'2 Real Estate Results, B'3 Results of Private Estate, this would come under the permutation. Transaction 8 is similarly treated. Transaction 9 is a mixed transaction. One branch of the Agency is

				ECONOMIC BALANCE.				PERMUTATIONS.	
No.	Date.	DESCRIPTION OF TRANSACTION.	TOTAL.	Proprietor. AA^1		Agents and Correspondents. BB^1			
				Dr.	Cr.	Dr.	Cr.	Amount.	Develop.
1	2	3	4	5	6	7	8	9	10
		First Article	1 140,000.	.....	140,000.	140,000.		....	......
		Second Article	1 15,000.	15.000.	....	....	15,000.	....	......
		Adding these together	2 155,000	15,000	140,000	140,000	15,000.	....	

FIG. 4.

		In Proprietor's Account		15,000.	15,000.			15,000	A
		Same in Agency				15,000	15,000	15,000	B
		The result	2 155,000	.....	125,000	125,000	....	30,000	AB

FIG. 5.

		(Entry on Single Line)	2 2,400.	1,200.	1,200.	1,200.	1,200.	....	

FIG. 6.

		(Final form)	2 2,400	.....	....		....	2,400.	AB

FIG. 7.

		Article 1	1 3,950	.....	3,950	3,950	....	....	......
		Article 2	1 4,000	4,000.	....	....	4,000.	....	......
		Subtract	2 7,950	4,000. 3,950.	3,950. 3,950.	3,950	4,000.	....	......
		and				3,950	3,950	3,950. A 3,950. B	
		We have the result	7,950.	50.			50.	7,900.	AB

FIG. 8.

		(Totals resulting from entries)	188,260	850.	126,590	126,590	850.	60,820	

FIG. 9.

		(First entry)	2 155,000	.....	125,000.	125,000	....	30,000	AB

FIG. 10.

		(New figures)	2 154,762.57	.....	122,645.33	122,645.33	....	32,117.24	AB

FIG. 11.

			..	....	.....	122,645.33	138,703.95	16,058.62	....

FIG. 12.

FIGS. 4 TO 12, INCLUSIVE, REFERRED TO IN TEXT.

first head. Therefore this entry would be as follows:

Agents and Corre- { Cashier
spondents { Commercial Results } Dr. 310

Proprietor { Cash
{ Interest } Cr. 310

In the Journal account B is debited and A is credited this sum, and there is no debited and another credited, but not to an equal extent. The two articles are the following:

1. { Ag'ts and Correspondents (Cashier) Dr. 3,950
{ Proprietor (Cash) Cr. 3,950

2. { Proprietor (Bills Receivable) Dr. 4,000
{ Agents and Correspondents (Paoli as debtor on note) Cr. 4,000

Pursuing the same method as with entry No. 1, we would obtain the figures shown in Fig. 8. Of the two original amounts, the smaller is doubled and placed in the permutations..2x3,950= 7,900. The difference in A Dr., and B Cr... 50.

and both in the Total............... 7,950.

The principle is precisely the same as in Entry No. 1.

Transaction 10 is another example of

ECONOMIC BALANCE.

DIFFERENTIAL.		INTEGRAL.	
Proprietor.		Agency.	
Dr.	Cr.	Dr.	Cr.
($Cr.\ ^{Agency.}_{Dr.}$)		($Cr.\ ^{Proprietor.}_{Dr.}$)	
1	125,000	140,000	15,000
2		1,200	1,200
3		2,500	2,500
4		3,000	3,000
5		1,000	1,000
6		500	500
7	310	310	
8	160		160
9	50	3,950	4,000
10	30	2,000	1,970
11		200	200
12		900	900
13	700	700	
14	640		640
15	550	550	
16	740	740	
	1,590	127,330	156,710	30,970

FIG. 14.

the same rule. Transaction 11 is an interior change not affecting the proprietor. Bianchini assumes a debt formerly owed by Carli. While this might be treated as a permutation of the Proprietary Account also, it is given as an instance of a transaction affecting only one account. The amount is entered singly in the permutative column, and singly in the total column (No. 4).

Transaction 12 is also an interior change affecting the integral accounts with the Proprietor only. There is no change in the agency, and his warehouseman is responsible for just as much value as before, but there is a change in the kind of value from woolens to white goods, although the total of merchandise is the same. Therefore it is referred to A^2, A not being affected. Marchesini refers this to A, which makes it appear on both sides of the merchandise account, contrary to the usual rule.

Transactions 13 and 14 are simply modificative. Transaction 15 is the result of an inventory. The Proprietor finds that the actual amount of his merchandise is $56,250, and the account A^2 only calls for $55,700. There must, therefore, have been a profit of $550. which is added to the agency and the proprietor's accounts.

Transaction 16 is a permutation, which affects the differential accounts only, and hence is marked A' and B'. It will be better understood when the developments are studied. The totals resulting from these entries in the Journal are shown in Fig. 9. It will be seen that the Proprietor

DEVELOPMENT A INTEGRAL.
Values Composing the Patrimony.

Number	MAIN ACCOUNT.		SUB-ACCOUNTS.				
	Proprietor.		A-1.		A-2.		Etc.
	Dr.	Cr.	Dr.	Cr.	Dr.	Cr.	
1	15,000	140,000					
...		1,200					
2	1,200	2,500					
3	2,500	3,000					
4	3,000	1,000					
5	1,000	500					
6	500	310					
7							
8	160						
	etc.	etc.					

FIG. 15.

and Agency accounts are exactly in counterbalance, and that the total column is the sum of all the debits or the sum of all the credits, plus the permutations. Thus:

Proprietor, Dr.....	850	Proprietor, Cr.....	126,590
Agency, Dr.....	126,590	Agency, Cr.....	850
Permutations......	60,820	Permutations......	60,820
	188,260		188,260

It seems to me that the Logismographic Journal does not tell its story simply and clearly. Let us take up the first entry (Fig. 10). It is possible to deduce from this the facts that the resources are $140,-000, and the liabilities $15,000, but it does not strike one very forcibly at first sight. Let us test the matter by presenting the figures in Fig. 11.

Can the reader tell at sight what are the assets and what are the liabilities in this case?

This is determined only by dividing 32,117.24 by 2..................... 16,058.62

120

Having thus ascertained the amount of the liabilities we

add to it.......................... 122,645.33

in order to learn the resources.. 138,703.95
and add again.................... 16,058.62

to obtain the proof of the total column 154,762.57

Is not this artificial in the highest degree, and if the object of accounts is to give information, is that object fulfilled?

Compare the form of Journal shown in Fig. 12. Here I have discarded the columns "Numbers and amount of articles in double entry," and also the permutation column, opening only four columns instead of six and using in this particular case three instead of four. I should treat the following entries in the same way. In Fig. 14 are a few of them under an amended heading. In this I have constructed the Proprietor's Account differentially and the Agency Account integrally. These two developments are acknowledged by the authors of logismography to be the most indispensable, but it will be objected that if the Proprietor's Account be stated only differentially, it cannot be developed integrally. I say it can, although I think it useless. By the simple device of transposing the columns of the Agency, we have the entire account of the proprietor, as I have intimated by the words "Proprietor, Dr. and Cr." ready for integral development. We may start our development A integral as shown in Fig. 15.

The Strong Room of a New York Bank

The means and methods of guarding treasure are at present receiving attention not only in a scientific, but also in a popular way. The following extract from C. D. Lanier's article in Scribner's Magazine contains a number of particulars that are likely to be read by many with interest.

No little dramatic interest is latent in these huge boxes of heavy masonry of the dimensions of a large room, with their thousands of interior safes, each with its own locks of various complexity and strength. In a single vault on Broadway there are 15,000 compartments from a size just sufficient to contain a dozen railroad bonds to the huge caverns of masonry that hold tons upon tons of silver and gold. The main doors which furnish entrance to the great box are the points on which the utmost mechanical skill is lavished. No burglar would ever think of trying to effect an entrance through the walls. If he disposed of the watchman who tramps around the outside in a little alley between the outer walls of the building and the vault, it would require days to drill sufficient holes to take a solid piece out of the wall. But if a burglar can only overcome the lock of one of the main doors, there is the entrance ready made. These doors are marvellous. One of them weighs fifteen tons. They are constructed by welding together layers of different hard metals, sometimes seven distinct kinds, so that if an ingenious burglar finds a way of piercing the first, an entirely different problem confronts him at the second, and so on. At any moment his drill is likely to make connections with an electric alarm, which not only raises the guards of that vault, but tells the watchmen of half-a-dozen others, some a mile away, that trouble is at hand. But even if the lock were overcome the monster doors would not open, because a large section of the stone floor has to be sunk down by an electrical device before the bottom of the door is above the masonry. Just above each main door appears an ominous-looking pipe; it can, in the event of burglarious efforts, belch forth boiling water and steam on the assailants below.

Notes

"Serving the Mail-Order Buyer" is the title of a little pamphlet by Charles J. Shearer, formerly advertising manager for Strowbridge & Clothier, Philadelphia, which has been issued by the Advertising Agency, Philadelphia. It contains just that character of advice and direction which firms in various lines of business find of advantage in adding to their equipment a mail order department and extending their enterprise to include a mail order business. The under current of the advice presented turns largely upon the character of the advertising to attract inquiries. Mr. Shearer has been a very successful man in building up a mail order business for the concern with which he has been connected, and he draws largely for the material of his pamphlet upon his experience. It is something that every business man will profit by examining.

We have received from F. S. Thompson, Public Accountant and Auditor, St. John, N. B., a copy of his report made to the Municipal Council of Cumberland County, upon the books of the treasurer for the period of 1880 to 1897. The report has been very carefully prepared, and is an analytical, as well as a comprehensive statement of what the accountant has found in the books referred to.

APPRECIATION FROM THE POINT OF VIEW OF THE CERTIFIED PUBLIC ACCOUNTANT

John R. Wildman

APPRECIATION FROM THE POINT OF VIEW OF THE CERTIFIED PUBLIC ACCOUNTANT

By JOHN R. WILDMAN, *Haskins and Sells*

The certified public accountant's interest in the subject of appreciation is a practical one. He is forced to consider the matter in connection with his review of accounting and his certification of financial statements.

The facts are, whether or not such procedure is justifiable, that physical property and intangible assets frequently are revalued by, or at the instance of, the owners of such possessions who attempt, in various ways, to give expression to the estimated increases in value. The certified public accountant, therefore, is confronted primarily with a condition; not a theory.

The authority for the restated value may be either a report of independent appraisers, or a resolution of corporation directors.

Inasmuch as the certified public accountant does not attempt to act as an appraiser, to pass judgment on the work of such persons, or to assume responsibility for the values which they fix, he accepts their judgment and qualifies his statements accordingly.

Inasmuch as corporation directors, in some jurisdictions, are empowered by statutes to fix values, and even though not specifically so empowered are within their corporate rights in so doing, the accountant usually takes the position that he must accept their judgment when they revalue assets, provided there is no fraud involved and they officially record such acts in the corporate minutes. In such cases the accountant places the responsibility on the directors by proper explanation in his statements.

The occasions for revaluations which give rise to estimated increases in values are various. One corporation may wish to bring out a bond issue. Another corporation may wish to offer an issue of preferred stock. Still another company may see in the procedure an opportunity to overcome a deficit in capital, thus preparing the way for future declarations of dividends payable in cash. A fourth concern may wish to use the restated value as a basis for depreciation and thus increase the charge for depreciation against earnings.

In one particular case, a company owning city realty considered using an appraised valuation for the purpose of restating its land and building values, crediting the estimated increment in land values to surplus available for cash dividends. This was done on the theory of equalizing the increase in value among the stockholders over a period of years, rather than giving the benefit of large profits to the shareholders at some future time when, and if, the profit might be realized.

In another case, a company having on its balance sheet a large amount of deferred charges which had accumulated as the result of numerous refinancings, caused certain intangibles to be revalued, credited the amount of the increase to capital surplus, and wrote off the deferred charges against such surplus.

Cases, illustrating the use which is made of asset revaluation in order to take advantage of an estimated increase in the value of such assets, might be continued at length. It is doubtful, however, if a continuation would develop uses substantially different from those already described.

The principle is well settled, and is specifically exemplified in cases such as the one involving the directors of the American Malting Company (65 N. J. Equity 375), that anticipated profits may not be made the basis of dividends payable in cash. In that case, quoting from the opinion written by Judge Clarke, "These contracts were to deliver at a future time a product not yet made from raw material, not yet purchased, with the aid of labor not yet expended. The price agreed to be paid at that future time had to cover all the possible contingencies of the market in the meanwhile, and might show a profit, and ran the chance of showing a loss. When the sales actually took place they were entered in the books. But to calculate months in advance on the results of future transactions, and on such calculations to declare dividends, was to base such dividends on paper profits—hoped for profits, future profits—and not upon the surplus or net pofits required by law. It does not seem to me that you can 'divide,' that is, make a dividend of a hope based on an expectation of a future delivery at a favorable price of what is not yet in existence, under the statute."

The principle is generally accepted, and is supported by Jennery v. Olmstead (36 Hun 536), that a rise in market prices over the cost of commodities carried as current assets does not justify a credit to profit and loss, or an increase in earned surplus. In the case of Jennery v. Olmstead, the court had to pass on the question of whether an increase in the market value of United States bonds, than which nothing could be more marketable, was a proper credit to profit and loss. The court held that it was not.

In further support of the principle that unrealized increment does not constitute a profit distributable in the form of cash dividends, might be cited Marks v. Monroe County Permanent Savings and Loan Association (52 N. Y. St. Rep. 451, 22 N. Y. Supp. 589), in which it was held that unearned discount was not so distributable.

The statutes of Ohio (General Corporation Law of 1927, Section 8623-38) require that "Cash dividends shall not be paid out of surplus due to or arising from (a) unrealized appreciation in value of or a revaluation of fixed assets * * *."

In the outstanding case of Eisner v. Macomber (252 U. S. 189) the United States Supreme Court held that in order to be subject to taxation, income must be shown to have been "derived" from capital, and not merely a "growth or increment of value in the investment." * * * "Enrichment through increase in value of capital investment is not income in any proper meaning of the term." This case, of course, will be remembered as the one in which stock dividends were declared by the Supreme Court to be non-taxable.

In another case which arose in connection with the Profits Tax Laws, the United States Supreme Court held in the case of La Belle Iron Works v. United States (256 U. S. 377) that appreciation could not be included in invested capital.

If contractual rights to receive in the future, amounts in excess of cost, or an opportunity to realize profit through resort to a ready market, do not warrant the recognition of increased asset value, it does not seem that any opinion expressed by, or in behalf of, the owner of property, can effectively increase the value of such property to the same owner.

The conclusion well may be reached, therefore, that an estimated increase in the value of assets, even if the estimated increase is recorded in the books of account of an enterprise, does not increase either actually, or constructively, the surplus available to that enterprise for distribution as cash dividends.

Exception to the foregoing conclusion possibly may be taken on the ground that it is not applicable in a case where one corporation

owns all, or a sufficient amount of the stock of another corporation
to direct the application of surplus profits, and periodically revalues
its investment in the stock of the subsidiary company. Such circumstances seem not to indicate an exception to the rule which excludes
appreciation from earned surplus. Revaluation on the basis of net
asset values of subsidiaries, where warranted by circumstances of
control, is but another way of giving expression to a result which
would be achieved by consolidating the accounts of two companies.
That this procedure may result in an amount of surplus greater than
that of the parent company alone, does not place the parent company
in the position of having taken credit for unrealized appreciation.

The question may be raised, next, as to whether the procedure of
increasing the book value of an asset, increases the capital account
of an enterprise. The value of capital to an enterprise is determined
by its earning power. Capital being but a collective term compre-
hending ownership of, or an equity in, the assets of an enterprise,
the earning power inheres not in the capital account, but in the substance by which the capital is represented. To answer in the affirma-
tive the question of whether increasing the book value of an asset
increases capital, it must be shown that the asset which has been
raised in value has increased earning power which justifies the value
assigned to the asset.

Physical property in the form of buildings and equipment scarcely
may be considered to be capable of producing any favorable effect
on earnings. On the contrary, the older such property becomes, the
greater, frequently, becomes the burden on earnings. Consequently,
such property does not meet the test which justifies an increase in
asset value and in capital.

Land, under certain circumstances of location and demand, may
increase in value, but the increase is a theoretical one requiring an
exchange in order to make it effectual. In the hands of the same
owner and without improvement, usually it has no increased value
in use.

Mineral deposits are analogous to land. Their value in use continues the same. Their value in exchange requires a transfer of
ownership, before an increase in value may be recognized.

Values in ore bodies, or other natural resources, established by
discovery and engineering appraisal, constitute an exception to the
foregoing statement, in that they represent added wealth which finds

its rational place in capital, and is justified by increased value in use, with the consequent effect on earnings.

Nature, also, is responsible at times for increment which it seems must be recognized. Probably no one would maintain that the natural increase in timber, live-stock, or nursery-stock should be ignored in any attempt to portray, by means of accounting, conditions and operations of enterprises dealing in such resources. On the contrary, it seems but reasonable that the accretion should be admitted to a place in the inventory of assets, with the consequent effect, as the case may be, on capital, reserves for unrealized increment, or profits.

Coming finally to intangibles, it is apparent that some enterprises possessing rights under contracts which have been undervalued, or not previously valued, or having franchises, patents, trade-marks, copyrights, etc., acquired at nominal cost, may enjoy profits in excess of those which are normal for their particular line of business. Under such circumstances, it seems that the owner of such intangibles would be justified in attributing the excess profits to such assets, and in placing on them a value commensurate with their earning power. In cases where the increased earning power has been demonstrated to have continued over a reasonable period of time, and is sufficiently permanent to warrant it, it would not seem irrational to raise the book value of the asset and credit the amount of the increase to capital. The effect, incidentally, would be to adjust the future return on capital so that it would tend to conform to the rate assumed as the norm.

There are at times circumstances involving land which create a situation analogous to that in which the capitalization of intangibles is warranted. Where capital, represented by land at cost returns a profit substantially and continuously in excess of normal, it does not seem illogical to increase the land value and the capital so that the future percentage of return on the increased amount of capital will approximate a normal rate of return. This is not on the theory that the value of surrounding lands has increased and created a possibility of sale at a profit, but that the owner, by reason of the increased earning power conferred on him by a fortunate purchase, is entitled to capitalize that increased earning power. Thus, it seems that the situation becomes analogous to that involving intangibles.

The preceding discussion of appreciation in its relation to capital seems to warrant the conclusion that an increase in the book value of an asset does not justify an increase in capital account unless the asset has increased value in use. Increased value in exchange does not constitute grounds for increasing capital.

Common law and specific statutes, in some jurisdictions, may deter those charged with the direction of corporate enterprises from paying cash dividends out of anticipated profits, or estimated surplus. There is little, if any, regulation, however, outside of that employed by the Interstate Commerce Commission and the various public service commissions, over the bookkeeping of corporations.

If a corporation desires to give expression to a theoretical increase in value of property, there is little an auditor can do to prevent such practice, except to inform himself thoroughly on the subject and exercise his logic and moral suasion in the premises. He can and should, however, refuse to certify to a statement in which the expression of increased value results in a misleading representation with regard to surplus, or to capital.

Justification of the practice of recognizing appreciation is attempted at times on the ground that the increase in value will be recovered out of future earnings through increased charges for depreciation.

This theory is fallacious, in that if the proportionate credit, representing a decline in unrealized appreciation, is properly applied, that is, as an offset to the depreciation charge, the net result will be the same as if depreciation had been taken on the property value before it was increased.

The effect of charging an increased amount of depreciation is to show the realization of a fictitious profit on property at the expense of future income. The result is doubly misleading. Net income from operations has not, in fact, been reduced; neither has a profit been realized through disposal of the property.

This argument is in no sense a criticism of the practice now prevalent of having property appraised by qualified appraisers. For purposes of insurance, appraisal is a proper procedure. For purposes of negotiation incident to a sale of property, or recapitalization involving the entry of new money into an enterprise, appraisal is pertinent and logical. For the purpose of creating a surplus to be distributed to shareholders in the form of cash dividends, appraisal is impertinent and unsound. If an appraisal *relating to property which is subject to depreciation,* is used to create a surplus which will be apportioned by means of a stock dividend, the procedure is not only unsound in that it erroneously assumes an increase in capital, but it is misleading in that it conceals the burden which is placed on future earnings through the increased depreciation charges which must follow.

The contention sometimes is made that the cost of replacing property having increased because of a rise in the general level of prices, property values should be marked up in order to protect invested capital against a sudden and unexpected charge in the event of severe property loss. Such procedure, being accompanied by an increase in the periodic charge for depreciation, has the advantage, it is claimed, of providing for the extinguishment of the property on the basis of replacement cost while protecting the original capital against impairment in case of extraordinary loss.

The fallacy in this theory, as it relates to capital, is that the property value will be extinguished with equal certainty on the basis of original cost and the corresponding periodic charge for depreciation, and capital will not become impaired. Depreciating property on the replacement basis is tantamount to anticipating an increase in surplus or in capital and attempting to make good the realization of the increase out of future earnings.

Directors who fear extraordinary property losses should arrange for insurance on the basis of replacement cost as long as such cost is above original cost. If directors consider it desirable to provide a reserve against extraordinary property losses, they should create it through a special charge against surplus, rather than misstate the net profits by excessive charges for depreciation.

If a corporation decides to increase its capital by means of an appraisal of property, perhaps no preventive can be imposed. Such steps should be taken, however, with the knowledge that if the property is of a depreciating character, the increased depreciation charge will result in decreased future net earnings in an amount equal to the depreciation on the appreciation. This effect is one especially worthy of consideration in its effect as between present and future shareholders. Those who buy shares, the capitalized value of which in part is based on appreciation of depreciating property, must expect to suffer the consequences of reduced future profits, and perhaps reduced dividends.

The power to prevent a corporation from writing up the value of its property, where prevention is desirable, obviously, is beyond the

control of the accountant. But the right is his to determine the kind
of financial statements to which he will attach his certification. It is
his duty to refrain from certifying to financial statements which are
misleading. Applying this formula, consideration may be given to
the various treatments of appreciation in an attempt to discover what
constitutes a misleading statement.

Property clearly described on the asset side of a balance sheet as
being carried at appraised value should mislead no one. Intangibles
so described should be equally clear. Earned surplus which contains
an undisclosed element of appreciation is misleading, and the inclusion of appreciation under the general caption of surplus is a mis-
representation.

While it may seem sufficient in giving effect to appreciation to
differentiate it from any earned surplus by showing it as "capital
surplus," or "surplus arising from appreciation," all the reasoning
heretofore applied seems to lead to the conclusion that appreciation
does not, in fact, give rise to surplus of any kind. Under such circumstances, it appears that the credit for appreciation may not be
described in any way on the balance sheet as surplus, without danger
of misleading the reader.

Almost equally dangerous is the practice of including the credit
for appreciation in the capital account, without disclosing the fact,
in cases where corporations have shares of no par value. The impli-
cation exists, where such stock is involved, and there is no question
of stated share value, that the capital account represents the amount
of consideration received for the stock, plus such amounts as the
directors have authorized to be transferred from surplus thereto.
The inference may be drawn, therefore, that such capital is based
on closed transactions, and is not dependent in any part upon future
earnings for its establishment.

No one should be misled with respect to the credit for appreciation,
in its relation to capital and surplus, if an amount equal to the estimated appreciation is placed in an account by itself, stated on the
balance sheet in a separate caption above the capital stock, and ap-
propriately described. A descriptive title which would be universally
acceptable is difficult to find. Judging the matter from the standpoint of what must transpire if effect is to be given to appreciation,
and it is to be treated correctly in its relation to the asset, to capital,
to depreciation, to earnings, and to surplus, the element seems to

stand out clearly as an estimated increase in value which has not been established by realization, or by earnings. Consequently, it may be described accurately as "Unrealized appreciation" or "Unearned appreciation."

The conclusions reached with respect to appreciation are as follows:

1. The recognition of appreciation in accounts generally is unsound from the point of view of economics.*

2. Appreciation does not increase capital, except in cases of newly discovered value, and of increased intangible or other asset values which are supported by indisputable earning power.

3. Appreciation should not be recognized unless it is justified by newly discovered value, or by increased value in use. Value in exchange does not justify its recognition.

4. Appreciation is not recognized by the profit economy, which requires that there shall have been a closed transaction before gain or loss may be determined.

5. The recognition in accounts of appreciation as creating a realized and distributable asset value is contrary to common law, and to some statutory law.

6. Profits, ascribed to appreciation, are excluded from income which is subject to Federal taxation.

7. Appreciation does not give rise to surplus which may be distributed in the form of cash dividends.

8. Appreciation does not give rise to earned surplus.

9. Appreciation may not be shown as having given rise to surplus of any character, without danger of being misleading.

10. Appreciation should not be given effect in a balance sheet, except as an estimate of unrealized value, in the nature of a reserve which may be shown either on the side of the liabilities or as a deduction from the corresponding asset. If shown on the side of the liabilities, it should appear above the capital section of the balance sheet, and in any event should be described as "Unrealized appreciation," "Unearned appreciation," or by means of some caption equally clear and accurate.

11. The theory that appreciation may be recovered out of earnings by increasing the charge for depreciation is erroneous.

*A study of the subject of "Appreciation" by graduate students under Professor A. C. Littleton, in the College of Commerce and Business Administration, University of Illinois.

12. The amount corresponding to depreciation of appreciation periodically deducted from unrealized or unearned appreciation, in cases where effect has been given to appreciation, should be applied as an offset in reduction of the charge for depreciation, so that the effect on net profits will be the same as if the charge for depreciation had been based on the value of the property prior to the introduction of appreciation. Stating differently, depreciation of appreciation should be charged against "Unrealized appreciation."

DEPRECIATION AND OBSOLESCENCE AS AFFECTED BY APPRAISALS

John R. Wildman

DEPRECIATION AND OBSOLESCENCE AS AFFECTED BY APPRAISALS

BY

John R. Wildman, C.P.A.

New York City

If a dollar of capital is invested in property, and the property has a known life of one year, and the capital is to be kept intact, a dollar of value must be included in cost within the period of one year, and recovered as an element of the sale price. Such is the theory of depreciation, reduced to its simplest terms.

If the property in which the dollar is invested has a possibility of becoming unsuited to its use sometime prior to the expiration of its otherwise estimated life of one year, shall the dollar of value be included in cost and recovered as a part of the sale price during the first six months of the year, or during three months, or during what period? Such is the problem of obsolescence.

If there is a possibility that at the end of a year it will cost a dollar and a half to replace the property, shall a dollar and a half be included in cost within the period of the year and recovered as an element of the sale price. Or should the investor be satisfied to recover his dollar from the buyer, and bear the risk of an increasing price level himself? Such, briefly, is one of the most highly mooted questions which arises in connection with appraisals.

The profit-economy under which business is conducted contemplates that the purchaser of goods shall pay the seller a price which results from adding to cost a margin for profit. Physical property which, through its use, contributes to the production of goods or services, rightly may be regarded as depreciating in value, and the loss in value properly may be considered to constitute an element of cost. In a well managed and successful business enterprise, the loss in value of the property passes into the cost, is recovered from buyers as a part of the price which they pay for goods, and returns to the enterprise in the form of a receivable, or in cash. Thus, the capital of the enterprise is maintained intact.

In due course, if the business continues, the physical property will have to be renewed. Into this situation the price-level obtrudes. If by the time replacement of the property is demanded prices have risen, the purchasing power of the dollar will have declined. The dollar originally invested then may purchase but eighty cents worth of property. In other words, the dollar may purchase but four units, whereas originally it purchased five. There has been no change in the investment of capital, but the things which it will purchase having increased in price, the dollar of capital has to be satisfied, as it were, to be represented by fewer units of physical property.

The effect on subsequent cost is not altered. Future customers will pay the same amount for the replacement of four units of property, only at a higher rate per unit than those in the first depreciation age. And so the process may continue, governed always by the price-level. Over sufficiently long depreciation periods there may be several counter-balancing changes in purchasing power. A depreciation program designed to provide for higher replacement costs may be entirely upset by falling prices long before the time to replace arrives.

Is it the part of wisdom and good judgment to attempt to give effect in present costs to future variations in the purchasing power of the dollar? If one foresees that the replacement of plant facilities twenty years hence will have to deal with the problem of reduced purchasing power, and further, if one can estimate with sufficient accuracy what the reduction will be to warrant such action, then one must load his costs in the meantime so that at the end of the period he will have recovered enough more dollars to replace a like amount of plant at higher prices. While this has been going on a credit equal to the amount of loading presumably will have been accumulating, constituting, in effect, an addition to capital at the expense of customers. It must not be forgotten that the customer pays. If costs are loaded, the customer pays for the loading. If the profit-ratio is established on a basis of loaded cost, the customer not only contributes capital to the enterprise but pays an added price for the privilege.

2

If one's consciousness is affected by the question of economic justice, here is a matter for earnest consideration. If in this age of fair but stern demand for maximum profit, economic justice is but another term for social sentimentality, there is still the question of competition to be considered. In any system of scientific price-fixing, prices, perforce, must be higher if provision is to be made for property replacement at higher levels. The concern with loaded costs conceivably may be at a disadvantage in a field where competition is a factor in the sale of goods. Where is the economist, or the cost-accountant, so clever that he can persuade management knowingly to adopt a loaded cost as a precaution against possible dollar-depreciation, when by so doing resulting prices will defeat sales?

Admittedly, property-depreciation on the basis of original cost must be recovered out of sales, if capital is to remain intact. Admittedly, a margin for dollar-depreciation must be established in some manner, if property is to be replaced in kind and will be purchasable at time of replacement only on a higher price level. But, it must be known first that such condition will exist. Also, it must be known when the time and what the level will be. The thought of such procedure in relation to physical property is a suggestion to the imagination which leads on to the application of the principle in all the ramifications of accounting and ends in complexities which are alarming to the average mind.

The subject of obsolescence presents problems not unlike those of providing for dollar-depreciation. The theoretical effect of providing for obsolescence is to increase the depreciation rate; a shortening of the natural life by applying a factor to cover a sudden death. The high prices of some and low prices of other radio apparatus is a case in point. Not long since it was said that the average life of each new invention in the field of radio was six weeks. Whether or not that figure is accurate, manufacturers of radios must needs load their costs to provide for supersession. As a result, prices of the most modern sets are high. Those who fail to take account of this peculiarity in their line and are unable to dispose of their volume in time, are forced to sell their goods at the buyer's price, wherever, if at all, he may be found. Manufacturers of radio sets who employ highly specialized machinery, adapted only to certain work, are

3

faced with the same danger. Depreciation due to natural causes must be supplemented by a provision for obsolescence. As a consequence, the depreciation rate is increased and the effective life is shortened.

If the uncertainty of obsolescence is linked with that of dollar-fluctuation, the difficulty of practical application becomes complicated in the extreme. Stated in terms of cost accounting, the provisional charge for replacement must comprehend a base rate for natural depreciation, plus two supplementaries: the first for obsolescence; the second for dollar fluctuation. If one is to be meticulous in his calculations, he must, in addition, give effect to the purchasing power of the dollars which the residuum will produce at the time of replacement.

Let it be assumed, for the purpose of clarifying this somewhat abstruse suggestion, that a given unit of property costs $100.00 and has an estimated natural life of twenty years, with a residual value of 10%. The normal rate for depreciation thus becomes 4½%. Next, 3½% is added (arbitrarily) for the obsolescence factor. This results in a loaded rate of 8% and an effective life of 12½ years.

The price-level 12½ years hence is estimated to have increased 25%, so that property of like kind for replacement purposes will cost $125.00. The residuum will be converted into dollars at the then prevailing rate and thus will have a purchasing value of $12.50. The amount to be recovered out of earnings during the period of 12½ years will be $112.50, calling for an annual replacement charge of $9.00.

The composition of the $9.00 annual replacement charge is as follows:

Normal property depreciation	
(4½% of $90.00),..........	$4.05
Provision for obsolescence	
(3½% of $90.00),..........	3.15
Provision for dollar depreciation	
(2% of $90.00),.............	1.80
Total,.................	$9.00

The effect of carrying out this program may be seen from the following tabulation:

Recovered (in cash) from customers:
  As normal depreciation,..... $50.625
  An obsolescence,.......... 39.375 $90.00
  As dollar depreciation,......   22.50 $112.50
Recovered (in cash) from sale of
    residuum:
  As original investment,....... $10.00
  As appreciation,............   2.50   12.50
Total amount available for re-
  placement purposes.......... $125.00
Original cost of property to be
  replaced,...................   100.00
Remainder,................... $ 25.00

An analysis of the remainder shows that it represents an addition to asset value of which $22.50 has been acquired by assessing trade debtors, and $2.50 resulting from an increase in the value of the residuum. Whether or not there is a difference in the character of these two items need not be argued. The gradual sale of an asset at a price in excess of cost seems not to differ from a sudden disposal on the same basis. It is interesting to observe, however, that this increase in value is permanent in character. It is to be reinvested in property and is about to start through the next depreciation cycle. The effect is an increase in capital.

The foregoing study is premised on certain assumptions. The price-level will rise. It will rise 25% in 12½ years. The property will cost more to replace. The annual amount of normal depreciation in the next cycle will be more, because of the increase in value. Invention still may hold the fear of obsolescence over the heads of the managers. And perhaps prices will continue to rise.

But, on the contrary, those who attempted to forecast the effect of obsolescence in the first instance may have been wrong. Invention may have lagged. A unit of property fully depreciated at the end of 12½ years, with the aid of reasonable maintenance, still may be functioning as efficiently as ever, and continue on to a ripe old

5

age, in the guise of an invisible asset.   One or more of several hundred unforeseen and as yet unheard of possibilities may so affect the economic fabric of the country as to result in a decline in prices. It is conceivable that the replacement fund recovered out of earnings might not be needed at the expiration of the depreciation period, and might, in fact, due to a decline in the price-level, have a replacement value far in excess of its dollar amount.   Such are some of the problems which grow out of attempts to give effect to uncertain factors, such as obsolescence and fluctuating prices.

Appraisal, if an accountant might venture to state his understanding of the word as used in a technical sense, is a systematic study of the quantity, quality, cost, and condition of the units comprising property, and of their utility as a whole, from which is established a value in terms of current prices.   The various kinds of value need not be discussed here, inasmuch as such differentiations result in different amounts and not different effects in relation to depreciation and obsolescence.

Appraised value, for the purpose of this discussion, will be taken to mean reproduction cost, less accrued depreciation.   More specifically, it may be stated as the cost of replacing as of a current date, the same quantity and quality of units of property in the same physical condition as those involved in the original cost.   In other words, if the identical property had been installed originally at cost prices now prevailing, and had been depreciated over the same period and at the same rates as the property in question, what would be its present value?

During an ascending price-trend, appraisals establish values which are in excess of cost and, consequently, force consideration of the effect which the increase in value has on capital, surplus, insurance, taxes, depreciation, costs, selling prices, profits, borrowing power, and property turnover.   Conversely, a declining trend raises questions of relationship affected by the decrease in value.

Appraisal automatically introduces the fluctuating-dollar factor. Management may ponder long and well before deciding the question of whether to order a policy which takes into consideration changes, from time to time, in the purchasing power of the dollar.   Management which has had its property submitted to appraisal, and has adopted the resulting value, has no choice but to consider immediately the problems which are presented by the application of that factor. It may or may not concern itself with property replacement at levels prevailing twenty-five years later.

The pressing questions, in most cases nowadays, grow out of increases in value, because of the marked rise in the general price-level over the past fifteen years. Reproduction costs now generally are higher than at any time during that period. They have been rising consistently, except for a temporary decline about 1920–21. Reproduction costs applied now to units of physical property acquired during the past fifteen years usually result in higher asset values which call for consideration.

Appraisals which bring about increased values raise, first, the question of what is to be done with accrued depreciation in excess of that for which provision has been made. If a piece of depreciable property which cost $100,000.00 has been depreciated for two years on a ten-year basis, the amount for which provision should have been made is $20,000.00. If, at the end of two years, that same property is appraised at $150,000.00, the accrued depreciation for the two-year period will amount to $30,000.00 and what to do with the difference of $10,000.00 is a question which forces itself on the attention.

The opportunity to recover it from past customers obviously has gone. The declining purchasing power of the dollar, corresponding to the rise in prices, would make it appear that adequate provision for property replacement had not been made in the past and that this newly discovered additional loss should be charged, in case there is no surplus, against capital account. But no one does that.

Nor are there many cases where the additional loss suffered is charged against earned surplus, on the theory that costs in the past have been under-charged. If there is a capital surplus, real or imaginary, the additional loss may be charged against that account. But in the majority of cases, probably, the loss is absorbed in the property account as an offset to the gross increase in value. In other words, property which, except for the application of accrued depreciation, would have had an increased value of $50,000.00 now, on the basis of depreciated reproduction-cost, has an increased value of $40,000.00.

The increase in value also raises the question of depreciation treatment in the future. Perhaps of all the questions involved in appraisal this is the one most vigorously debated. That this should be so is quite natural, in that one's judgment may be influenced by the point of view from which the problem is approached, or one may be led to wrong conclusions from failure to consider all angles of the problem.

As a premise, let it be assumed that depreciation is an invisible decrease in property value which, unless capital be allowed to become impaired, must be included in cost in order that it may be recovered from customers as a part of the sales price. Thus, every door to the replacement of property value is closed except that which leads to the customer.

The questions which now arise include particularly the following: "What is the purpose in making a charge for recovery?" "Is it to accumulate a sufficient number of dollars to replace property identical with that now in service at prices determined by the present level which is higher than cost?" "Is it to keep in the enterprise an amount equal to the number of dollars originally invested?"

These naïve questions have been sufficiently troublesome to divide the Supreme Court of the United States. Were it not for the fact that two learned justices have dissented from what seems to be the general view of the courts, one would indeed have great assurance in undertaking to argue the matter.

In a considerable number of cases it has been held, in substance, that the present value of property constituted a proper rate-base. Out of this we read that the depreciation provision should be based on reproduction cost, less accrued depreciation. If this is the correct application of many court decisions, including several of the United States Supreme Court, and if these decisions are sound, there would seem to be no point in pursuing the matter further.

But Mr. Justice Holmes and Mr. Justice Brandeis, in the frequently quoted case of Southwestern Bell Telephone Co. v. Public Service Commission (262 U.S. 276; reversing 233 S.W. 425—Mo. 1921), seem to have held to the contrary. In that case, while the majority favored present value as the proper basis, the key-note of that opinion being that it is "property, and not the original cost of it, of which the owner may not be deprived without

8

due process of law," the Justices in the minority opined that the capital actually and prudently invested, rather than the present value of the property, should be taken as the rate-base.

It is conceivable that a rule might apply where property is to be taken by right of eminent domain, or damages are to be allowed for trespass, or reimbursement is to be made for loss, which would be different from that which is applicable where property is consumed in service. An enterprise whose property is seized lawfully, is severed from its property as of a current date, and has no choice but to submit. Incidentally, it is obliged to take what the law allows. The only rational measurement of value is that based on current prices. But if the amount happens to be less than the appraised value carried on the books at the time of seizure, will the difference be assessed against customers, or carried over as a deferred charge and gradually recovered in that manner? Does a property loss not compensated by insurance constitute a proper charge against future operations? Are trade customers chargeable with a loss from trespass?

It does not seem unreasonable to assert that the entrepreneur is entitled only to have his original capital kept intact, on the basis of dollars invested, where the enterprise is a continuing one. Such is the basis of all his obligations. He does not undertake to so compensate long-term creditors that the dollars he pays back to them will buy as much as those he borrowed from them. He does not guarantee that the dollars which he pays for interest will be increased in number from time to time, in the event that the purchasing power of a dollar declines with an ascending price-level. Why then should the entrepreneur ask of customers that they insure him, by paying higher prices for goods, against a decline in the purchasing power of a dollar when the time arrives to replace his property?

With the door closed to the replacement of property values, except that which leads to the customer, where will the entrepreneur who is faced with decreased purchasing power of his dollars, when, and if, such is the case, when the time arrives to replace his property, obtain the necessary funds? This question may be dismissed promptly by a scriptural answer, "Sufficient unto the day is the evil thereof." And it need not be considered facetious to suggest that he may contribute more capital, or mayhap borrow, in order to replace his plant in proper physical proportions. If he has deep-seated convictions that additional funds will be needed for property replacement at enhanced values, he may make a charge against surplus profits in the meantime, thus keeping in the business an amount sufficient to cover the increased cost. In an extreme case, the reserve so created may be specifically funded and any temptation to use the funds for purposes other than replacement of property so avoided.

In pointing toward a conclusion in this discussion, obsolescence being regarded as a charge supplementing depreciation, no specific cognizance will be taken thereof, further than to observe that where property values are based on appraisal which is in excess of cost, any loss through sudden obsolescence has the appearance of being greater in amount than it is in reality.

Appraised values for borrowing, insurance, trespass, condemnation, sale, consolidation, stock issues, and similar purposes seem logical and consistent. When used for recovery purposes they appear to work an economic injustice; to consumers when there is a rising price-level; to investors when prices are falling, because of the fluctuating dollar value on which they are predicated. When appraised values are made the subject of periodic application in a rapidly fluctuating price-level, the result is a jagged series of charges for depreciation. It has been said of those who favor cost as a basis for depreciation that they are not consistent in the application of their cost theory, inasmuch as they price inventories at the lower of cost or market, but would not so price fixed property. Fixed property is not comparable to merchandise which is on the eve of passing into the market. A decrease in value due to an increase in the purchasing power of the dollar has no more effect on investment in property than a temporary decline in stock market prices has on investment securities. Carried to its logical conclusion, the fluctuating purchasing power of a dollar ends in an absurdity. Its value in terms of prices, particularly at some distant date, seems too uncertain to warrant adoption in any scheme of charges affecting current operations. But one may give due effect to appraised value for the proper purposes of capital borrowings and financing, sale, insurance, consolidation, etc., without having to involve operations. This, obviously, is done by crediting any increase, due to appraisal, in the value of property over cost, to a reserve for unrealized appreciation and subsequently charging against this reserve the depreciation on appreciation, when depreciation on cost is charged to operations.

The effect of appraisal on depreciation is dependent, in the last analysis, on whether the charge for recovery is based on replacement of property, or on the preservation of investment. It is to be hoped that, ere long, the Supreme Court will see the greater wisdom of the latter basis and offer a better guiding rule, by handing down a unanimous decision which will confirm the sound judgment of Justices Brandeis and Holmes.

NOTE: Since the foregoing was written, the United States Supreme Court has handed down a decision in the case of St. Louis & O'Fallon Railway Company v. Interstate Commerce Commission. This decision, based on the merits of the particular case, seems to hold that the commission erred in determining the value of the O'Fallon property because it failed to "give due consideration to all the elements of value recognized by the law of the land for rate-making purposes," among which is present cost of construction, or reproduction cost. Three justices dissented: Messrs. Brandeis, Holmes, and Stone.

ADDRESS OF THE PRESIDENT

John R. Wildman

American Association of University Instructors in Accounting

Address of the President

John R. Wildman, New York University

It seems to be the proper thing to begin a meeting of this kind with the address of the president. While I have no desire to inflict upon you any long drawn out speech, I had thought it incumbent upon me to review the work of the year and point out some of the problems which will confront us as a result of changed conditions, and to make some recommendations for the future based upon the experience of the past year.

I see some familiar faces and many unfamiliar ones. This is the second annual meeting of the association. The association was organized last year at Columbus at the same time as the meetings of the American Economic Association. This association decided at that time to hold its meetings at the same time as the meetings of the American Economic Association, and in that way it became more or less affiliated with the American Economic Association. There was considerable discussion at the time as to whether it was desirable, but it seemed to be the thing to do. I believe we have received, by reflection perhaps, some prestige from the connection. It has helped to strengthen this association and given us a place in the sunlight. We have been taken seriously and have been very kindly treated by our relatives and friends, and I feel that our favorable reception was due in large measure to the relationship.

According to our constitution, the objects of the association are:

(1) To advance the cause of instruction in accounting.

(2) To offer an opportunity for the discussion of subjects of interest in the fields of accounting and accounting instruction.

(3) To promote more intimate and cordial relations among instructors in accounting.

7

(4) To institute plans tending toward the standardization of accounting courses in institutions of university grade.

(5) To formulate a policy with regard to transfers of students of accounting from one institution to another.

If we attempted to measure our success during the past year according to these standards, I feel frankly that the result is none too satisfactory. I think we have aroused some interest in the subject of accounting and some interest in the association as evidenced by the fact that previous to this meeting we had seventy-one members widely distributed among the schools and universities giving instruction in accounting. About twenty-five per cent of that membership is from one university, but that perhaps is to be expected owing to the nature of things. Perhaps the largest school in the country and the largest staff of instructors might be expected to furnish a large quota of members in an association of this kind. Notwithstanding this fact, the balance of the membership is well distributed geographically.

People are taking us seriously. They are asking what this association is. Is it an outgrowth of the American Economic Association or is it a new growth? I think it is a hopeful sign when people talk about us.

I believe the cause of instruction itself has been promoted, even though no collective progress has been apparent. There must have been a good deal of individual progress growing out of the contact of the instructors one with another last year. I think we have cause for congratulations that even a small amount of progress has been made. I know I have felt it in my own case. The meeting last year was very helpful to me. I am sure it has been the same with other individuals. We had a most interesting and helpful meeting. I have been told a great deal of benefit was derived from it.

Acquaintanceship has developed cordial relations. No feuds have developed. No factions have sprung up. As far as I know, there is no politics. I, for one, hope we may go along without any of this; that we may go along as a large group of friends.

The committees appointed last year were four:

(1) Standardization.
(2) Correlation.

8

(3) Nomenclature.

(4) Reciprocity.

I must be frank to say that I do not know how much progress the committee on nomenclature has made, because I have not been able to get any information from that committee.

The committee on reciprocity has made some progress. It has done a considerable amount of work, but the report from the committee has not yet reached me, and according to a letter from one of the members, it will be only a tentative report.

The committee on standardization is represented by a report, and the committee on correlation is represented by one of the members who is ready to present a report for the committee.

I feel very grateful that even two committees have brought in reports during the year. Obviously any attempt as yet to provide for the transfer of students would be premature. Before we can discuss any kind of a logical transfer of students we must settle the question of standardization, and correlation, and many other matters.

I have no desire to present any alibis nor regale you with excuses. You all know what havoc the war has worked. It has been exceedingly difficult to accomplish things this year, particularly on account of the wide geographical distribution of the members of the executive committee. The changed conditions such as we have at the present time have already brought us new problems. Our falling off in students is causing and will cause changes in the arrangements and number of classes. The changed needs of students may demand a change in material. The demand for trained men in accounting was never any greater than at the present time. I have observed during the last six months the advertisements for accountants in the New York papers, and I have never before seen so many appear. This is a good indication of the activity in the field. I know from talking from other practitioners in New York that they have never been so busy.

Of course many calls have been made on the big men in the profession for Government assistance. Many of these have been obliged to give up their practice entirely. The older men in the profession are moving up and making opportunities for the younger men. Work incident to the war has so increased as to present to

9

us a demand for material in the shape of young accountants which we have never been called upon to face before.

This as about all I have to say in retrospect. With regard to the future, I would like to make one or two recommendations if I may.

It seems to me that the most important thing is the election as president of an active, energetic man who will rise to the situation confronting us, keep in touch with the developments and have the energy and enthusiasm to urge us forward. This is a very critical time for this association. It may very easily lapse into inactivity unless someone with plenty of energy takes it in hand.

I think one of the things which will be in order during the next year will be a membership drive, if for no other reason than to keep the association alive financially.

I believe we need, from a geographical point of view, a more cohesive executive committee. It would be well, it seems to me, to have all members of the executive committee selected from the same part of the country in order that they may get together and have real meetings instead of having to carry on their work by correspondence. If the work must be carried on by correspondence, it is much easier to do so when the men are within two or three hundred miles of each other.

I think there is another thing to which the association should give some attention, that is the possibility, during the continuation of the war, of having informal meetings. I have experienced great difficulty this year in arranging a program. I have had three or four arranged, and the last one has been to some extent upset. This suggests to me the desirability of devoting the remainder of this session to round-table discussion. I think that we should devote our attention to some special line, taking up some particular work and concentrating on it. One of the most important things is the correlation of the universities and the high schools which I suggest for your consideration.

I cannot close without paying my respects to the members of the executive committee and of the other committees for their work during the past year and to thank them for their coöperation.

THE DEVELOPMENT OF
CONTEMPORARY ACCOUNTING THOUGHT

An Arno Press Collection

Baldwin, H[arry] G[len]. **Accounting for Value As Well as Original Cost** *and* Castenholz, William B. **A Solution to the Appreciation Problem.** 2 Vols. in 1. 1927/1931

Baxter, William. **Collected Papers on Accounting.** 1978

Brief, Richard P., Ed. **Selections from Encyclopaedia of Accounting, 1903.** 1978

Broaker, Frank and Richard M. Chapman. **The American Accountants' Manual.** 1897

Canning, John B. **The Economics of Accountancy.** 1929

Chatfield, Michael, Ed. **The English View of Accountant's Duties and Responsibilities.** 1978

Cole, William Morse. **The Fundamentals of Accounting.** 1921

Congress of Accountants. **Official Record of the Proceedings of the Congress of Accountants.** 1904

Cronhelm, F[rederick] W[illiam]. **Double Entry by Single.** 1818

Davidson, Sidney. **The Plant Accounting Regulations of the Federal Power Commission.** 1952

De Paula, F[rederic] R[udolf] M[ackley]. **Developments in Accounting.** 1948

Epstein, Marc Jay. **The Effect of Scientific Management on the Development of the Standard Cost System** (Doctoral Dissertation, University of Oregon, 1973). 1978

Esquerré, Paul-Joseph. **The Applied Theory of Accounts.** 1914

Fitzgerald, A[dolf] A[lexander]. **Current Accounting Trends.** 1952

Garner, S. Paul and Marilynn Hughes, Eds. **Readings on Accounting Development.** 1978

Haskins, Charles Waldo. **Business Education and Accountancy.** 1904

Hein, Leonard William. **The British Companies Acts and the Practice of Accountancy 1844-1962** (Doctoral Dissertation, University of California, Los Angeles, 1962). 1978

Hendriksen, Eldon S. **Capital Expenditures in the Steel Industry, 1900 to 1953** (Doctoral Dissertation, University of California, Berkeley, 1956). 1978

Holmes, William, Linda H. Kistler and Louis S. Corsini. **Three Centuries of Accounting in Massachusetts.** 1978

Horngren, Charles T. **Implications for Accountants of the Uses of Financial Statements by Security Analysts** (Doctoral Dissertation, University of Chicago, 1955). 1978

Horrigan, James O., Ed. **Financial Ratio Analysis—An Historical Perspective.** 1978

Jones, [Edward Thomas]. **Jones's English System of Book-keeping.** 1796

Lamden, Charles William. **The Securities and Exchange Commission** (Doctoral Dissertation, University of California, Berkeley, 1949). 1978

Langer, Russell Davis. **Accounting As A Variable in Mergers** (Doctoral Dissertation, University of California, Berkeley, 1976). 1978

Lewis, J. Slater. **The Commercial Organisation of Factories.** 1896

Littleton, A[nanias] C[harles] and B[asil] S. Yamey, Eds. **Studies in the History of Accounting.** 1956

Mair, John. **Book-keeping Moderniz'd.** 1793

Mann, Helen Scott. **Charles Ezra Sprague.** 1931

Marsh, C[hristopher] C[olumbus]. **The Theory and Practice of Bank Book-keeping.** 1856

Mitchell, William. **A New and Complete System of Book-keeping by an Improved Method of Double Entry.** 1796

Montgomery, Robert H. **Fifty Years of Accountancy.** 1939

Moonitz, Maurice. **The Entity Theory of Consolidated Statements.** 1951

Moonitz, Maurice, Ed. **Three Contributions to the Development of Accounting Thought.** 1978

Murray, David. **Chapters in the History of Bookkeeping, Accountancy & Commercial Arithmetic.** 1930

Nicholson, J[erome] Lee. **Cost Accounting.** 1913

Paton, William Andrew and Russell Alger Stevenson. **Principles of Accounting.** 1918

Pixley, Francis W[illiam]. **The Profession of a Chartered Accountant and Other Lectures.** 1897

Preinreich, Gabriel A. D. **The Nature of Dividends.** 1935

Previts, Gary John, Ed. **Early 20th Century Developments in American Accounting Thought.** 1978

Ronen, Joshua and George H. Sorter. **Relevant Financial Statements.** 1978

Shenkir, William G., Ed. **Carman G. Blough: His Professional Career and Accounting Thought.** 1978

Simpson, Kemper. **Economics for the Accountant.** 1921

Sneed, Florence R. **Parallelism in Two Disciplines.** (M.A. Thesis, University of Texas, Arlington, 1974). 1978

Sorter, George H. **The Boundaries of the Accounting Universe** (Doctoral Dissertation, University of Chicago, 1963). 1978

Storey, Reed K[arl]. **Matching Revenues with Costs** (Doctoral Dissertation, University of California, Berkeley, 1958). 1978

Sweeney, Henry W[hitcomb]. **Stabilized Accounting.** 1936

Van de Linde, Gérard. **Reminiscences.** 1917

Vatter, William J[oseph]. **The Fund Theory of Accounting and Its Implications for Financial Reports.** 1947

Walker, R. G. **Consolidated Statements.** 1978

Webster, Norman E., Comp. **The American Association of Public Accountants.** 1954

Wells, M. C., Ed. **American Engineers' Contributions to Cost Accounting.** 1978

Worthington, Beresford. **Professional Accountants.** 1895

Yamey, Basil S. **Essays on the History of Accounting.** 1978

Yamey, Basil S., Ed. **The Historical Development of Accounting.** 1978

Yang, J[u] M[ei]. **Goodwill and Other Intangibles.** 1927

Zeff, Stephen Addam. **A Critical Examination of the Orientation Postulate in Accounting, with Particular Attention to its Historical Development** (Doctoral Dissertation, University of Michigan, 1961). 1978

Zeff, Stephen A., Ed. **Selected Dickinson Lectures in Accounting.** 1978

DATE DUE